OLE MAN (ON A) RIVER

Kayaking the Mississippi River
From Source to Sea

Ken Robertshaw

Ole Man (on a) River is the work of Ken Robertshaw who asserts the right to be identified as the author of this work in accordance with the Copyright, Designs and Patents Act 1988 and it may be not be reproduced, in part or in whole, including photographs, without the express permission of the author.

Published by Ken Robertshaw
January 2015

Web: www.mississippichallenge.co.uk
Facebook: mississippichallenge2014

All profits from the sale of this book will be donated to The Theodora Children's Charity

Further details can be found about their activities at
www.theodora.org.uk

An illustrated lecture is available from the author who would be delighted to attend your organisation to present it to you. If you have bought this book at a jumble sale more than 5 years after the date of original publication that offer may not still be available.

Ken Robertshaw is a native of Halifax, England where he lives with his family. He is a former Police Officer having served 28 years with the West Yorkshire Police, retiring as an Inspector.

Over the years he has been involved in many charitable events including playing in a squash relay for 15 hours and driving a Heavy Goods Vehicle carrying goods to assist in the relief of orphanages and hospitals in Romania, following the collapse of the government in 1990. He paddled a kayak with members of his Police team for 12 hours in 1980, which did nothing to prepare him for this adventure.

He joined the Rotary Club of Halifax in 1993 and served as President of the club in 2003. Along the way he has been involved in many different projects mostly concerned with the development of young people. He ran the Rotary Youth Leadership Awards programme for the Yorkshire area for 16 years helping young people who have demonstrated leadership qualities to improve their skills. He has also participated and led similar courses on an International basis in Australia, the USA and Sweden.

He was elected District Governor for Rotary International in Yorkshire in 2007 and has chaired Rotary International in Great Britain and Ireland national committees for Leadership Development and Training and Vocational Service and has served on the Rotaract committee.

He became a supporter of The Theodora Children's Charity in 2005 when he first came across them and has been involved in fund raising for them for several years.

At almost 60 years of age he has no intention of slowing down and looks forward to his next challenge. If he gets permission from the wife!

You may be interested in his previous expedition when he drove a dog sled team across the northern latitudes of Europe, 350 kilometres above the Arctic Circle, to raise funds for the charity, which can be found in his book entitled

"6 Dogs, A Sled and Me!"

No expedition of this type can take place without the support of many people.

First place goes to my wife Pauline who gets the biggest thank you. Once we had overcome her initial objections she became a fervent supporter spending hours feeding stories to media outlets and never loosing faith in the belief that they would run the story. Some did, some didn't. Their loss.

A close second goes to my family for putting up, not just with my absence, but also the worry they must have experienced as they followed my progress on a computer screen whilst hearing reports of bad weather and, on one occasion, riots in a city where we were headed.

I am also grateful to my friends who supported my family while I was gone and to those individuals who sent email, Facebook and text messages of support throughout the journey. The horrors of the electronic age that Winston and Julia became paranoid about have turned to benefits they could not have dreamed of.

The President(s), as the expedition period covered two Rotary years, and members of the Rotary Club of Halifax for their personal and financial support.

We are also grateful to FIFA World Cup and English Premiership referee, Howard Webb, for agreeing to be our Patron for the expedition. These ex coppers are everywhere it seems.

This book has been made readable thanks to the editing skills of Denise Firth. You will probably be as thankful as me.

There are many other people that gave support of one sort of another and if I have forgotten you it was not intentional and I hope you will understand.

For equipment we are grateful to the following for their support: -

Taylor Made Safety (Halifax) for their support with expedition clothing
Reed Chillcheater – Buoyancy aids, spray skirts, paddles and dry bags
Eddyline Kayaks - Kayaks
Vango – Tents
Ben Aaron – Custom made carry bags
Global Telesat Communications – Spot3
Power Traveller – Power Gorilla and Solar charger
Stuarts Hardware, Burrwood Accident Repairs, and Keep Safe Storage, all from Halifax, for their financial support
250 Squadron (Halifax) Air Cadets for the loan of training equipment.

Without any doubt the biggest of THANK YOU's goes to Jim Lewis of Grand Rapids, Minnesota who ensured we got off safely (and more), Bob White of Minneapolis, Minnesota for turning up at the right time, John Sullivan of La Crosse, Wisconsin for going the extra mile to help us at a time of need, Tom Drennan of St Louis, Missouri for the shelter, The Treischmanns of Lake Providence for the rest day and ringing round, Carl Michel for his organisation and my Louisiana Rotary Family of Doug, Gloria, Marguerite and West for all their support.

The assistance and kind words of every person we met on the trip shall never be forgotten, often without us knowing or remembering your name. If I have missed anyone I apologise but the gratitude is still there.

In memory of
Rotarian Eric Daniels
Adventurer, Friend and Mentor

Table of Contents

Forward -
André Poulie, Founder Theodora Children's Charity   9
Howard Webb, Patron to the expedition   11
Prologue   13

Expedition Research   17
Training   21
Planning   25
Things get serious   31
More Training   41
Final arrangements   53
And so it begins   59

Week 1 Lake Itasca to Grand Rapids, Minnesota   69
Week 2 Grand Rapids to Little Falls, Minnesota   83
Week 3 Little Falls to Lake City, Minnesota   93
Week 4 Lake City, Minnesota to Pleasant Valley, Iowa   121
Week 5 Pleasant Valley Iowa, to St Louis, Missouri   141
Week 6 St Louis, Missouri to Memphis, Tennessee   159
Week 7 Memphis, Tennessee to Newton Bend, Mississippi 177
Week 8 Newton Bend, Mississippi to Belle Chase, Louisiana 195
Week 9 Belle Chase, Louisiana to Mile zero,   221

Physiological and Psychological effects   233

Ken Robertshaw is an incredible man. He has shown that no matter what life throws at you, there are enormous adventures to be had. I am the Founder of the Theodora Children's Charity. The charity brings music, magic and laughter to over 30,000 sick, disabled and terminally ill children across England. Ken's incredible adventures have helped us to send our professional performers, called 'Giggle Doctors', to the bedsides of children who need them most.

Ken's spirit and attitude embodies the values at the very heart of Theodora: life is precious and every moment counts. He has shown what amazing things can happen once you get out of your comfort zone. Ken lives in the moment, not the past or the future. Like The Theodora Children's Charity, Ken looks for sources of happiness in order to enhance life and cherish every moment. Who knows what tomorrow holds. Today is all we have.

Ken is above all, an adventurer. He's brave, he takes risks. At the same time, he realises how precious life is and makes sure that he never puts his life at risk. Reading Ken's book one becomes profoundly aware of the lengths he went to in order fight against the odds. How many of us would be so brave, I wonder?

One must surely take one's hat off too to Grace, for taking on this incredible challenge. She fought against the odds and never gave up despite the numerous different things that made every attempt to stop her in her watery tracks! She'll no doubt act as a huge inspiration for all the young people she works with.

Everyone at Theodora and I are all so very grateful to Ken and Grace for all that he has done to raise money for us. We'd also like to thank all Rotarians who helped him realise his dreams and also you, Reader. Buying this book will help us to touch the life of another poorly young patient in hospital.

This book is a joy to read and an inspiration for anyone looking to undertake the project you've always dreamt of...and particularly, if it is to support a worthy cause.

André Poulie, 6th January 2015
Founder, The Theodora Children's Charity

When I heard about Grace and Ken and their plans to kayak the entire length of the Mississippi River I was full of admiration for their intentions. When I learned that neither of them are experienced kayakers I was amazed at their enthusiasm and drive.

When it comes to physical undertakings their expedition must surely rank as one of the toughest, not just physically but mentally as well. I looked at a map and wondered how they were going to find places to stay, where they would eat, how they would resupply and those were the easy elements. When I looked at the vast wilderness areas they would be travelling through I realised that they would depend on each other for days on end and that they really had planned an epic journey.

To say that they are something of an 'odd couple' is not an understatement, where else would you find a 22 year old Sports Coach and a 59 year old former Police Inspector and sharing an adventure such as this? They took on all aspects of the journey without any support from major sponsors and struggled to gain recognition in the media but they did not give in and have raised a staggering amount of money in the first 6 months for their charity The Theodora Children's Charity, a small organisation that helps entertain children in hospitals and hospices around the UK.

Their connection comes through Rotary International, an organisation well known for supporting worthwhile causes, whose members are frequently described as 'ordinary people doing extraordinary things'. That is certainly true of Grace and Ken except I would never describe them as 'ordinary' after following what their journey down the spine of the USA.

I was delighted to be asked by them to be patron of their expedition and am proud of their achievement. I hope you enjoy reading of their adventures as much as I did.

Howard Webb
FIFA World Cup and English Premier League referee
Patron to the Mississippi Challenge

Prologue

It all started because I couldn't sleep!

Pauline and I spent January 2012 visiting friends and relatives in Australia and, unlike previous visits when we had gone via Singapore, this time we had chosen to fly with Asiana Airlines, a South Korean company. Not that this was any less of a journey time, but it was a couple of hundred quid cheaper, and it gave us a chance to visit somewhere different. Seoul is certainly different and one of the coldest places I've been.

Considering that 2 months later I would be sleeping in a tent in the Arctic regions, that is quite a statement. And it's true. There again I was wearing specialist clothing in the Arctic that would have looked silly on the streets of South Korea's capital city.

So why couldn't I sleep? Well dear reader if you have ever taken a long-haul flight you will know what I mean. Try as I may, I have never managed to sleep on an airplane, with not more than short naps and with an 11+ hour flight, things get a bit wearing. So when I get home I try to stay awake till "a proper bedtime" but invariably fail and as a result go to bed early and end up wide-awake at 4:00 am. Some call it "jet-lag", others "travel shock" whatever it gets called, it takes a few days to get over the long trips.

It was the second night after we had returned that found me wide awake at 4:00 am so I got up rather than risk disturbing Pauline. Once up and around with a cup of tea, I began to watch a Wildlife programme on one of the all night channels. This one happened to be about the Mississippi River, exactly what, I can't remember but I recall thinking "I bet that kayaking the Mississippi River is quite an adventure". Thinking back, Helen Skelton from BBC TV's Blue Peter, had recently been featured in a documentary where she had kayaked the Amazon so that's probably where the thought came from.

Enter good old "Google" (where would we be without it and who did we ask before it came along) and the search term "Canoe the Mississippi". I was not surprised that there were quite a lot of references, people hold festivals on various sections, there are clubs at various points and the different States all make mention of Recreational Kayak and Canoe access. What did surprise me was the relatively low numbers of people that it reported as having done the whole length in one go. Don't get me wrong, there are quite a few but not as many as I thought.

Thoughts of the Mississippi left my head completely as I headed to the gym where I was training in preparation for participation in an expedition driving a dog sled team from Tromso, Norway to Kiruna, Sweden. I was taking part to raise funds for the Theodora Children's Charity; a charity that supplies specially trained children's entertainers to work in hospitals and hospices. They do a superb job bringing laughter to children in circumstances where there is not a lot to laugh about and along the way prove that laughter really is the best medicine.

I first came across The Theodora Children's Charity when preparing for my year as District Governor for the Yorkshire area of Rotary International and am proud to say that as a result of the support of Rotary Clubs in Yorkshire, we have been able to introduce them to the Bradford and Leeds areas. Details of The Theodora Children's Charity cane be found at the end of this book.

Following my expedition to travel across the Arctic areas of Northern Europe I wrote a book of my experiences *'6 Dogs, a Sled and Me!'* and produced an illustrated lecture for a wide variety of organisations. One of the groups I spoke to include my friend Grace Alsancak and her family. Grace and I first met when she was an attendee on a Rotary Youth Leadership Awards (RYLA) course that I was in charge of. As one of our outstanding graduates of her course, she was selected to be part of a small team that undertook an exchange with a Swedish Rotary District to experience leadership training under differing cultural and legal frameworks.

Grace is a former competitive diver, as in high and springboard, and is now a coach to aspiring future champions. It was during the UK half of the exchange, she persuaded me to learn how to dive off the 5-metre board at the local swimming pool. That's a long way down trust me, and if you want to see how I got on, you need to access YouTube and search for "Ken's High Dive Challenge". I take no responsibility for injuries sustained while you laugh at me.

Not only that but she is also something of a kindred spirit as she is not one to turn down a challenge or an experience. Shortly after her return from Sweden, Grace took part in a charity challenge climbing Mount Kilimanjaro, Tanzania. Apparently she saw a flyer at University one day and signed up the next.

Anyway, back to the evening of the talk and when the formal presentation ended I asked "Any questions?" after the usual "How do you go to the loo?" and "How cold is -25°C?" Somebody said, "After such an adventure what are you going to do next?" Heaven alone knows why but I immediately said "I'm going to kayak the length of the Mississippi River".

In a flash Grace said "Cool, I'll do it with you". Everybody laughed, including me, and we moved on to other questions. A few days later Grace rang me up and said, "I was serious about the Mississippi, were you?" Well with a challenge like that what else could I do but start the research in earnest.

Expedition Research

At this point all I can say is thank goodness for the biggest library in the world and her curator; The Internet and Google. It certainly gave me access to a wealth of information. There were a number of 'blogs' and websites started by people who had undertaken the journey either in total or part; maps produced by the Minnesota Department of Natural Resources (DNR) and the US Army Corps of Engineers (USACE) and various US Government and State departments websites promoting safe boating practises, campsites or simply tourism.

My first step was to seek out the maps that cover the route to try and get a sense of what the route would be and how we would navigate the river. Ed Stafford, the first person to walk the length of the Amazon said that navigation on a river is easy. Keep the river to your left and follow it downstream. Perhaps something of a simplistic view but good advice, not very practical though. In his book he described how he encountered flooded areas that made the river several miles wide covering an area of 700 sq. miles. Not something that maps can cope with. Then again maps of the Pantanal in Brazil are hardly what you pick up from the local petrol station, so I suppose he had a point.

Maps of the Mississippi River are a different thing. Basically the river is divided into three parts. From its source in Lake Itasca through the Minnesota headwaters/National Park area to the St Paul/Minneapolis, Minnesota area; from St Paul/Minneapolis to Cairo, Illinois and from Cairo to the Gulf of Mexico.

Maps from Minnesota Department of Natural Resources cover the first stage. There are 9 in total and they cover all the recreational waters in the area and give details of not just the river but also the campsites, launch points and access roads. These maps are really aimed at people using parts of the river for a day out or perhaps a trip from A to B and back. They are not the most detailed maps I have ever used and the scale is strange. Don't get me wrong, they are detailed in terms of the route the river takes and very useful, but not quite to the same standard as the Ordnance Survey maps we use in the UK and they don't carry the same amount of information.

One feature they do report is the dams used to generate hydroelectric power and the subsequent collection pools that precede them. More about these later.

The second two sections are mapped by the USACE who have overall responsibility for maintenance of the Mississippi as a commercial waterway. Strangely, navigation and river safety aids are the responsibility of the US Coast Guard who do not produce any maps of the river. The USACE maps are very detailed, especially in and around the lock systems and power plants, but only for River Traffic. There is little or no detail about towns along the riverbanks, in fact they hardly show more than the name and then only linked to a commercial dock, if there is one. Even the big cities such as St Louis and Memphis are just shown as built up areas just at the side of the waterway.

The Mississippi carries commercial traffic in the form of barges as far north as St Paul/Minneapolis, Minnesota, hauling all manner of goods, and between St Paul/Minneapolis and Cairo, Illinois there are locks to account for the drop in the river. The USACE also regulate the depth of the river on this area by controlling the amount of water flowing through dammed areas, this also has the benefit of assisting with flood control. From Cairo to the Gulf of Mexico there is no requirement for locks as the drop is sufficiently 'flat' but there are still flood defences in the form of earthen banks, called 'Levees', or steel walls that they maintain.

My research indicates that the locks are free to use and open to all craft, not just commercial traffic. I have no doubt that they are much bigger than the ones we see on the canals of the UK but will work on the same principle.

To say that the 3 sections of mapping are weighty is an understatement, when printed out; they fill a lever arch file and weigh a couple of kilos! There is no doubt that we cannot undertake the journey without these maps but weight and space will be a limiting factor. One option is to divide the book into three sections and find helpers that can meet me at set points to relieve me of a used section and swap me for the next one. If we do this then I should be able to find assistance from the various Rotary Clubs along the way. Another option is to download them onto my Apple MacBook and refer to them each night for the next day's journey. I will be carrying it anyway so might be able to use a technological solution.

I also consider obtaining a set of maps from US mapping company Rand McNally for each state we pass through but on checking the scale and detail discard this idea as they are road maps and give insufficient detail on the river.

The next part of my research is information from people who have done it. The first was Guy Haglund, who seems to be permanently on expeditions, he not only gave me some sound advice on where to find information, but who produced a day-by-day itinerary for his source to sea journey which has proved absolutely invaluable.

Guy travelled alone and completed in 65 days, including a couple of rest days and a day lost to bad weather. He was the inspiration for setting the target of 60 days to complete; with 2 of us to egg each other on and share tasks at campsites we believe this to be achievable.

Research about the flow of the river shows it varies from 2-3 mph in the upper areas to 5-6 mph in the lower reaches. As you read this you probably think that we would be able to sit and let the flow take us and still make progress. Remember that thought for later in this journal.

Now comes the big question – how long is the Mississippi River? Good question and the answer depends on who replies. The US Army Corps of Engineers only measure to Grand Rapids Minnesota, the US Department of Interior supplies three figures, one includes major tributaries, one the 'recognized' course and one that includes part of the Missouri river. The Minnesota DNR gives a figure of 2350 in one publication and 2500 in another. The only thing everyone agrees on is that it starts at Lake Itasca, Minnesota.

Whatever the distance you settle on the Mississippi is rated as the 4th longest river in the world, and there is some argument about that as well. What is not in dispute is the fact that it carries over 41% of all rainfall to the east of the Rocky Mountains and from the eastern half of Canada. That is a lot of water.

For our purposes we settle on 2350 as being the figure we are aiming to cover. This works out at an average of 40 miles per day. Every day. For 60 days. Without any days off. Say it quick and its not too bad. Now for the bad news. Guy Haglund only managed 12 miles one day in the headwaters area and several around the 25 mark, due entirely to the low flow, tree falls, vegetation and general meander of the river. This will mean some adjustments for us, as undoubtedly we will have the same type of problem.

Training

The next stage in my preparation was to find out if I had, or at least could learn, the skills to actually do the journey. At this point I need to mention my wife Pauline. Some would say the long-suffering Pauline.

Understandably she was sceptical at first but as I began to do more research she begins to voice some serious doubts. She openly tells me that she thinks, "You are too old, it's too far, it's too dangerous" but stops short of actually asking me not to do it. Later, as I get closer to setting off, she is actually very supportive and makes suggestions based on her research about the trip.

It was obvious that fitness would be a factor, this was covered by my late-in-life conversion to gym membership, I'd kept it up from the Arctic trip and am in pretty good shape overall The specific fitness would be tackled later with the help of the trainer at the Queens Sports Club, Halifax, Brian Rayner. Brian was Senior Mr Natural Universe at the age of 58 and 10 years later is still in great shape, he has been fantastic in advising me, and driving me on in training sessions.

The next factor is kayak skills. I'd done a bit in the Scouts and in the early 80's had done 10 hours up and down the canal with some Police colleagues to raise funds for a charity but other than that – NIL. As my son commented to some of his USA work colleagues when he told them of my plans "No, he has no experience of kayaking, it wouldn't be much of a challenge if he knew what he was doing would it?"

Fortunately, I know a man that has! Pete Richardson is one of the Waverider/Awesome Adventure team that I have worked with for years on the RYLA courses and is a former kayak instructor for the British Army at the Guards Adventure Training Wing. Not only that but he still instructs and keeps his qualifications up to date. It was obvious to me that I needed to know if an expert like Pete thought I could develop the skills and if he said "No" or I felt that it was beyond me then I would abandon the challenge.

So Pauline and I invited ourselves down to Devon to see Pete and the rest of the Waverider gang. True friends that they are, Paul and Jacqui Findlay left a key for their house under a rock and Mo Morris, another member of the Waverider team, came to have a brew with us till they got home from a walk. Did I say friends? I should say family.

So there I was on a cold, damp Saturday morning (well what else did you expect in Devon in late September?) pulling on a wetsuit while sheltering round the back of Pete's van in a car park before setting off out into the Bristol channel in a 15 foot sea going kayak.

Pete's brief from me was simple. If he said, "You can't do it" then I wouldn't. The sub-text was he had to reassure Pauline. Probably more than me. Ten minutes into the session he pulled alongside and said "You'll be right" and we then launched into how to spot deep and shallow water, wind direction, navigation and hazard avoidance and paddle technique.

Before we finished, he had one last trick up his sleeve – capsize recovery. He tipped me out without warning to see how I fared. I obviously did all right as he declared that I was "OK". Praise indeed.

As he commented afterwards, capsizes rarely come out of the blue, there is some factor that is in play and builds up to falling out. We then went through recovery techniques, including climbing into the boat while afloat and staying upside down, being rammed by your buddy and pulling yourself upright using their boat. Sounds scary but really is quite fun!

End result – go away and train and you will be fine. I found out later that Pete took Pauline to one side, dropped the humour and told her not to worry – I had done OK and had the right attitude for the task in hand.

That evening we all went out for a meal in the only town in the UK to have an exclamation mark as part of its place name, Westward Ho! The explanation for this is simple really.

The village name comes from the title of Charles Kingsley's novel *Westward Ho!* (1855), which was set in nearby Biddeford. The book was a bestseller, and entrepreneurs saw the opportunity to develop tourism in the area. The Northam Burrows Hotel and Villa Building Company, chaired by Lord Portsmouth, was formed in 1863 and the hotel they built was named the Westward Ho! Hotel, and the adjacent villas were also named after the book. As further development took place, the expanding settlement also acquired the name of Westward Ho! So the exclamation mark is an intentional part of the village's name. It is the only such place name in the British Isles.

Saint-Louis-du-Ha! Ha!, Quebec, is the only other town in the world that shares the distinction of having an exclamation mark in its name.

Whilst this has nothing to do with kayaking the Mississippi it does show that the USA is not the only place with strange place names, look up Waterproof, Louisiana and Intercourse, Pennsylvania as examples.

During the meal we catch up on family stuff, RYLA stories (this was the first year for 17 years that I had not been involved) and general chitchat. Nobody mentions the challenge. That is until Pete's wife says, "So when are you setting off on this trip then?"

I don't know which surprised me most, Pauline's' lack of reaction or me saying "I hadn't really thought about that" which was true, I hadn't. I decided there and then that more research was called for.

The following day was the journey home. Fortunately, Pauline tends to sleep a lot when in a moving vehicle, trust me she has slept through the most magnificent scenery that Europe has to offer, so instead of "discussing" the proposed journey I get time to think about it.

I start to mentally list equipment, time schedules, support options, costs, emergency procedures, techniques, possible problems, fund raising. Every time I think of something and run through it another topic pops into my head. I decide that the time has come to write everything down and form a document that can be used as a planning tool

Back at home I quietly start to research the challenge further and actually find that my confidence increases as my knowledge grows. Just looking at the maps gives me better insights into what can/will/might happen or what will be an obstacle and where help can be found.

Planning

I have this idea that we could use a mobile home as a support vehicle, running it with a combination of Pauline, Grace's parents and other helpers at various points. The first obstacle is cost. There is no second one, this idea is a non-starter.

I then think about using a car and having Pauline et al set up/take down campsites and shuttle us between sites and start/finish points on the river. Although not Pauline's favourite option as she is not keen on driving in the USA, I persuade her that if others join in, it is possible. Then cost arises again and this option is put in doubt. It is finally killed off when a detailed study of the maps shows that there will be significant numbers of days when we will not be able to make use of a support vehicle. After careful consideration the cost outweighs the benefit and the proposal is discarded.

As the next few weeks pass I am out at various events giving talks about my dog sledding experience and raising further funds for the Theodora Children's Charity, through donations and sales of my book. I decide that 31 October 2013 will be the close of the fund raising, just so it has a definite date and I can produce a balance sheet than any other reason. The appeal actually raised a total of £15,000 with over £13,500 going direct to the Theodora Children's Charity after operating costs had been deducted.

It is at these talks that the question "What are you going to do next" arises. Now, and with a more confident air I announce that I <u>will</u> kayak the length of the Mississippi from Source to Sea. The reaction ranges from "WOW" to "Some adventure that will be" through to "Are you mad?" to "I wish I could do something like that".

Pauline is present at one such event and is asked, "Are you doing it as well?" Answer "NO" and "What do you think of the idea?" The answer is sometimes a raised eyebrow and a shoulder shrug, sometimes she says "I'm not happy but can't stop him", sometimes she just says nothing and looks at me.

Tonight it was a combination of the eyebrow and shrug with a look at me. This does not bode well. Nothing is said that evening but the following day out it comes "Ken, I don't think you should do it – it's too far, you're too old and it's dangerous".

My response is simple, "There are people that are older than me that have done it, it's as far as it is and I will train for it. I'm doing it!"

From that point on I was committed even more than before and in truth was looking to prove to myself that all the things she had said were not true. An even bigger truth is that I did, and still sometimes do, wonder if I can do it. The only way to find out is to try.

I also call to mind the saying "The more you tell me I cannot achieve something, the more it makes me determined to do it".

November is a month that has seen us take a long haul/long time holiday and 2013 was no different. A tour of the South Eastern USA is settled on, giving us a chance to see parts we have not visited before, meet up with old friends, make some new ones and grab some sunshine. Travel tip; there is not much sunshine in the Tennessee Smokey mountains in November!

We visited North Carolina to meet up with Graham and Barbara Wilson whom we met through Rotary. Graham was a District Governor at the same time as me and we met purely by chance at one of the dinners at the RI Assembly in San Diego, an International training event for the Rotarians elected to the Position of District Governor. As we approached the table, Graham looked at my name badge, which states country and club name as well, and declares "Halifax! I was born in Halifax". As he has (almost) an American accent I say, "No, not Nova Scotia – we are from the original one in England". "Yes" he declares "The one in England, Halifax General Hospital, Dryclough Lane". It turns out his father was in the British Army and was posted to Halifax. It was only later in life that he emigrated to America.

Graham had arranged for me to speak at three Rotary Clubs about the dog sledding and when done they all ask what my next challenge will be. When I tell them of my plans I get similar reactions to the ones in the UK. I discover that if someone from the USA tells you that you are mad to take on one of their rivers, then it is time to realise that it is something out of the ordinary. I did meet one man who had done part of the river though and his only comment was "You'll have a great trip".

An endorsement at last!

As we move towards Louisiana and our Rotary friends/family we have to cross the Mississippi a couple of times as it winds along the state borders of Mississippi and Arkansas. On one such crossing we can see about 2 miles in a straight line in both directions and the river is a dark, slow moving, tremendously wide smooth swathe that cuts through banks lined with trees some 50 foot tall. It looks a little daunting to see it like this. Pauline watches it slide past the window as we drive over the bridge, turns to me and says, "You ARE mad". In my defence it was just getting dark, was starting to rain and nowhere looks like paradise in those conditions. I don't say anything.

A week later we cross the river again, only this time in bright sunshine and the river sparkles with a million diamond-like pinpoints of light dancing on the surface. Being in Baton Rouge where ocean-going sized ships are moored offloading cargo of every shape and size offsets this. No comment is heard from the passenger side. Or my side.

During our stay in Louisiana my good friend Doug and his wife Gloria treat us to their usual hospitality that sees us overfed and well watered. This year Doug has a real treat – I got to sell hotdogs at the Neville High School football game on Friday night. He didn't mention that we would be with family in Shreveport and that the game was in Monroe, an hour's drive away. But it was huge fun, even if half the customers didn't have a clue what I was saying nor me them.

Doug assures me that when we get to the Louisiana state border as we travel the Mississippi River that he will be there to greet us. Of that I have no doubt. Its just the size of the welcome party that worries me and how far down the river will they stalk us in a boat, taunting us with cold beverages just out of reach. Did I say he was a good friend?

We move a little further South to Moreauville to another branch of my USA 'family', Marguerite and West Constantine. They own and run a goat farm and one sideline is that they get parties of school kids looking round and finding out about farming as a career/lifestyle. Imagine the scene: - A school bus pulls up in the front yard and discharges some 30 7 year olds who are split into groups to visit the various parts of the farm including hand/bottle feeding the baby goats. Suitably excited they then get served a cold drink by a man and woman who 'talk funny'.

When they are all together, Pauline and I are formally introduced as coming from England. My 'sister' (it's a long story) Marguerite asks the children "How do you think Mr Ken and Miss Pauline got here?"

One small child immediately puts his hand up and when pointed to, stood up and said "On the Mayflower" which proves that a) he paid attention in class about thanksgiving and b) we look older than we thought!

We continued on our journey meeting up with friends from Rotary in Florida before we finally leave the sunshine, hospitality and sightseeing to return home for Christmas.

In the last few weeks before Christmas I manage to see Grace and put to her the actual magnitude of what we have proposed and the research I have undertaken. Two months of hard work, accommodation in tents frequently 'wild' and perhaps difficulty finding towns to re-supply. Couple this with preparation, sourcing kit and funds, training and work. Written like that sounds more daunting that I had imagined.

Neither of us is put off, so we agree that Christmas needs to be got out of the way and planning and training needs to start in January.

HAPPY NEW YEAR!

2014 arrives with record flood levels in many parts of the country with some small UK rivers resembling the Mississippi, well that's what the media report. Obviously they haven't seen it.

Also in the news are reports that In the USA they are having extremely low temperatures and high snowfall; I am hoping it doesn't adversely affect our planned trip later in the year with floods. On the other hand if the snow melts slowly enough the flow rate may increase and help us along. At this stage it is not clear.

I am once again in the gym 3 times a week and Brian Rayner, my trainer, works out a programme for me that concentrates on core strength and stamina. There are sessions when I think he is trying to kill me. Still it must be doing me some good; at least that's what I tell myself.

I continue to research the route and people who have done it in the past and find that it is a highly travelled waterway. Commercial traffic is a major user with huge barges travelling as far as Minneapolis. Recreational watercraft are abundant in the Minnesota Natural Parks, using lakes and rivers for all manner of travel as the whole state seems to be one big natural playground.

One highlight of the research is talking to a chap called Matt who, with 2 friends, did the journey in 2013. He proves to be a great help mostly by putting our minds at ease over such things as rapids (not that big), locks (bigger than imagined but safe), wildlife (only saw one bear ½ a mile away) and campsites etc. along the route (plenty). This reassurance is good to hear, especially as he admits to only really training for a couple of weekends before they set off! If they survived, so can I!

Things Get Serious

During January, we start to lay down the communications infrastructure, a webpage is registered, Facebook and Twitter accounts opened and emails set up. Don't be over impressed by this, Grace did most of it; I just tagged along and paid the bills. With the webpage on-line Grace proposes that we see if we can obtain a couple of kayaks to do a short video that can be published on YouTube to help promote us. I manage to scrounge an afternoon's use of 2 small craft, which are really designed for white water use, from the Scouts at a local center.

The result? Laurel & Hardy would be proud of us! Grace goes round in circles while I zigzag like a drunk on ice. Much hilarity ensues and the resulting video, whilst not an Internet sensation certainly got quite a few views. We can only get better; well that is the opinion of the majority. I'm not too sure.

February sees us reach a couple of major milestones in our planning. Pete Richardson has secured an invitation to Devon to meet Chris Reed from Chillcheater who has indicated the he may be able to offer us some sponsorship. Chillcheater is a small but well know company in the sea kayaking fraternity who produce a range of clothing that is designed for the extreme cold temperatures found in the waters around the UK, they have even outfitted expeditions that have travelled in the Greenland area. Not sure that we need protection from cold to that degree but they also produce spray skirts, buoyancy aids, dry bags and all the other safety gear we will need. They are also importers for Eddyline Kayaks and Swift Paddles, equipment that is made in the USA so they know their products well.

It also sees us secure sponsorship from a company in Halifax, Taylor Made Safety, which produces work wear with custom embroidered logos. They offer to supply shirts and hoodies emblazoned with logos to promote our challenge. This is a big boost for us as it's starting to feel real – other people now think we can do it!

The trip to Devon see Grace and I travel down the night before, she was working till 19:00, and stopping halfway before continuing on after a very early start.

Because it is arranged in a rush, I can only get a hotel with one twin bedroom. I check with Grace who sees no problem. Pauline comments "What will people think when they see you?" I reply "They won't see us sharing a tent for 2 months!" Pauline shrugs and says, "Don't snore – poor Grace!"

This is the first time it actually strikes me that there is an age gap of 36 years and that Grace could almost be my granddaughter. Many times in my life I have had friends that have been older or younger than me and I have always accepted it as human nature to find common interests that cross age and gender barriers or even that some people have a connection that goes deeper still, often without knowing why.

The difference is that I have never set out on an expedition to track a huge distance in a simple craft powered by muscles only with anyone before.

Do I care what people think of the age and gender difference? No, not one iota. Grace is a kindred spirit and ready to accept a challenge in life. Perhaps a few more 'Ken & Grace' teams in the world would see less friction between people in social, employment, political or cultural groupings.

Despite the weather and the typical British traffic hold ups we arrive at the appointed time and place to meet Chris and what a super guy he turns out to be. He is already captivated by what Pete has told him about us and our challenge and has started to put a sponsorship package together. He offers discounts on clothing and equipment as well as some very sound advice on the equipment we will need and the ways in which we can get the best use of it. He also offers advice on the type of kayak he suggests we use in terms of size as well as other technical specifications. His recommendation is the Eddyline Journey.

He has already started the discussions with his partners, Eddyline, to see if he can secure equipment from them at a discounted price. To cap it all he has a friend/customer who uses the type of kayak he recommends to us and he has arranged for us to visit him and see them, so off we go.

It turns out that the friend is Austin, a former RAF Squadron Leader (Air Traffic Control) who lives high on a hill with magnificent views over the

Bristol Channel and inlets and is another top bloke.

He is the proud owner of 2 Eddyline 'Journey' kayaks and allows us to pore over them. At 16 feet long and 2 ½ feet wide, they have storage bins fore and aft, deck lines and clips for extra storage in deck bags, an adjustable seat that allows for storage behind the paddler and storage in front of the paddler's feet. The hull is designed so as to give optimum stability whilst maximising speed for the effort expended. It also features a drop-down 'skeg'; this is like the keel on a sailing ship and acts as a fixed rudder. This provides straight-line stability. Unlike the boats in the aforementioned video clip!

I can't decide if it looks huge or tiny - huge because of its length and features; - tiny because of the entry hole for the paddler and the realisation that it would be 'home' for 2 months.

One thing is large – the price tag! It might be what the experts are recommending, and nothing they have said so far leads me to believe that they haven't anything but our best interests at heart, but at almost £2,000 each they are expensive.

As we have a coffee and a general chat it becomes apparent that Austin, Chris and Pete are very knowledgeable and experienced and have undertaken many trips to a huge variety of locations over the years. The one they haven't undertaken is the one we are planning so it comes as no surprise to find out that they would come with us if they had the chance.

We round off the morning with Chris giving us catalogues and ideas about kit and he promises to be in touch as soon as he has worked out prices for the kit he supplies and any response from Eddyline.

One of the other reasons for the visit was to have a session with Pete on rescue techniques. Thankfully he has arranged for use of an indoor swimming pool from another contact. February in the sea is not my idea of fun.

The boats he has brought to the pool are about 12 foot long and a bit more like what we will use. This is the first time we have been in a kayak and worn spray skirts. These are neoprene covers that fit around the paddlers' waist with a strong elastic band that stretches over the access hole and snaps on to the rim to make a seal. The aim is to provide a seal that will prevent water entering the cockpit as this would not only be uncomfortable but would make the boat unstable if it filled up. They also keep water out when the boat capsizes.

The spray decks have a tongue at the front, which, when the kayak inverts, is pulled and allows the paddler to 'fall' out of the boat. This is the easiest way to exit the craft, although not the driest, and allows the paddler to recover the boat by holding on to it and swimming to the bank. The drawback is that the kayak fills with water that has to be emptied out. It also has the potential for losing equipment stored in the boat.

The next technique is to remain in the craft, leave the spray deck attached and right the kayak, using a combination of buoyancy, arm power and your partner. This is a relatively easy technique but it does however require good teamwork.

On inverting – DON'T PANIC. Reach to the bottom of the kayak, which is now where you used to be, on the surface, and bang on it to attract attention. Then wave your hands in the air back and forth. This is where the teamwork comes in. Your partner paddles up and puts the nose of their kayak against your hull in a position where it can be grabbed by one of the hands you are waving. Once you have hold, pull on your partners boat and raise your knee under the lip of the seat area to push in the direction of rotation. This combination of factors will right the craft.

This technique depends on being close together, attentive and keeping a clear head. The key is not to panic; 30 seconds is not really is a long time and one that anyone can hold their breath for. It's all about trust in your partner's, and your own, abilities. If you are unable to right yourself then there will still be time to revert to 'Plan A' and exit the boat underwater.

Pete then saved 'the best' till last. How to fall out, remove water from the kayak and get back in. In deep water. That sounds like fun; or hard work depending on your point of view. OK, the falling out bit is easy and staying afloat is helped by the kayak and the buoyancy aid so there is not much effort expended in treading water.

Emptying is not too bad either. You float alongside your kayak and your partner lifts the bow/stern out of the water and rests it on their craft, which causes most of the water to run out before the boat is righted. So far, so good. Then you have to push up out of the water and lie across the kayak deck; swivel so that you are lying along it but face down and facing the back; wriggle about till you can put your legs into the cockpit; slide yourself into the foot well then turn around and sit down.

Another method is to push up and lie across the deck then get into a seated position astride it before wriggling into position where you can swing your legs up and into the cockpit to allow you to sit down into it.

Saying that these techniques are hard does not do justice to the word 'HARD' – it took some practice but we did it. You really do need to see the video to appreciate the difficulty of it. What you cannot see is the bruises I gathered from this session.

All of this led to the formulation of: -

EXPEDITION ORDER NO. 1
DO NOT CAPSIZE.
EVER.

Please bear in mind that when we were training the pool was indoors and heated and the kayaks were empty. On the trip it will be in cold, open water with flow. Water is always colder than the air temperature and deeper water is colder still. The kayaks will be loaded and have deck cargo and although wearing flotation jackets we will also have clothes on. Capsizing will be enough of a challenge; loss of equipment would be a huge blow to recover from.

As well as vital personal safety training it reinforces our view that the expedition is best tackled in two separate craft rather than a two-man boat. The argument for a two man craft centers around use of the power generated by the occupants working in tandem but I believe that this is outweighed by having two sets of equipment, such as tents, and food and being assured that we will have shelter and be able to eat in the event that we lose one kayak.

The day is rounded off with McDonald's burger and chips (the first I have ever had) and a chance to meet up with my mate Paul Findlay, the chief instructor for the RYLA activities. Paul is excited about the opportunities the expedition presents in terms of Grace speaking to the RYLA groups as a living example of just where opportunity can take you if you only take it. This is a vision I share, as I really want to use the experiences I have had to try and enthuse young people into doing more with their lives. Having Grace do the same will have a much greater impact, as they will see that adventure activities are not just something adults with time and money can undertake.

Both Paul and Pete are full of advice not just on paddling techniques but also practical tips on equipment that we will need. One of the biggest pieces of advice is to practise with kit before we set off so that we know how to use it and are thoroughly familiar with it. It's too late to learn when you need it for real. One piece of advice is to make sure that equipment that will be worn is broken in. OK, so buying a buoyancy aid and wearing it while training to break it in was one that I had thought of, but breaking in the paddles? How do you break in a glass fibre tube? Surprisingly this was exactly what happened, more of that later.

Paul and Pete and the other bits of advice keep flowing. A lot of it is simple but stuff that can easily be overlooked or not even considered. It is conversations like this that save lives, using the knowledge of people that have experienced the same or similar rather than trying to guess. Some of the things they tell us are: -

- Carry a large sponge to remove water from the bottom of the boat – it will weigh next to nothing, never break down and is cheap.

- Carry a knife that has a saw edge to get out of tangles, cut firewood, ropes and the like. Fasten it to the life jacket and hope you don't need to use it.

- Eat all day. Energy bars, nuts, fruit, anything – just keep replacing the energy source.

- Carry a couple of tarpaulins and rope. The uses for these seem endless – spread out on wet ground as an extra layer to sit on/ pitch tents, suspend a rope and throw the tarp over it as an extra shelter, use it as a windbreak or an emergency shelter. Grace comments that she has seen a video of three blokes sheltering under a picnic table during a storm with water coming through the gaps. Throw the tarp over it and hey presto instant small house.

- It can be used to cover the kayaks more to keep rain/animals out of the cockpit but also to help hide them from prying eyes. A tarpaulin is probably the cheapest but most versatile piece of kit we will have.

- The list continues, first aid kits, hats that have cover for the nape of the neck, neoprene gloves for cold days, dry bags inside dry bags for important stuff, Tupperware boxes in various sizes.

- Have a spare set of paddles and choose the same make as the ones we have so that they are interchangeable.

- Perhaps the biggest piece of advice is to double up on important stuff like tents, food and water containers. At the expense of less important items; like clothes

The one thing that comes through is that they believe in us and that we can do it. And not just physically, they tell us they know that we can survive the endless boredom that we will encounter and have the right mental attitude. Having backing like that means more to me than pledges of money.

All too soon we are back on our way home through heavy rain, heavy traffic and monotony. As we track along, Grace nods off, just like Pauline so I'm used to sleeping passengers. I am struck by the similarity of the journey home and the expedition. Two people travelling in the same direction but not really together, in the sense that they communicate but not all the time and not unless they need to, the direction is governed by the road/river, the pace dictated by traffic/water flow and the unending sameness of the view. Perhaps long distance driving is good mental discipline training for expeditions like ours.

Sitting here writing my journal I remember what Paul Findlay said about what would be our biggest danger and threat to our safety. Not lack of experience, weather, wild animals, river traffic or equipment damage but a single word. Complacency.

Accidents happen because people get sloppy, take short cuts and, worst of all, start to believe that it won't happen to them. Until the day it does.

Never take each day as the same as the last one, never believe that what you did today will be what you need to do tomorrow; never assume that just because you haven't needed a piece of kit that you won't ever need it and always be aware that the way something happened last time may not mean that it will happen that way again.

All of what I have cautioned against are normal human traits. We get used to things, we get comfortable, and we establish routines. On occasions we perform our lives to a never changing script and forget to look around once in a while to see what is going on.

When I first started to attend to and investigate road collisions in the police, complacency was probably the biggest cause of the incident. People would undertake the same journey hundreds of times without anything happening till the day something was different and they didn't react.

We used to say that if you dug a hole in the road 10ft x 10ft x 10ft and surround it with a million lights and cones, the person that drove into it would be the bloke who's house it's outside 'because it wasn't there yesterday'.

Perhaps the lesson in this is to live life like every day is going to be different and try to make it be so if you can. We all have commitments of one sort or another, jobs, family, friends, hobbies; I think the trick is to not let them become habits or routines, or worse still, self-imposed prisons. Simple things like taking a different route to or from work, write a letter – *a proper letter, on paper, with an ink pen* – to someone that you haven't seen for a while or just sit in a different chair while you watch TV, all these little changes make a difference to you as a person whether you realise it or not.

Look around you and see how many things are the same every day, at how predictable people are, how you conduct each day. Then apply Paul's warning word – complacency.

For us on the journey down the Mississippi it could mean damage to equipment and the end of the expedition, injuries or worse still, death. In life it could mean a self-imposed sentence of mediocrity.

I'm not sure which I think is worse.

A few days after we had visited Chris at Chillcheater he offered us a deal on the buoyancy aids and paddles that is too good to refuse so we take him up on the offer. It's getting even more real now; we have equipment! Not only that but a couple of local firms have pledged support that will cover the purchase of the paddles.

More Training

Just before we went down to Devon we borrowed two 10-foot kayaks from the local Air Cadet Squadron so that we could do some proper training. The loan included paddles, glass fibre one-piece things that were actually quite light, or so we thought. At the end of the first training session we both had blisters on our hands and arms that felt like they would drop off.

After a couple of sessions with these paddles the first pieces of our sponsored equipment arrived.

We are now the proud owners of 'Swift' paddles. Talk about make a difference! For starters, they have a carbon fibre shaft with thermoplastic blades and weigh *less* than two pints of beer. They are jointed in the middle to allow the blade pitch to be altered to suit individual styles and come apart for storage/transport.

The blades are actually 'handed' and shaped to give maximum pull for minimum effort. No blisters, not as much arm/shoulder ache and we move through the water faster and further with each stroke. As we use the paddles more we develop our technique and the aches and pains subside. I wonder how far we will get down the river before they come back.

With the purchase of life jackets and paddles and the borrowing of kayaks from the air cadets comes the chance to use the local canal as our training ground, as we don't have a suitable river nearby. This actually has unforeseen benefits. The lack of water flow requires us to walk at all times and helps build technique whilst the unchanging scenery prepares us for boredom.

What does surprise me is the life that inhabits the banks and undergrowth's. Ducks and geese are much in evidence and there are obviously fish as we see the occasional dead one floating on the surface and quite big ones too, bigger than I expected.

As the time passes the ducks and geese can be seen herding their young in little flotillas as they paddle along looking for food. As we approach, the ducks dart for cover of the bank and overhanging greenery with, occasionally, one of the parents adopting the "I've got a broken wing – chase me" act to lead us away from the chicks.

The geese are a different proposition. There are often several families together and the young are surrounded by 2 or 3 adults and shielded from view while the other adults arrange themselves on either side of us, hissing and spreading their wings. Some even climb onto the towpath to put themselves above us. They look as though they mean business and could probably do quite a bit of damage with a peck from a hard beak or a thump from a wing. We prefer not to see if this is true and paddle past avoiding eye contact! Let's hope this method works for the wildlife on the Mississippi.

The canal was, of course, primarily designed for the carriage of goods and as such does not always pass through picturesque postcard parts of town. OK, at various points there are well-kept locks and marinas and even some residential developments making good use of old industrial buildings or land but in the main they pass through lots of nothing surrounded by overgrown banking.

In some ways, I can accept a level of neglect, times have moved on and the waterways are no longer a viable method of transport for industry, and as such do not attract the finance needed to maintain them to a high standard.

What I am appalled to see is the deliberate and cruel neglect of the environment. Everything from old mattresses and fridges to plastic bins and scrap metal thrown over walls so that it adorns the banking, rotting slowly and polluting both visually and literally. On the water itself, there are cans and bottles, old footballs and literally thousands of plastic bags. Blocks of foam insulation float about and the ubiquitous supermarket trolley stands at a drunken angle like some sort of mesh ship sinking below the surface.

All of this is bad enough but the worst visual assault is the graffiti on bridges, warehouse walls and even lock notice boards. None of it is interesting in the way that "John and Mary forever 1939" would be as a possible social comment as some young man goes off to war or even artistic like the works of Banksy.

No, these are multi-coloured scars that make no sense, convey no message but merely serve to disfigure everything.

The hand of man at work again despoiling the very place they call home. It may not be on the scale of open cast mines or pumping pollutants into the atmosphere but it serves to underline, even on a low level, just how little some people care about the planet we inhabit.

And to what purpose? Mining and logging at least serves some purpose, albeit at the expense of the people it intends to serve in the long run. But graffiti? Is it freedom of expression? Underground art? Social comment? I'd rather see political slogans such as the ones on house wall ends in Belfast than these illiterate daubings; at least they have a perceived message.

On occasions these messages can provide humour on an intellectual level as was evident when a gable end in Belfast was adorned with the slogan "ULSTER SAYS NO" during some debate on unification in the early 2000's. Some wit appended "But the man from Del Monte says YES" in a parody of a fruit canning company advert some years earlier. Not to be outdone, some wag added "And he should know because he is a true Orangeman" – a reference to the loyal orange order, staunch advocates of the Ulster state and links with the UK – now that is graffiti that serves a purpose, laughing at the political and ideological stupidity that prevents people living in peace.

Anyone caught despoiling the environment in this way should be made to remove it. With toothbrushes. Theirs.

One of our early training trips we set out to travel from Sowerby Bridge to Brighouse, a distance of some 10 miles. In itself, not a huge journey, but one that involves negotiating numerous locks. Although we have both joined the British canoe union to allow us access to the waterways, and give us a large amount of insurance cover, we elect not to use the locks themselves but to portage (carry) the kayaks around them as this will give us much needed practice at getting in and out of the boats and negotiating obstacles while conveying them.

One lesson we do learn is that a set of portage wheels will prove invaluable in the upper areas of the Mississippi where there are lock systems to allow the barges access to the towns and cities. I am not sure how much use they will be once out of the lock areas, as we will be pulling out of the river onto reed and grass banks. I suppose it depends on the terrain.

As well as portaging, another consideration about using the locks on the Mississippi is timing. Although kayaks have the right to use them free of charge, commercial traffic takes precedence. This inevitably will lead to delays that will eat into the day's travels thus dictating that portage may be a faster option. We will take each one as it comes.

On the training portages we learn some valuable lessons about carrying boats. The ones we are training with are only 10ft long and are not loaded with anything like the amount of equipment we will be carrying while ours will be 16ft long and our entire worldly possessions will be in them, including drinking water which weighs in at 1Kg for every litre and we will probably carry about 15 to 20 litres each.

The first lesson we learn is getting the boats out of the water, <u>without</u> letting them float away. It should be easier on the riverbank as we won't have to climb up walls like the edge of the canals but nevertheless we still have to keep hold of them. Second, we might, and I stress MIGHT, be able to carry both at once on a straight section and for short distances but as soon as there is any obstacle or bends in the path it is back to one at a time.

Third, and most important, if someone offers to help, accept it. From hauling you out of the boat to lifting it out of the water and carrying it, if they want to help, let them. It really is surprising how often offers of help are made which in turn leads to a conversation about what we are doing and why. On some occasions it even leads to donations being made which just goes to prove how generous people are, both physically and financially.

As we plough up and down the canal the number of people that are walking (with or without dogs), running (with or without dogs), or cycling (with or without dogs, see a pattern developing yet?) are almost without number and many of them speak to us to ask where we are headed. The look on their faces when we say "We are training to travel the length of the Mississippi river" is great fun and for those that then say "On the canal?" to which we reply "No the real thing" it's almost laughable to see their reaction.

By now we have heard nearly every reaction: "Wow", "What" and "Why" are the most popular with "What an adventure" and "You're brave but mad" running close by. Everyone wishes us well with some even sounding envious.

I have put some small posters on the hatches giving details of what we aim to do and Grace produces some banners for the side that read MISSISSIPPI CHALLENGE 2014 and 2350 MILES 60 DAYS. Once these are affixed the comments and questions come even faster.

The training continues and we start to have regular contact with some fellow canal users, not something I suppose will happen as we travel the river. The route we use may be boring and repetitive but we cheer ourselves with the knowledge that every paddle stroke takes us nearer our goal.

As we paddle about we talk of all sorts of things, some of them even concern our impending journey. One question we ask is how many paddle strokes will it take us to complete the journey?

So dear reader, how many do you think it will take? The total river distance is 2350 miles and we will measure strokes each side, as in left paddle, right paddle, left paddle = 3 strokes; write your estimate here _____. The answer is at the end of the book – NO CHEATING!

One thing we discuss is the tactics of the actual journey. Although setting off in August and travelling into early October, we anticipate that the weather will be hot with occasional rain and some storms.

One tactic we agree on is to set off early in a morning, the aim is 07:00, to then paddle till 12:00 and if possible find somewhere that we can buy a meal, if not then cook one. We will then stay out of the heat of the day and set off again no later than 14:00 aiming to make camp about 19:00. This will give us 10 hours of travel per day and when we have a decent river flow speed to assist us will allow us to cover considerable mileage, hopefully higher than the minimum 40 per day we need to cover. That's the aim; we will see what the reality is.

We also practise fastening the boats together, both fore and aft and side to side as well as passing things back and forth. One thing we discover is that wind can assist as well has hinder and we talk briefly about trying to sail. I'm not sure that it would be a good idea as it would take a lot of practice and might even work against us or push us into danger. I do consider using an umbrella positioned between us when we sit side by side and rest, to make use of the wind, like a sail. We will have to see.

As the practise continues I start to feel more fluid in my paddle action. One day, I was alone, as Grace had to work; I set myself a target of 3 hours non-stop to see if I can handle the constant effort. I manage 2 ½ hours as Pauline rings me to tell me we have visitors. In that time I have covered over 10 miles and only paused for about 15 minutes in short spells, mostly to tell people what I am doing, and at the end don't feel as though I have over exerted or done too much. Even better as the day goes on I do not stiffen up or feel sore, even better still, there are no effects the following morning. I hope this is the case on the river but suspect it will not be.

At the beginning of March we sit down and look at the start date. My work commitments take me to the middle of July and Grace has been accepted as a volunteer at the Commonwealth Games in Glasgow and doesn't finish until the end of July so the decision to settle on August turned to be the right one. As a result of checking flight times and costs we book flights that will take me to the USA on 1st August to do the last minute shopping and for Grace on 5th August so she can rest between the games and setting off. The actual date for us to start the expedition is set for 7th August.

So, We have a website: www.mississippichallenge.co.uk, a Facebook page: Mississippichallenge 2014, a Twitter feed #Mississippi 2014 and have business cards we can hand out, have placed posters in various places and lots of word of mouth. We even have videos on YouTube that Grace has produced, admittedly they provide a laugh at our expense but it serves to get us known. We have the flights booked and some of the equipment we will need. What we don't have is kayaks or somewhere to stay before we start out. Minor detail.

Promoting the expedition is proving to be hard, very hard as no one seems to be interested. I begin to think that most people think we are joking or are doing it on the canal or a rowing machine. I start a series of press releases and look for an angle that should help when inspiration comes from The Rotary Club of Halifax's' Annual Charter

Dinner, a black tie affair and the most unlikely setting for thinking about a long distance kayak journey.

The guest speaker for the evening was Howard Webb: the FIFA World Cup final referee in 2010 and one of the top referees for the English Premier League. Like me, he is a former policeman, as is his manager, so when I make an approach asking him to be patron we already had things in common. His first reaction was in the "wow" category and he seems genuinely amazed to hear of our plans. He agrees to be our patron and we set up a photo call in a couple of weeks.

Howard is a really nice guy and offers to lend his name and mention our challenge to as many media people as possible but we are fully aware that the 2014 world cup is looming large and the Premiership title race is hotting up and that is his day job and primary concern. Still any help his name brings will be most welcome.

I knew that promoting the expedition would be hard but didn't realise how hard. It's almost as though people don't believe us or think it's a joke. The local newspaper, The Halifax Courier, once a daily, now a weekly, prints my initial submission but uses a photograph from my dog sled trek in the arctic. They also use my press release featuring Howard Webb but only after six attempts of submitting it and it being ignored. I later found out that the journalist I was dealing with had left the paper yet his email was on their website and was still live. At least it contained all the information as they printed it exactly as I sent it.

And don't get me started on other news outlets; press releases have been sent to just about every newspaper, both regional and national, with no response at all. Local TV and radio has the same result – nothing.

Yet everyday media outlets fill page after page with bad news, hard luck stories, speculation as to what various celebrities are doing or getting sentenced to or in the case of footballers, how much they are paid or who they have bitten this week.

Nothing at all about the achievements of ordinary people. Exam results are met with "They aren't as hard as they used to be" instead of praising the kids for their hard work; A young person who is a rising sports talent in anything other than football is ignored; The philanthropic works of Rotary clubs, and others, is given little or no comment.

At the other end of the scale 'celebrities' get huge coverage for whatever they do. Whilst I do not underestimate the physical effort they put into a task, the scale of media promotion before and after the event overshadows anything that 'ordinary' people do.

Promotion of our challenge and the obstacles we face is becoming something of an obsession with me. Celebrities have teams that plan everything, obtain all the necessary permissions, book hotels on the route and even publicise their passing through. At the event they will have doctors, physiotherapists, cooks, support workers, vans full of spare gear and the ubiquitous film crew.

What have we got? A website we design and manage, social media feed we update, constant emailing out of information (that gets ignored) and as much word of mouth as we can manage. We also have jobs, families and other tasks that need attending to.

Who do we have? Our families and friends and each other. That's all.

Does that make our expedition any less notable? No, but it makes it harder for us to keep enthusiastic about it all. Rotary has a strapline of "Ordinary people doing extraordinary things" which I believe describes our challenge to a tee. And yet my own Rotary District Executive team declined to promote the event through our own internal network. An event that is being undertaken to support a charity established in the county by Rotary through fund raising I and others have previously undertaken, a charity that the same Rotary District supported for inclusion in the National Rotary database of supported charities, a charity that supports children from our District at a time when they are ill, frightened and away from family.

So, dear readers, if you get the hint that the lack of support is a factor causing some concern then you are right.

What makes it worse is that when an 'ordinary' person is doing something and, sadly, dies then the media pounce on it, and turn it into a story. The result? Huge donations and pages of stories but at the expense of the individual. What a sad state we are in when a death generates more interest that a challenge. Grace and I joke that if an alligator attacks us, we really do need to make sure it's on film!

Then all of a sudden things start to pick up, mostly as a result of friends in Rotary circles. The first is a live interview with Radio North Highlands on their weekend magazine programme (thanks Liz) followed by Bolton FM featuring us on their drive time programme (thanks Alex) who also want to feature us again before we leave and a couple of times live while on the trip. Phoenix FM and Calderdale Hospital Radio (thanks again Alex) do pre-recorded interviews. What a boost that is for us, at last, someone is promoting us. Might not be much but it's a start.

Then completely out of the blue, we are contacted by a researcher from BBC Radio Leeds who has found out about us from our Facebook presence. At last, media interest.

So, duly booked in for a slot at 08:45 on a Tuesday morning I battle the commuter traffic along the M62 only to be told when I arrive that because of the guilty verdict being handed down to Rolf Harris (celebrities again!), my interview will be recorded and broadcast next day. True to their word, they did broadcast on the Wednesday at 06:55 but it's probably been the biggest audience so far.

The good news continues that week when Chris Reed calls to tell me that Eddyline have offered to assist with a substantial discount on the price of the two Journey kayaks we will use, not only that but they have also offered to make them with a slightly thicker underside to withstand the rigors of portaging. This brings the price down to a level that can be funded in advance of sponsorship to the required amount and is a great boost. We take them up on the offer and they increase their support with an offer to deliver them for $200 to an address that we nominate at least one week before we set out on the trek. Things are really looking up.

Away from the difficulties of promotion and attracting sponsors the gathering of information before starting continued and every source was approached with an open enquiring mind. One of the biggest questions was: what permissions, visas or other licenses do we need?

Licences are easy. The Minnesota Department of Natural Resources requires a permit be obtained for craft using their waterways. Cost is minimal and they can be obtained at the Driving Licence issue office. The bad news is that a U.S. address is required so more work is needed on that. For the States below Minnesota, it is not clear, so again, more work.

Visas are not so easy. For entry into the U.S. the basic requirement is an ESTA, which is valid for 2 years and obtained via the Internet. This is a way of matching individuals to their other visa requirements, which vary according to the country of residence/departure.

For UK nationals, there is a 'Visa waiver scheme' that allows for entry and a stay of up to 90 days without formal application to an embassy or consulate, all that is needed is a customs declaration form and a form for the immigration service, both of which are handed out by the airline during the journey.

For the 90 day 'waiver scheme' the purpose of the journey can be tourism or business but it is unclear what parameters are put on these. Is the expedition tourism? Is the fund raising element business? What if we plan to take longer than 90 days? What if we end up taking longer? The government website for US Immigration is very comprehensive but, sadly, covers everything but the questions I need answered.

Enter Rotary connections. A friend of mine in Louisiana, Bill Gates (yes the Bill Gates, well he is to me) is a US Marshall with the Department of Justice and manages to answer the questions for me. Basically, call it tourism and if people want to donate to the charity that's fine.

As for periods longer than 90 days there is a tourism category for 6 months that requires copious form filling and an interview at the US Embassy. The 'waiver scheme' 90 days cannot be extended unless there are emergency reasons, such as unforeseen illness, or factors outside of our control, such as a transport strike on the day of departure or weather related delays.

At most basic, once the licence is obtained and visa entry granted, the river is open to all, although just how we obtain a licence is not yet clear. Some advisors say don't bother with a licence, "Just play the Brit card and they will leave you alone". Not entirely happy with that one.

Tucked away in a small corner of a big document is a single line that states "The Minnesota DNR recognise licenses from other states and countries for craft not registered or originating from Minnesota". As we are registered members of Canoe England, former the British Canoe Union, this will cover it. Or at least give us an excuse.

Final Arrangements

I have been seeking accommodation near to the start and find that there is an International Youth Hostel at Lake Itasca that has been used by several teams setting out down the Mississippi. An email conversation with the manager ensues and we have accommodation prior to the start and a place to have the kayaks delivered. We plan for me to stop overnight in Minneapolis on arrival and then hire a car to collect stuff prior to Grace's arrival. I will then return to the airport to collect her and the Youth Hostel manager offers to help take the car to the local rental office. This will mean extra expense for a one-way rental but is something we have to face.

Then came the bad news, Sara, the manager of the Hostel has broken her shoulder in a mountain bike accident and will be off work and unable to be regularly contacted. Not something that will actually stop us but does put a bit of a spanner in the works. I try not to worry about it and just get on with everything else.

One of the pieces of research we did led us to join a Facebook page called "Mississippi River Paddlers" a site set up specifically for people who use the river for recreation either in sections or its entirety. Set up by John Sullivan most of the subscribers are travellers such as Grace and I, but there is a central core of 'River Angels' who offer to help paddlers as they pass through. They offer accommodation, trips to stores, help with repairs, all manner of assistance and all without charge. They are all keen 'river rats' and just love to help anyone if they can. Altruism is alive and well.

One such 'Angel' is Jim Lewis from Grand Rapids, Minnesota who contacts me with an offer of an information sheet that he has put together as a result of his experiences over the years, I eagerly accept this; local knowledge is the best after all. This quickly followed up with an offer that I literally cannot refuse.

He offers to collect me from the airport, then Grace a few days later, give us accommodation at his home prior to setting out and take me/us to shops to buy equipment and supplies. AND he immediately states that he wants nothing for this other than reimbursement of fuel costs. What can I say but 'yes' and 'thank you'.

After the accident that puts Sara out of action his offer could not have come at a better time. He even asks about kayak purchasing and offers to take us to local suppliers who are known to offer discounts to teams such as us. When I tell him of our sponsorship deal he is impressed and immediately offers to arrange to be in to accept delivery.

It wasn't until a few days after accepting his offer that I found out that Grand Rapids is a 3½ hour drive, in each direction, from Minneapolis. And he is offering to make the journey twice for total strangers. Apparently there is a saying describing the people from this part of the world, Minnesota Nice. Never has a saying been so true.

The preparation is going well; the kayaks that the Air Cadets lent us have proven invaluable and the slack watered dull canal has served its purpose. But with 4 weeks to go we step things up a notch not just with training but also with equipment purchases.

We get an offer from a company called Vango, who manufacture tents to supply us with equipment at 50% discount in return for use of our images and write up for publicity. No problem there so we order two, two man tents working on the principle that if we have to share then we will have room.

Next on the list is a power pack and solar recharging panel that is obtained direct from the manufacturers, Power Traveller, also at a healthy discount so that we can keep cameras, phones and laptops charged up and useable. Called a Power Gorilla it is quite heavy and not something I would want to carry on a foot based expedition but does seem to be rugged and versatile.

The final piece of technology we opted to use was a GPS tracker called a SPOT3. This ingenious piece of kit will send out a signal that is linked to a map allowing family, friends, sponsors or just interested people to follow our progress. It also has the facility to send two messages to up to 10-email address each (one is end of day the other at a special point in the journey) and two emergency messages. The first is a sort of "I'm OK but need you to ring me" type of message to selected people whilst the other is an automated SOS signal that goes to a monitoring station that can see our location to within 10 square metres and who then contact the appropriate emergency service to dispatch help. Supplied by Global Telesat Communications at a discounted price it is a wonderful way for people to be assured that we are safe and well and to follow our progress.

Pete Richardson, the kayak trainer, came up from Devon and brought a 15ft sea kayak with him. Not the same as ours but close enough. WOW, what a difference! So much easier to paddle and so much faster. We do some fag packet maths and find that it is some 30-40% more efficient. We calculate this by observing that with equal paddle stroke length and number, Grace manages to pull away from me when normally I leave her behind, and it is not just a small lead, but considerable with each stroke. This bodes well for the journey; all we need to learn now is learn how to handle an actual river.

After the weekend with Pete, things get incredibly busy – we have visitors from the US on a Rotary Exchange visit. Doug and Gloria Seegers are some of our best friends in the world – Doug was my opposite number on the Rotary International Group Study Exchange programme in 99/2000. We were both Club Presidents in 2003 and have both been District Governors. Not only that but he comes from Louisiana and will be a huge support for us on the last leg of the journey. I have no doubt this is not the last time I will mention him.

I also have a busy time with work that sees Pauline and I being needed at various places at the same time as well as juggling staff at other sites. And then I have a couple of very dark days as I appear as a witness in a court case against a man who assaulted me. This particular episode in my life put the whole expedition in doubt as things could have gone very wrong. This is not the right place to discuss it but I know one thing – I am glad to be going away with that particular episode of my life behind me.

In the last 10 days before setting off the final packing began in earnest. All equipment that has been bought new has been played with and checked out, equipment that is my own that I am taking is checked to ensure that it is in working order and then the packing starts.

Everything is laid out and gone through to ensure that it really is necessary to be taken and as a result some clothing is discarded. I can always find a cheap pair of shorts and a tee shirt for paddling in if mine become worn out and 'normal clothes' will only be seen by people we meet on the river once so they won't know I only have one set!

With the final sort out comes bad news. The paddles wouldn't fit in the biggest bag I had. A quick trip round various sports stores proved fruitless and then I hit on it – Ben Aaron, shoes, boots and military surplus suppliers for 4 generations would have what I need. Well, not quite. The longest duffle/kit bag was still too small so he put 2 together stitched on some extra straps and we had a custom made piece of kit.

The paddles were wrapped in bubble-wrap, put inside the buoyancy aids and then inside the sleeping bag. My sleeping mat round the handles and the space taken up with my tent and a few other bits and bobs to even out the weight between this and the holdall I am using for the other stuff. Next problem. I now have 2 bags. It actually works out cheaper to take it as a second bag on the flight rather than ship it, all I have to do is pay $100 at the check in desk. It turned out to be just as simple as that and as both bags were soft they even got manual handling as 'fragile' rather than automated. Do airports do 'Fragile' for bags?

Lulled into a false sense of security, I relax on my final weekend and start to develop toothache. This got progressively worse until on Monday I relent and book an emergency appointment with my dentist, except he's on holiday, so I get a stranger. A prod, poke and x-ray later he declares nothing found but suspects a receding nerve under a capped tooth. He prescribes sensitive toothpaste, avoid aggravating it and come back on Thursday. I arrive home shortly after to find that the washing machine has died in spectacular fashion, showering rust all over a load of clothes. THEN our son, Kenneth, is opening the drawer under the gas hob in the kitchen and because a corkscrew is sticking up it catches and dislodges the hob!

Does Ranulph Fiennes have to put up with domestic stuff like this I wonder?

A bit more running about over the next 2 days; mostly last minute stuff, like buying and fitting a new washing machine which entails altering the pipes of course, brush teeth four or five time a day, refit the gas hob and have it checked, send out invoices so that we have some money coming in from customers and make sure that the SKY+ recorder is set for my favourite programs. Back to Ranulph Fiennes and normality?

In and amongst I manage to fit a visit to RYLA in to see the gang, especially Pete and Paul. A few last minute words of encouragement from Peter – mostly "Rotation", which is a reference to paddling technique and a lot of good wishes from the team, set me up. Pete really does look like he wanted to come with us but I will keep him updated on our travels.

And then the final, final pack; electrical stuff in hand luggage, everything else in the kit bags. Pauline looks at it all and says, "I hope it all fits in the kayak". She hopes!

And So It Begins

1/8/14
I don't get much sleep on my final night at home and not just as I am up at 4:30 to be off to the airport. My daughter, Rebecca, takes me as Pauline does not want to be over emotional at the departure point, plus which our grandson Thomas is visiting from about 9:00 so she wants to go back to sleep. Her parting words are "Don't be planning anything else while you are away"

At the airport I encounter a first for me, the gates are not even set up, never mind open so I wait patiently to one side. A family joins me and we watch as people walk down the aisles only to be turned back. We try not to laugh. In true British fashion a queue starts to form with my new friends at the head. They offer me a place in front of them but I decline, no sense in moving heavy bags till I have to. Rebecca takes a place in the queue for me but then as the lane is opened the family and the group behind call me across and insist that I go to the front.

As we wait, again, they ask what I am doing, obviously curious about the kit bags and the clothing logos. The surrounding 20 people who hear the response all look amazed when I tell them. I still can't get used to reactions when people hear of the trip. Is it really that strange?

Check in is easy, even if I have to lug the bags to the special handling area, which is good really as they might even survive the trip. Security, now that's a different ball game. The queue is immense and slow moving and I can't help but think that it is a target in itself. I don't suppose I'm the only one to think that. I just hope that the bad guys don't think it through to planning stage. I don't have the answer; I just hope the authorities have.

Because of press & TV warnings about the security requiring travellers to have everything fully charged and capable of being turned on, all I have to do is get everything out for x-ray. Great, that is until I can't find the power pack and solar charger. A few seconds panic later, I find that they have dropped to the very bottom of the bag. Typical!

So, here I am in the classic "Hurry up and wait" at the airport, drinking tea and writing my journal.

The time passes well as I am not only busy writing and reading emails and text messages from friends but also receiving phone calls, notably one from the 2014-15 District Governor, Rod Walmsley, up extra early so that he could catch me before I set off. Time for one last brew then it's time to board for New York, my first stop.

Well that was boring. 7 ½ hours sat in a battery hen sized seat watching films and nodding off, followed by a grilling at immigration, everything out of the bag at security for an examination of the electrical equipment and then a schlep around Newark airport as the gate had changed. The original was 'C' – nice and airy with a choice of eating-places. The new one is 'A', bus station sized, hot, crowded and one eating place which has the slowest bar service in the world. How long does one beer and one glass of water take! 0/10 for service so far. I hope I can stay awake till the next flight leaves!

Then along comes another change, this time a delay of an hour which is promptly followed by changing back to the original, followed by getting on the plane 20 minutes after scheduled departure. THEN we are pushed back and get parked up for half an hour while a slot is sorted out for take-off. The Wright Brothers never had this problem.

I sleep rather fitfully on the flight, mostly due to the bickering kids behind me, the eldest of whom needs telling – very forcefully – that screaming "I hate you and I'm going to kill you" to her sister on an airplane in the USA is not a very clever idea.

As we approach Minneapolis I get my first clear view of the Mississippi and immediately start to recognise parts of the map detail. I can scarcely believe that Grace and I will be travelling along the very stretch of river I am looking down on in about 4 weeks. It looks serene and almost still, save for a few white plumes as it breaks over sandbars and rocks close to the shore. As we turn for the final approach I see what can only be described as a barge parade where what seems like a hundred or more of these river going giants are strapped together like some sort of square island. Even from this far up they look huge. There and then I formulate

EXPEDITION ORDER 2
KEEP AWAY FROM THE BARGES.
ALWAYS

The airport is nice and airy with no sense of rush, unlike New York, and I get the idea that even though servicing a big city it's more like the airport at Monroe, Louisiana. Then I get to the baggage hall which spews luggage onto the smallest carousel I've ever seen (they're bigger in Monroe!) with everyone crowded around them and, which is worrying, there are rows of unclaimed bags. There is a young man struggling to move them out of the way but he seems to spend more time adding to the pile rather than finding their owners. As with Newark, I have to go looking for the paddle bag but at least here it is handed to me personally not just left by a counter.

Reunited with both bags I make a quick call to Jim and make my way out to the pick-up area. WOW I thought that Budapest Railway Station was the only transport hub organised on Chaos Theory lines! There are three lanes of traffic with people running out to their lift whichever lane it is in, cars suddenly swerve to the kerb to collect passengers and their bags. But as always there are scenes of family reunions, lovers being reunited, businessmen being whisked away and, because this is America, Uniformed Military Personnel coming home on leave and being greeted by everyone.

After a while, I find Jim Lewis, or to be precise he finds me, and the greeting is just like, well how me and my mate Pete Brearley would greet each other, a quick handshake, throw the bags in the car and say "Good to see you" then set off. It's like we've know each other half a lifetime, not corresponded on email for a couple of months.

The drive is 4 hours – 4 HOURS! This guy has made an 8 hour round trip to pick up a complete stranger and offer hospitality and help because he can. Why can't the world do more of this instead of fighting and arguing about things that happened in the past the truth of which has probably been lost anyway? We chat, laugh and generally the journey goes well and I manage to stay awake. I meet Sharon, his wife, but as I have now been out of bed for 26 hours, I immediately crash into bed.

2/8/14
I wake up at 6:30, having had a bit of a lie in compared with the previous day. No doubt it will catch up later in the day. The day is spent unpacking my bags and checking everything, what a relief it all

got here ok. Then the real prize of the day, I get to unwrap my kayak.

At 16 foot in length she is long and sleek and bright yellow and very, very shiny! I have already decided to name her OLLI, which is short for "ONE LIFE LIVE IT", and I must say I think it suits her and me I suppose.

Around lunch time Jim and I go shopping for various bits and bobs and although Grand Rapids is a fairly big town he seems well known. In fact the lady at the hardware store says "Hi Jim, not seen you for a while, have you been ok?" which only serves to reinforce my view.

After the shopping, we load various kayaks, including OLLI onto the car and trailer and set off to meet up with Jim's friends, 'The Itasca Kayakers', for a trip out onto one of the nearby lakes. Well actually two lakes as we set off on 'Little Trout Lake' and then into 'Big Trout Lake'. Not that well named, as I didn't see any fish at all.

OLLI is very stable and quick and easy to paddle even unloaded and riding high in the water. I need to make some adjustments to the seat and foot rest positions but overall she is superb. A large motorboat powers past leaving waves that are about 2 foot high and coming sideways at me and OLLI just rode over them like they were little ripples. Several of the group are casting admiring glances and even ask about how she handles as we travel along. As if I know the difference!

We pull up on an island that has a deserted set of buildings that had belonged to some wealthy family from Chicago in the 1930's and were used as a summer home, and have a group picnic. As we are sitting around we are hailed by some passing canoeists who shout, "Is that your yellow boat right out there?" pointing to a lone boat floating steadily away from our island. PANIC! OLLI is one of two yellow boats in our group!!! We all run to the water's edge and with great relief find that its not mine but one of the other (more experienced) member's of the group.

As we paddle back I chat to Betsy who seems very interested in OLLI and asks for a quick spin in her. I oblige and this leads to a conversation about how much would she cost, I tell her about the list price and the deal I got and that ideally I would like to get as close to that as possible and I get an idea that she may just make a bid. Jim tells me later that he has let people know that both kayaks will be for sale on completion of our expedition.

I finally get to bed at 11:30 and go out like a light.

3/8/14
I sleep till 8:30, which is absolute BLISS the downside of which is that it leaves me with a head that feels to be full of cotton wool. Jim and Sharon head off to church and I tackle sorting and packing OLLI. First things first, I adjust the seat and foot rests, check out the various lines and elastic straps, apply the sponsors stickers and then set to and get all the gear into one place and start to pack it into the dry bags.

At first I thought that I just wouldn't have enough bags but as I started to pack stuff down and squeeze all the air out of the bags it starts to disappear. Even the MacBook, still in its neoprene sleeve, then a zip lock plastic bag goes into a dry bag that still has room for the Power Gorilla and a few electrical bits and pieces fits.

Once everything is all packed up I start to find that it is going in to the boat quite easy and soon have everything in. So from thinking that it won't fit to finding that I still have room for food is a great feeling. Mind you I have only packed an absolute minimum of personal gear. I have a spare set of clothes for paddling, a set of 'nice' clothes for times when not on the river, waterproofs and a wash kit. The rest consists of first aid kit, basic survival equipment, phones, cameras, Leatherman tool and other assorted bits and bobs that might be needed along the way.

Working on the principle that I have left something out I go back to my room to check that I have everything and look at the clothing, equipment I am not taking and the bags I carried everything over in. I obviously cannot take them with me so decide to mail everything to my friend Marguerite in Louisiana, which is where I will ultimately end up. Not just because the river ends in Louisiana but also because she has offered to coordinate our recovery from mile zero.

I turn my attention to a few other practical details like fastening the knife to my life jacket, making and fitting tether lines for the boats and securing the deck bag and tarpaulin before stopping for lunch when

Jim gets home. He is surprised that the gear all fitted in the boats as he admits that he has been concerned that space would be an issue when he first saw them.

After lunch I take everything out and check it again before repacking the boat and find that I have even more room now I have had another shuffle. Jim and I then have a session with the maps and my first big surprise arrives. He plans out that we can be back at Grand Rapids 8 days after we have set off, which is far faster than I thought. Not only that, but he has made his plans fit us being here, so we can have a bed/shower. What a true friend he is turning out to be.

Tonight they have invited friends over for dinner. One of the guests is Brian Smith, a former RAF Officer from York, who is a long time kayaking buddy of Jim's. I met him back in the UK while planning the trip, as he was the organiser of a successful attempt to set a speed record for traveling the Mississippi in the 1970's. A lot of what he told me still holds good today but, as with my other military friends, it is his encouragement and belief in our abilities that is most beneficial.

The other guests are all part of the team that did the journey with Jim a few years back and they are all most supportive of our challenge. It is no exaggeration that we laughed the night away. With stories about kayaking and several tall tales I feel really at home with the crowd. Not exactly an early night but great fun.

4/8/14
I managed to contact Pauline via FaceTime after breakfast and even got to see Thomas and Kenneth so a good start to my day.

Jim has an '87 Corvette Stingray that is pressed into use as we head out for the day. He wants to visit someone selling a rifle of a vintage he is looking for and to introduce me to his friend, Chuck from Spring Rapids Paddle Store at Mountain Iron. And another great guy. We ask if he has a set of portage wheels and he stops everything to seek out a lightweight pair and when he does he declares "no charge, just get 'em outta my barn!" I protest, he insists but eventually I win and pay the princely sum of $5 for them; apparently this is typical of his generosity, Minnesota Nice at work again.

We head home for lunch and then go shopping for a few essentials, a pay as you go USA network phone, some extra rope and karabiners and a few other little bits. Then its home again to have an early dinner. The original plan was to have an early night but, as usual, we get talking and it's soon getting late. All in all an easy day but productive nonetheless.

There is no doubt in my mind that Jim has been an invaluable resource and is truly passionate about helping people in his sport of choice. Tomorrow he is going to take me to Lake Itasca Hostel, then to Minneapolis to meet Grace. How many people do you know would do all this for a stranger?

5/8/14
We make the trip to the start of everything for Grace and I, Lake Itasca. On the way into the park we visit Coffee Pot Landing which is likely to be our first campsite and the first thing I see is a beaver dam right across the river. It looks like a pile of twigs but when looked at closely is quite a sturdy structure. I look forward to a closer look when we get back.

The main reason is to meet up with Sara Parthun at the Headwaters Hostel who initially was a great help with accommodation and offers of storage. She has recovered from her pushbike accident but explains that her correspondence dried up because she was unable to use the computer and do much for herself. It was at the same time that Jim stepped in so perhaps I do have a guardian angel. As a thank you for her initial offer I take her a policeman's helmet and a copy of '6 Dogs', only to find that she is married to an ex-cop and is utterly delighted with the gifts.

After a short visit we go to the visitor centre, the park is huge and has miles of hiking and biking trails as well catering for water sports, and I get a full set of the DNR maps. The staff are wonderful when I tell them of the trip, wonderful in the sense that they don't raise an eyebrow but do wish me luck.

First stop is the launch point, wide-open and beautiful vistas; the second stop the "actual" source. It just looks like a small stream that runs off the side of a lake. There is a small series of stepping-stones that have obviously been augmented over the years and a pool that then dramatically narrows.

The stepping-stones are about 10 yards wide, the pool perhaps slightly more and about 15 yards long and it then chokes to about 3 yards wide as it disappears off into the greenery rounding a corner and disappearing from view. There are people walking across and having the obligatory photo taken but not a single kayak to be seen.

Not much for something that is actually classed as the fourth longest river in the world, which is over a mile wide in places. Tall oaks from little acorns grow though. Oh, I forgot to mention the depth. The pool would be about mid-calf and as the channel narrows it actually gets shallower.

Then we spot the first problem. There is a bright orange plastic net strung across the channel with a big sign that reads "KEEP OUT – ESSENTIAL WORK IN PROGRESS".

I had been told that there was work being carried out but thought it was on paths and bridges and didn't really affect the river but as we look around it obviously does as we see it again in a couple of places as the river meanders through the prepared park area. This is something of a dilemma, we could duck under it and go on our way, and risk upsetting the authorities or we can review an alternate point in site and miss out about 2 miles.

Jim and I discuss this for quite some time. It is obvious that the closure is primarily for the paths but does affect the river and I am of the view that it is not worth upsetting the authorities for the sake of 2 miles. We are not buying local permits but will use our Canoe England membership as boat registration, this is covered according to the website but I just don't want to give some 'jobsworth' an opportunity to spoil things. I can just hear him saying "You aint goin nowhere till you get that permit and add $200 cash as a fine for ignoring the signs" and then still have to move put in points!

We are still discussing this when we arrive at the airport and the decision is made to use the alternate. Sad thing to greet Grace with I know, but it's as well she knows about it from the start.

Jim takes me on a route to Minneapolis that eventually tracks the river and it is more like a proper river now.

We stop at a town called Little Falls to look at a dam and see the portage area. I am quite surprised to see that it is well constructed and designed for easy access; obviously a lot of people travel this way. The rest of the day is spent travelling down to meet Grace via an outdoor shop to buy a portage cart. More expense. We pick Grace up and she looks exhausted, in fact she does sleep most of the way home. It is really good to see her and I am relieved that she got through everything ok.

Another late night and not a very restful one for me. I just want to get going.

6/8/14
Not a good start to my day after another disturbed night, I'm starting to feel anxious and doubt is creeping in. I almost find myself looking for a reason not to do this. I seem to have spent most of the night holding an internal argument. Commitment is the winner.

Grace looks refreshed but confesses that "head of cotton wool" feeling. We chat about the start and agree that it's not worth it, so the alternate it is. We also discuss other stuff that Jim has mentioned and that, we agree, is good information. We look at Grace's boat and I busy myself with a few bits and bobs and then start a map check.

Tom Drennan, a Rotarian from the St Louis area, is introduced to me by email, and he not only agrees to look after a set of maps but it turns out that he used to work on the river transport system, so has lots of contacts. Another great piece of luck.

It is while doing all this that I think of my friend Eric Daniels, who sadly died in 2006. He was a true friend and helped me overcome some personal problems back in the late '90's. He was also my mentor in Rotary and instrumental in getting involved in RYLA. An extremely adventurous person, he would accept any challenge and whilst I wasn't, and probably still aren't, in his league he awakened in me the sense of adventure I had but that had been pushed down somewhat.

All I could think was how much he would have loved to do this or at least help in the planning and decide that the book should be dedicated to him. As I write it at the front of my notes, I start to cry. Silly really, because Eric wouldn't want me to be sad. As I sit and think how he would have been so enthusiastic and supportive of the expedition my spirits lift and I realise things are going to be OK.

The rest of the morning goes OK until I have a FaceTime with Pauline and tell her about thinking about Eric and have another cry about it all. She tells me that he would be proud of what I am doing just like she is. I suppose thinking about a good friend no longer with us was just the trigger for a lot of emotions about the whole trip.

The afternoon is taken up with food and last minute equipment shopping and then the final packing/loading of the boats ready to set off in the morning. A relatively early night and that's it – tomorrow we start!

Week 1
Lake Itasca to Grand Rapids, Minnesota

7/8/14
I wake up at 4:30 for a bathroom call but manage to get some "sleep" till about 6:00 when I get up and sort a final few things to be packed away, and then have a somewhat subdued breakfast and away we go.

We ride to Itasca State Park in almost silence. Even Jim is not his usual jokey self. We have moments but not like the conversations we have had over the past few days. The original plan was for a 10:00 put in but that has slipped before we get there. We do the obligatory photo call and look wistfully at the barrier. Somehow now I am here again it seems like cheating to go 2 miles down the road.

We ask one of the rangers if we can put in by the bridge that is downstream from the 'official' start point but still within the park area. 'No problem' is the answer so we do, watched by 20 or 30 people. When they are told what we are doing it draws admiration and applause. One girl asks if she can come with us. As we are about to set off and pass under the bridge I give the youngsters in the group my little *"Don't let anyone tell you that you are too old, young, fat, thin, tall or short to do something. If you want to do it, do it'"* speech which results in a round of applause.

Then we are off! As we enter the water we find that it is so shallow that we start out walking and pulling the boats behind us, which we do for about the first 2 miles. And you thought we were kayaking!

We had gone about 25 yards when the river started a left turn that would take us out of sight from the bridge when suddenly we hear a man shout "You won't make it". We are too busy trying to keep our footing to turn and identify him, and anyway a response would only give him some sort of twisted pleasure.

Eventually it gets deep enough to use the boat as intended, but it's soon back to walking. We then enter an area that is covered with tall and dense reeds and bulrushes. We cannot paddle through this for much of the time and have to resort to pulling ourselves through by grabbing the reeds and hauling on them. We cannot see where we are going, as the reeds are far higher than our heads and the water has no discernable flow.

The only way to judge that we are going in the right direction is to see which way the reeds under the water surface are pointing. This is purgatory. We have been going less than an hour when I reach into the water to pull myself off a rock and feel the end of my right thumb get sliced through by a sharp rock. It bleeds like mad and I have to make do with my hankie as a bandage until I can get at the first aid kit.

We have more paddling and walking. The scenery changes with each challenge, beaver dams, fallen trees, reeds, bulrushes, portage paths round blocked areas and the last one is a narrow meandering corridor of wild rice that is soul destroying. Grace is tired and it's her turn to cry. But she battles through. We start to talk and as she lets out her feelings things improve. At one point she says "They say the worst bit is with the barges, I'm looking forward to them now!"

We keep going and it almost seems never-ending until suddenly we find the landing sign; or rather we see it being used as a clothes drier. The owners are a couple of what people would call hippy or new age travellers but to us they are fellow river rats. Critter & Yvonne they are called, dreadlocks, piercings, tattoos; the whole 9 yards but fantastically helpful and supportive people. They help us drag the kayaks up onto the landing and carry the gear up to the campsite.

I cook as Grace puts the tents up and just before we retire for the night I start talking to Critter about their plans. It turns out they hitch hiked from Chicago and then bought or scrounged equipment they would need for their trip all the way to the gulf. They are in a canoe and openly admit that they intend to take their time, probably arriving at the end of December. I also find out that 'Critter' is actually called John. I am sitting near the campfire they have lit when he asks if I want a marshmallow, which I can see cooking on sticks. He asks if this is something we do in the UK, I tell him that with all our rain the answer is 'No', when suddenly I see that they have caught fire and Critter says, "Darn it I always burn them". He then picks them out and promptly puts it in his mouth blowing out a gout of flame! It turns out he is a fire-eater and puts on a show for us. I never expected that.

8/8/14
We wake up about 7:30 and potter about for a bit before having breakfast. Not a bad night's sleep. At least I didn't wake up in a panic wondering where I was and what the hell I was doing! We break down camp and pack up and then have to portage – a kayaking word for carry everything out of camp about 600 yards to a different part in point because of a beaver dam. This just adds delay to our start time. Still, we are on the water for 10:08 and the flow is pretty good.

It is as we set off that we have our first encounter with wildlife. A Bald Eagle, the national symbol of the USA, is disturbed from its eyrie and swoops down towards us from the top of an immensely tall tree. As he is almost directly overhead he wheels and circles around us before heading off downstream. Its as if he is confirming the direction of travel for us.

What a magnificent bird he is. The spread of his wings gives him the appearance of a small airplane while his grace and poise as he rides the air currents indicates the mastery his species have of the skies. When I look at this animal I find it inconceivable that the US Government had to place it on a register of protected species as it had almost been hunted to extinction. By their own citizens. It is their National Symbol and they hunted it almost to the point of extinction. I make no apology for repeating that statement. Whilst the population has increased it is still not back to the levels of yesteryear and there is a movement to have it removed from the protected list so that it can be hunted again.

Our aim is Pine Point landing, more of that later. Although we are making quite good progress things get slowed down by fallen trees, beaver dams and thick vegetation that blocks our way. The vegetation is just mind numbing. We dub it the 'Green Hell' and whilst not unpleasant in terms of hard work it is just a green wall that makes seeing anything impossible. Our first example of the mental part of the challenge being harder than the physical side.

We aim to pitch camp by about 17:00. Things seem to go well until we can't find the campsite at Pine Point. The map shows that we will have to cover about 18 miles and the site will be there or thereabouts. The figures on the map are only approximate, as the river meanders will change with time, rainfall and vegetation breaking free. We see what we think is the campsite, but it is a couple of miles short on the GPS so we continue and keep a look out. Grace finds an inlet that has obvious kayak marks but I am not convinced that it is the right one, so we keep going another 2 miles.

Trouble is we don't find the site we are looking for and it's too far to the next for safety. So we head back upstream. I am so mad at myself at this and when we get back to the one Grace found it's not what Pine Point is described as. Still it's a camp, is on a point and has a pine on it. We drag the boats up onto the riverbank and make our way up to the flat area to pitch the tents. When I look out from this vantage point, all I can see is a sea of green, which the river meanders through. The actual river cannot be seen at all, the only visible bit is the 20-yard stretch at the bottom of the hill. How much longer can this last?

Grace admits that the scenery is getting her down as it just does not change and offers no view of anything. I can't say it's doing much for me either. Suddenly we hear voices down at the bottom of the hill and Critter and Yvonne come into view as they negotiate the narrow channel. They too are not sure where they are so decide to join us. I return the courtesy they showed us and help them with the boat and gear up to the campsite. Critter produces my water bottle, which I thought I had lost and a karabiner that I didn't miss. Never judge a book by its cover.

I am talking to them both about their journey and they agree that the wild rice and bulrushes are well named as 'Green Hell' and ask if they have looked at where we will be going tomorrow, when they say 'No" I point out to the green carpet that stretches into the distance without a single glimpse of water. Yvonne puts her tongue out and blows a raspberry. Summed it up well I thought.

We have a meal of dehydrated something and turn in for the night. Let's hope we sleep well and get a good start, as our aim is to get to the town of Bemidji, which will be the first since setting off. This calls for another 20 mile or so day. I hope we can do it.

9/8/14
Not a bad night's sleep. I got up just after 6:00 to find that there was a mist hanging in the valley that gave it an ethereal quality, even more

so when the green carpet seemed to be on fire where the river wound through it with the mist rising along its route. Right from the start this day promised to hold nothing but boredom and unchanging green walls of wild rice. We knew that this would happen but when seen from above it really brings home how long it will last. We get packed up and on the river and Critter comes down to wave us off. Probably not to meet us again I suppose. Shame really.

The river meanders through the high vegetation and then we come to the floating bogs. These often have large chunks that detach and float downstream. So much so that the map mentions it. They list it as 'not dangerous but a navigation hazard'. That's an understatement as the river can literally change shape as you watch it with, what seem like, small islands floating at an angle to the direction of travel.

We pass a campsite called iron Bridge and it is beautiful. A couple of tables with benches in a cleared area and a three-sided hut for shelter. The grass even looks to have been mowed. It would have been a much better spot than we had last night but it was just too far away. Suddenly the river widens and we start to pick up speed so much so that, after 4 hours, we have done nearly as much as we did in total on day one. This gets us excited as we are now on track.

We round a meander and see a bridge that carries a road over the river. Civilisation does exist after all it seems. There is a man standing on the bridge with a camera and he calls out to ask if he can take our picture. He also asks where we are from and then wishes us well as we pass under the bridge and out of view.

A little further on there is another bridge and we see a family on the bank and the kids are climbing onto the bridge to jump into the river; a scene that could be recorded anywhere in the world. As we approach, the dad jumps into the river to swim with the kids and speak to us. We say our 'Hellos' and he tells me that he is a 'Savage Indian' so I tell him 'I'm a wild Englishman'. We laugh and after a few minutes move on. I wonder if these will be the strangest meetings we have. Probably not.

Progress continues apace until suddenly we enter a narrow channel that is lined with hundreds of trees. The bad news is that they not only line the way, many have been uprooted by the floods in spring and are laid across the river. The authorities have tried to ensure a path has been maintained by cutting the root end off but because they fall from alternate sides they have cut them in a zigzag pattern. Not only that but the distance between trees is often so close that turning a 16 foot kayak round the bend takes a lot of 'toing and froing'. Then there are the trees that have fallen since the work was done and the only way to get past them is to pick a way through the fallen crown of the top of the tree. Either way, between getting stuck or just having to negotiate them, we slow down to a crawl.

This is just so frustrating. We were making great progress, had left the mind-numbing wild grass behind only to have it replaced by a 3-dimensional puzzle.

The area is about 2 miles and takes us 2 ½ hours in time to pass through. Then as suddenly as it starts, it stops and we are moving again. The channel widens and we are heading along at a good pace, unfortunately through wild rice again. I see the top of a boat in the distance and realise that we are near to Lake Irwin, which is the precursor to Lake Bemidji, the first of the big lakes.

As we run in it is well after 16:00 so we decide to see if we can find a hotel in Bemidji itself. As we get close to the first lake I hear music and then as we leave the rice lined channel and enter Lake Irwin……. There are people sitting round tables and chairs drinking wine, playing volleyball and Frisbee – in fact the most bizarre thing you can imagine.

A group wave to us so we paddle over for a quick chat. It turns out that the lake is not very deep, it is actually a collecting pool for a hydroelectric plant not a natural lake, and has sand bars dotted all around that people use as picnic spots. They are amazed at two Brits setting out to travel the length of the Mississippi and declare that they wouldn't even do the upper reaches we have just travelled through, and they live right alongside it.

We cross the lake with wind at our backs, go up the short channel into Lake Bemidji and there is a Hilton Hotel just ahead on the right. We beach the boats and I walk in to the reception area, still wearing wet trousers and a floatation jacket and they don't miss a beat. The man on the desk tells me that they are booked up but that there may be room at their sister hotel, the Doubletree, next door. He rings to see if he can get a room while I walk round and repeat my entrance. Again a very professional response and an affirmative answer to my room request. It turns out that it is truly the last one they had as a few moments after I had confirmed I would take it, I hear the man next to me being told that there are no rooms available.

The room costs $199 and has a superb view of the lake. We shower, change and head out for dinner. Our first stop is a Dairy Queen across the road for an ice cream cone. How bizarre the day has been, only 4 hours before we had been stuck in trees without any sign of people at all and now we are sat watching cars whizz past and people strolling about on the lake edge.

We have our first real food for three days and then retire for the night. A good night's rest awaits I hope.

10/8/14
And it was a good night's rest. I awake just after 6:00 to find Grace sat up in bed. I had managed to get breakfast included, I should hope so at that price. So we filled up on bacon, hash brown and eggs and water, lots of water. I actually had to say to the waitress "no ice, you can get more water in the glass" which elicited "oh yeah, never thought of that" from her.

We pack up all our gear and cart it all down to the boats, I didn't want to leave anything in them the night before, Grace said "perhaps we aren't trusting enough", she might be right but I'm not taking the risk.

At the Hilton Hotel, next door, we went to the kitchens and they filled up the water containers for us and off we go, across Lake Bemidji. It's classed as a small one but still it was about 3 miles from the bottom to the exit, which we couldn't find at first. We asked some blokes who were fishing and they pointed it out. I asked what sort of fish they were after and they said a name I didn't catch and then added, "They're carnivorous and like fingers" I hope the cut to my thumb doesn't drop blood in the water and attract them.

Once back on the river we start to make good time. The banks are very pretty with trees (standing up), green patches (not overgrown) and plenty of boat landings and houses. Nice big houses. But strangely the whole place is deserted; Grace suggests they are still in bed.

This part of the river takes us past the Northernmost point so we watch out. After a while we actually see people and pause to talk to them. "Did you see the sign for the Northernmost point back there", "No" we chorus, "It's on the side of a white house up on the left side". No wonder we missed it, we were looking for a brown one like for campsites! The lady asks for my email and promises to send me a picture. I hope she does (she did). We soon reach our first dam that we have to portage round. The operation goes smoothly and the wheels work.
There is a family setting up to drift down the river on inflatable kayaks and tyre inner tubes, they are all ages from Grandma down. They ask, and we tell them, all about the trip and they offer to help with launching the boats and advice on crossing the lakes that we will encounter later in the day. They are the first of many people we would come across who help us in some way and then take details so they can follow us on our website and Facebook.

As we approach the next lake, Lake Stump, the green-hedged hell starts again and we get a bit disheartened. Fortunately it soon passes but brings back some bad memories. Stump is followed by Lake Wolf and Lake Andrusia. We do not have to cross these fully, just a bit across the bottom.

Then comes Cass Lake, which is huge and to make matters worse it is now raining and we hear thunder. We have no option but to start to cross as our target campsite is on the other side, but it's getting worse. I lead us to an island that is marked as private property but we shelter there anyway. Fortunately the rain eases and we set out again having decided to head for Star Island, which has a campsite and is just over half way across the lake. Star Island is so big that it has a lake of its own, it is the only one in the world that has this feature or so the guidebooks say. We didn't go and look for it.

After a bit of searching we find the campsite. There is a catamaran on the 'beach' and tents have been put up. Trouble is it looks like the inhabitants have been abducted as there are boxes of food and equipment open and scattered about. We decide on a spot and start to set up when a chap wanders in and says 'Hi'. Turns out his whole family are camped on the other side and it's full so he and his brother are camping here. The other tents are for college kids that staff a camp on the other side and they don't always get used. His name is

Bart and after a chat takes a photo for us, sets up his brother's tent and wanders off into the woods.

We eat and make up our journals while watching the sunset. I actually feel quite good despite the weather, as this is the farthest we've come in a day so far. Tomorrow we have to face the rest of Cass Lake and then the big one, Lake Winnibigoshish.

11/8/14
When I woke at 6:00 I could hear the wind lashing waves on the shore and realised that today would not be easy. As soon as I looked out and saw foot-high waves my thoughts were confirmed. I was walking to the Forestry Service toilet, yes they do exist, they're a sort of toilet pedestal with seat and lid that led into an enormous pit. Quite comfortable and a great view, especially of anyone walking towards you. As I walk I come across Bart doing his early morning yoga; I just wonder how can people bend like that?

After a quick breakfast a fast pack up is on the cards so we make a start. Bart's brother (I never did catch his name) appears and we discuss the wind. Being local he suggests we head straight across the narrow part of the lake and then around the north side of the shoreline. This will give us some shelter and reduce the size of the waves. As we set off my boat is swamped before I can get my skirt on, so I have to bale out and start again.

Once we set off it is a slog. We are travelling into a 5mph wind and the waves are 2 feet high. The route we have to take is almost 5 miles and it takes us 2½ hours of non-stop effort and rolling about on the waves. This is not fun. Navigation is not easy either because we swing about so much that we cannot always get our bearings. I hail a fisherman and ask for directions and he points us towards the exit channel and we are glad to get off the lake.

We get to the other side and rest for a while. We have a phone signal so I ring home and get to speak to my grandson Thomas who blows me a kiss. He will be 2 tomorrow and I will miss his birthday. Never mind, when he is older we can share adventures, but perhaps not this grand. Or perhaps they will be, who knows?

The portage point at this side of the lake is a campground and has a 'host' who is located at the entrance and takes the camp fees and does odd jobs. We replenish the water carriers and use their toilets and we come across the host's brother who is wandering the grounds looking round. As we approach him he tells us he is looking for a knife that he has dropped and asks if we have seen it. When we ask what sort he tells us that it is a 3-foot long machete. So how do you just 'drop' a 3-foot long blade and miss it? Time to go I think.

The river that runs to the next lake is another green hell and a couple of times we get led into dead ends as the reeds have moved about on the floating bogs making the actual route hidden. I work out that we won't have enough daylight to cross Winnibigoshish and suggest we find a campsite. There is one on the western shore that is actually more set up for RV's than tents. We meet a family on one of the RV stands who show us where the water, toilets and ranger station is. There are a couple of Rangers there who are just packing up for the day and they tell us to pick a site that is not reserved and put our money in the box. One of them says "Camping near the boat dock isn't permitted" but as we walk away our new best friend tells us that they will be gone in half an hour and won't be back till 8 am tomorrow.

We decide to take the risk of camping near the boat dock, my excuse will be I misunderstood the accent if challenged, and we have a really nice spot. As we have our evening meal I'm sat looking across the lake and think it should be twinned with the North Sea, it's that big. I cannot see the other side. The map shows it to be just over 13 miles across and 22 miles top to bottom. Everyone who writes about the lake will say that the wind will be a factor and even the map, which shows the route of the Mississippi going directly across from West to East, carries a warning that non powered craft should not attempt this route. It is recommended to go via the northern or southern shores but this would be a journey of over 25 miles, which would take at least a full day. More if the wind is from the north.

12/8/14
Not a good night. I went to sleep worrying about the park rangers coming and moving us off the site, which to be fair was the picnic area, got woken up by some strange animal noises several times and then the worst of all my pee bottle had leaked and made things smelly and

wet. Great!

I get up and out of the tent at 5:45 am to find that it is calm and still on the lake and that the sunrise is an amazing sight. I wake Grace up and after she has seen how the lake looks we decide to go for the straight across option, setting off as soon as we can before the day heats up and the wind starts. We have breakfast and pack up in quick time. The added benefit is that we will be gone before the rangers arrive.

The lake is calm with barely a swell and no wind as we head due east. After about 6 miles the wind starts to pick up and the surface of the lake is pushed about causing a swell to build up, steady at first with just a 2 foot swell but then, as the wind speed rises, it increased to 4 foot. At one point all I could see of Grace was her head and shoulders.

Occasionally, the waves would be breakers and the decks would get washed, thank goodness for the spray skirts or we would have sunk! As the wind starts up and OLLI starts to roll about I am glad of the inherent stability but unfortunately the water containers I have stowed behind my seat move and one of them ends up digging into my back at kidney height. I can't do anything about it and have to put up with it but it causes me considerable pain. We battle on reaching the other side unseated and elated.

While we were crossing the lake our first milestone, 100 miles, was reached so we celebrated with a song. I don't think we will be an Internet sensation when we post it on YouTube but it will give someone a laugh.

On reaching the eastern side of the lake we found the dam and discovered that the portage was a steep climb both out of and back into the route. By chance a man and his two strapping sons were on hand to help and we were soon up across the road, I think when I asked them using the words "Could you help me and my young lady friend" it had the desired effect as the two lads swept down the hill to Grace in a flash. They were big lads and carried the boats at a pace that was impressive and hard to keep up with. They chatted with us for a while before wishing us well and continuing on their journey while we had lunch before setting off again.

When we get onto the river we find it has real flow. We set off at 4mph and at one point actually reach 6mph. In total we covered 30.7 miles for the day, actually further than we had planned so that when we stop at the campsite for the night we are now a day ahead of schedule and our meeting with Jim on Thursday. We discuss the route tomorrow and decide that if we aim for another 30 miles we will be almost in Grand Rapids on Wednesday night so that we can relax on Thursday morning till Jim picks us up.

The campsite is at Leech Lake River Access which is also a boat ramp. As we are walking about the path appears to be moving! A closer examination reveals that there are hundreds of tiny frogs in the grass that get disturbed by our footfall. Just after we had finished our evening meal we are approached by a car and out jumps a lady who introduces herself as Sandy Bromenschenkel who is one of the River Angels from the Facebook page and who has been in contact via that site. She tells us she is following us on our webpage and the Spot 3 as well. She truly is an angel, offering to take clothes for washing or visiting the shops for us but best of all she tells us we will be treated to blueberry pancakes when we get to her house which just happens to be the first one we will see as we emerge from the wild rice meander we are currently in!

We make a date with her and turn in for the night. As I climb into my sleeping bag I look up and see that a small frog has managed to climb up between the inner and outer of my tents and is sat directly above my head. Hope he keeps quiet.

13/8/14
Not a bad night despite the rustling of animals outside the tent and the rain starting to fall. The rustling causes me to get out of bed about an hour after getting in, I was still awake and reading so it was not a problem, and hang the food bag on a tree just in case it is something slightly larger than the little frogs. Not disturbed at all for the rest of the night.

Up at 6:30 and pack up. Just a bagel for breakfast as we have the promise of food with Sandy. That turns out to be 12 miles and 3 hours away through yet another 'green hell'. There is not much to say about these stretches of the route. They are mind numbing with a never changing scenery of an even colour and tone and we cannot even hold conversations as we are frequently in a line rather than alongside. We just have to put up with it.

The journey was worth every inch. We approach her house and see a sign welcoming us by name at the end of her boat dock and she is standing in the garden waving at us. Sandy leads us up to the house and true to her word there is a table groaning under the weight of blueberry pancakes, fruit, yoghurt and, best of all, a pot of freshly made coffee. She is an absolute gem and after a few minutes her mother joins us. We all chat and eat and forget all about the river until it is time for us to get moving again. An hour of civilisation, not much in the grand scheme of things but its 60 minutes that we will never forget. Just before we leave she mentions that the county fair is on and would we like to go as where we will camp tonight is not far away. To put distance on the river into perspective the three hours it took us to get to her house from our campsite took her 10 minutes by road. We say yes but only if it doesn't put her out. I get the feeling she welcomes the idea.

We set off and are soon back to being the last people on the planet. The site of the Minnesota Power Station dominates our skyline for a long time as we approach the town of Cohasset and the Pokegama dam, our goal for the day. There is a lake to cross, or would be if it were not chocked with weeds and wild rice that have created a veritable maze of meanders which adds a couple of miles to the journey. We reach the dam and find that it's a US Army Corps of Engineers organised site with showers and toilets. Heaven.

I ask a passing ranger about camping and he points to the side of the portage point and tells us to pitch there but doesn't mention payment which is odd because behind the toilet door is a sign that says "showers $4 for non-campers". By the time we are cleaned up and start erecting tents the staff have all gone home.

We set up so that the tents can dry out and I call Sandy and leave her a message. I text Jim as to where we are and he tells us he will contact us tomorrow. At the portage point is a notice about a free ride to the next dam provided by the Minnesota Power Company. This is because the dam we are at, and the next one, are big hydro electric generating stations and the water is very rough and fast flowing at both sides and the USACE don't recommend putting in near either of them.

We decide to arrange that in the morning so that we can get the timings right. It is obviously the norm and will save us from being at risk. I just hope everything goes to plan from here on in as on Friday we will be on our own for real – Jim will be behind us and the safety net will be gone.

As I am writing my journal at a picnic table I calculate that the GPS device uses batteries at a rate of about 20 hours of continuous use. I start to do some calculations on how many I will need and where we will be able to go shopping when a chipmunk hops onto the table to visit me. Cheeky little blighter and my first close encounter with the local wildlife.

Sandy, her husband Jeff and daughter Emma, came and picked us up to take us to the county fair which was in Grand Rapids, almost 10 minutes away. What a difference car travel makes! Quite a spectacle, its a cross between a fun fair and the Halifax Agricultural show with stock car racing on the side. We eat burgers and wander around looking at the rides, sideshows and animal stalls while chatting with them.

One thing we learn is that with an average annual snowfall of between 8 and 9 feet nearly all cars are 4-wheel drive, they carry chains and it is not unusual to end up in a ditch at some point. Perhaps the most amazing thing is that the local authorities only close schools when the temperature drops to minus 50 Fahrenheit and that is because they don't want the kids to stand in the cold waiting for the buses. It's OK at minus 49 though.

We are in bed for 22:00 so a bit of a late night. But as we have a steady day tomorrow it's not that bad.

I'm looking forward to a bit of a steady day as a chance to rest my back, which is still hurting from the pounding it took on Lake Winnibigoshish. The list of my injuries looks like something that usually occurs over a longer period of time; Slice out of right thumb – inside first hour; bruised legs from pulling kayak in river, loosening toe nail on right foot – banged on rock; bruised back from badly placed bottle and insect bites. Lots of insect bites.

Week 2
Grand Rapids to Little Falls, Minnesota

14/8/14
A steady start to the day, I was not awake till 7:30 and pottered about till Grace got up about 8:00. We got packed up and at 8:30 rang the portage assistance service. The man on the other end of the phone merely asked how many of us there were, and if we were ready to set off. When I said we were he told us that our lift would be there in about half an hour, and it was.

The guy driving the truck was right on time and asked what our plans were for the day. Day! We had plans for the next 52 days! Not that he was surprised at that as he has probably seen dozens of people like us and heard the same story every time.

When we told him that we intended to leave the kayaks at the put in point downstream of the power plant and then go shopping he was a little concerned. He said that he was not sure that it was a good idea as it might not be a safe place for our equipment. I told him that we had a friend in town that we were staying with tonight so he offered to take us direct there and then, if we needed it, would collect us again in the morning. Service indeed. We took him up on his offer and he took us straight to Jim's.

After unloading the Kayaks from the trailer and pitching the tents to dry them out, we went shopping. We had to walk to the shopping area, about a mile away but fortunately downhill, and found a little café where we had breakfast before visiting CUB Foods and Walmart to stock up on PowerAde and packet foods. We found a Starbucks and a Pizza Hut inside the CUB foods shop and had another snack.

As I was queuing for my coffee I got talking to 2 complete strangers, it turned out that they were in the area on a cycling holiday. I asked if they had a vehicle with them, they had, and if they could give us a lift to Jim's, which they did. See there are nice people in the world all you have to do is talk to them and be friendly. Called Andi and Ben, they run us right to the house, which is just as well as we couldn't have carried all the stuff we had bought. As we ride along we tell them of our challenge and forthcoming journey and give them one of our cards and they promise to follow our progress.

The afternoon is spent cleaning boats, gear and clothes. A bit of rest and a long chat with Pauline on FaceTime does me the world of good. Once everything is dried off, and my tent has been cleaned and freshened up, I pack up so that only the food and a few bits are left to do. Grace has been talking to home and finishes to come and join us as we have been called for dinner.

And when she comes out she is full of smiles and news. Andi and Ben have made a donation of $200 via the Just Giving link on our website which is just fantastic, what faith they must have in us.

I check the maps and tell Jim that I am aiming for a 35-mile day tomorrow as the river runs quite fast. He is of the opinion that we can do it, which is praise indeed.

Dinner was good; Brian and Judy Smith joined us so it was a laugh a minute. I asked to say grace, which surprised a few people, and used a version of the Celtic grace that I had adopted to suit the river.
Not a good night's sleep – or at least I don't think it was – perhaps the dreams are too vivid.

15/8/14
I awake early and feel nervous. After today the 'safety net' of Jim Lewis has gone as we start to head south. He takes us to the put in point just below the power dam and after hugs and handshakes we set off. The river is flowing quite fast, which is as well because it is 8:50 and we have a long way to go.

The scenery is stunning but never changes, the banks are lined with trees of a uniform height and type, and moves slowly by.

We saw the Bald Eagle again and its almost as though he is confirming our direction and being our guide and guardian as we travel through his bailiwick.

There is really nothing much to remember about today. After we left Grand Rapids there was nothing to see. Nothing but trees, trees, trees and more trees. No houses, no towns, no campgrounds, no passing boats. Nothing.

Today is the first day we didn't talk about anything. At all. All day. Probably because our minds were numbed at the realisation of what now faced us and the lack of anything that we have seen to discuss. Not much to say about the day really, other than we found the campsite, pitched, ate and rested.

A big day today with a record mileage, not difficult but boring! As for injuries: my back still hurts and Grace has a knot in her shoulder. We have a packet meal, make up the journals and head off to bed.

16/8/14
Not a bad night apart from some *very* vivid dreams. At one point I swear we were being buzzed by a helicopter, Grace said she didn't hear anything, so she either was very hard asleep or I was dreaming. I suppose it was my mind making up for the tedium of the day's journey.

Today was another long one with nothing much to see but the river and trees. It's starting to get more than monotonous. Plenty of people commented that we would see some breath-taking scenery and it is. Except when it is always the same for hour after hour. All we had was steady paddling with occasional rests and floating along with the river. The only high spot was a slight narrowing that made the flow speed up, as a result we got up to 6-8mph, for about 100 yards. It will be nice when that happens constantly. The enemy here is boredom and with boredom comes complacency. I need to watch that.

We stopped at Sandy Lake Recreation Area and had to pay for a campsite tonight, $24, which is OK, as we haven't paid at the other 2 that we should have. Hope they don't catch us at the airport and make us pay before leaving! This campsite is a bit bigger than the ones we have used on the riverside up to now; it's actually more geared up to host huge mobile homes, or RV's as they are called in the USA. Strangely though it doesn't have any shops or eating-places. Perhaps it's their idea of roughing it.

The campsite is located up a side channel that connects the Mississippi River to Big Sandy Lake, we never did find the smaller version on the map so it's back to the (un) imaginative names. The site is administered by the USACE and at the office I meet a woman who is straight out of a film about the army. Let me explain. She wears a uniform, complete with 'Smokey Bear' hat, highly polished boots and every phrase she uses starts with 'Sir, Yes Sir'. She talks to me about our trip and exclaims 'Sir, that is one hell of a trip, Sir' and 'Sir, if we can help at all Sir, the USACE is here to help, Sir'.

I invite her to call me Ken and she says 'Sir, I was raised by my Grandmother who was a full Colonel and my Grandfather who was a Regimental Sergeant Major, Sir, and they would turn in their graves if I did that Sir. It's how I was brought up Sir'. I didn't ask again.

Today was the first time we went south more than any other direction. As evidenced by the latitude and longitude readings. We plan a short day tomorrow to have a bit of rest and, hopefully, cooked food from a restaurant.

17/8/14
We had a late start today as we 'only' have 20 miles to do to get to the town of Palisade and the river flow is quite good. My back still aches like mad, and is now showing bruises from the pounding I took while crossing Lake Winnibigoshish. It feels OK when I am resting, not bad when paddling but hell when lifting or getting up from a sitting position. As we left the camp a fellow camper that we met on arrival gave us $20 as a donation, so used to offset the $24 camp fee, a nice gesture.

The weather is not the brightest we have had as we paddle along and then as we are about 5 miles from our target the rain starts! This makes us thoroughly miserable and is not much fun. Then it started to thunder. Great!

We soldier on and just keep going until we get to the Bridge before the campsite at Palisade at about 3 pm. I read the map a bit wrong and declare we are looking for a boat landing in 0.1 mile. After about 10 yards Grace shouts, "Could it be this boat ramp here?" It seems tourist type maps are to be sworn at not sworn by all over the world.

We set up camp in the rain, using the tarpaulin to provide some extra cover over the doors of our tents. It's a bit of a Fred Karno's to be fair but it works. After a while the rain slows down a bit and we walk into town, to find it is the smallest place on earth. The sign as we enter the town limits declares "Palisade Population 174". Typical small town, rural America. The real heart of the country.

It might have a small population but it has two fuel stations and two cafes and one of them is open! Serving real food, hot coffee and it has Wi-Fi. We are in heaven! I can do my banking, send an invoice that is due, email friends and update all the social media stuff that people are following us via. It's after 10 at night at home but I still manage a quick FaceTime with Pauline. Grace does her thing with the social media stuff and speaks with her family. When she shows me the Facebook page I am surprised at how many people are following us and sending messages of support.

The special on the menu is Chicken with mashed potatoes, vegetables and gravy followed by blueberry pie, does life get any better? The waitress is a gem and doesn't hurry us despite us consuming more Internet than food.

We sit in the warmth watching the rain fall steadily and end up having a conversation with a young couple that come in with their two small children. It turns out that he is a contractor and they have moved to the area from Alaska for work and are building their own house in the town. Or they would be if they could get the rain to stop long enough for them to get the concrete slab for the foundations poured. Until they get the house up they are living in a tent on the site. Rather them than me.

Just before the café shuts it stops raining so we walk back to the campsite and turn in for the night.

18/8/14
It has rained for most of the night and when we wake early it still is. As the weather forecast is for thunderstorms and heavy rains it's not such a good idea to be trying a 35 mile leg or waving paddles above our heads while the lightening spreads across the sky. Add to this that my back is now stiff and Graces' shoulder is knotted up, we look at the maps and decide on a short day, 8-10 miles to make some distance but without putting ourselves at risk from the weather or injury. It goes against the grain but getting miles is not as important as staying healthy and safe.

The café opens at 7 am so we head back up for breakfast and a warm up. A different waitress but the same great service. We are joined by what is best described as an 'old man's parliament' who obviously meet every day for breakfast and they talk to us when they hear our British accents. One thing they want to know is why we don't have guns and hunting like they do. When I tell them that no one has guns and they are all but illegal to own they set off on a monologue about their 'right to bear arms'.

I never did get chance to tell them that we have nothing to hunt. The rain stopped so we leave them to their discussion and walk back to the campsite again.

We are there for about an hour when it starts to warm up and becomes sunny so we pack up and set off at 11 am. As we only have about 10 miles to do we dawdle along and reach our target of Willow River campsite at 1 pm. It turns out to be mosquito hell, I get bitten instantly and in several places, so we decide to make for the town of Aitken, which is about another 21 miles downstream. This will make it a 31 mile day. It is what it is so we just get on with it, arriving about 5:30 pm.

Things go great till the last ½ hour when the heavens open and the rains come back with a vengeance. As we make it to the boat ramp for the town campsite I fall in the mud and am covered in black smelly gloop, so I lay down in the stream of rainwater that is running down the concrete ramp to wash it off. This causes great hilarity for both of us and Grace video records it for posting on YouTube.

We shelter in the campsite toilet till the rain almost stops and using the tarpaulin again as an extra shelter we set up the tents and go into town to find a restaurant. A nice little Italian place is about to close but we find that a Subway, which is the only other choice, is open till 10 pm so we settle down for hot food cooked by someone else.

The young man serving on, Tony, is very friendly and talks to us about our trip. I ask if they have coffee only to be told that they don't serve it after 11 am. He obviously takes pity on me and makes a pot full. Just for me.

I ask if they have Wi-Fi to be told "No, but they do next door and I know the password". It turns out that next door is the local Verizon shop (a telecoms dealer) so we log onto their bandwidth and manage to catch up on email and website again. As I chat with him he tells me that he has dropped out of college as it wasn't for him. I also watch him as we talk and see that he has a great work ethic, he always finds something to do rather than stand idle and constantly asks if he can help us in any way. He goes on to tell me that he is inspired by what we are doing and is determined to find his path in life. I'm sure he will.

I am sitting enjoying the warmth and a cup of coffee when a Deputy Sheriff and a Town Police Officer come in. I show them my Retired Police Officer ID and we start to chat. After a while another Deputy Sheriff and a State Trooper join us. After we have talked for a while the State Trooper shows us a video taken from inside his car a few days ago when he hit a deer at 130mph. The deer and the car were in bits. He was lucky, very lucky. Occupational hazard in these parts I suppose.

I beg a ride back to the campground and the Deputy Sheriff obliges. I take a photo of Grace being stuffed in the car, much to her delight. As we ride back to the campsite he tells us that all the Police Officers we met were the total night shift on duty in the County tonight. Even less than we have back in Halifax, but then it's not as heavily populated and they do have guns! He told us he would 'swing by a couple of times' to check on us during the night, just to make sure we would be OK.

Fed, watered and updated, we plan a big day tomorrow as the weather is supposed to improve, so it's time for rest.

19/8/14
Up at 6:00 to find that someone has parked up next to the toilet! Not that they shouldn't but it seems an odd place for that time in the morning. As I walk towards the car I notice that it has quite a lot of aerials on the roof so thought it might be a plain police car. But no it is an old man who has stopped on his way to somewhere to use the facilities. At least I hope he was doing that, bit early for anything else.

We pack up, have a bagel with chocolate spread for breakfast, that's a phrase that is going to get repeated a lot, and then set off. We know we have a long day and the weather forecast is not bad so we just get going. We settle into a rhythm but it is soon apparent that it will be another long boring day. And it is. No let up from trees, very little flow and nothing, absolutely nothing to see.

This is mind numbing. The scenery simply glides past without any change. The trees seem to be of uniform height and species, colour and spread. They come right down to the waters edge and screen our view of the rest of the world. There could be anything just beyond that fringe and we wouldn't have a clue.

There is a short rainsquall that passes without making much of a mark on us. Perhaps you can tell the limit of my boredom when the best bit of the day is managing to use the Porta Loo without getting out of the kayak, or spilling, not once but twice! Whoopee (that was a pun!).

The worst bit was getting complacent about things, something that I have already commented on earlier and something I knew I would have to guard against. Let me explain. I need to get at the sunscreen so I open my deck bag and get it out. I don't take enough care to keep the opening at a minimum or even to have the bottom lip pulled up and as a result my camera slides out of the bag and into the river. It floated for a few seconds, temptingly just out of reach as it goes behind me, Grace tries to get to it but again it is just out of her reach as it sinks. Not a chance of getting it back so I shrug, apply the sunscreen and keep paddling. No use crying over spilt milk, just use it as a lesson and don't do it again.

Grace got very down towards the end of the day and started to talk in a defeatist manner, like not being able to continue. I know it's being tired and bored of the same view that's talking not her, as she really is one of the most determined people I know.

I also know exactly how she feels as the same thoughts have crossed my mind but I know we will overcome it.

How can such chocolate box beautiful scenery be so boring. It was a big day today in terms of miles covered and mental barriers overcome.

We had selected a campsite some 40 miles down the river called Half Moon. When we got to the area we could see the sign showing where it was but could not get to it because of reeds and wild rice, the green hell again. Fortunately there was a boat ramp on the opposite bank that had enough land for us to pitch the tents on. Right next to a sign that declared 'No Camping'. We are becoming regular little outlaws!

20/8/14
We had been warned about the dangers of wild camping and how animals are attracted to the smells emanating from the tents and the food stores. We had been told about how they will literally tear everything apart to get at the smallest morsel. We had been told that we needed to take precautions to ensure that our food store was far enough away from us so that we would be safe from attack.

What we hadn't been told was how we could defend against those sneaky little animals that don't tear everything apart in a frenzy, but creep into the store bags and silently munch away on our bread store! Yes, the chipmunk was back. And the littler blighter had steadily eaten a line down the stack of bagels. Breakfast was not the biggest meal we had had but it probably was his!

The rest of the day was one of contrasts. At the start I proposed to Grace that what we needed to do was talk more to each other to stem off the boredom. The subject does not matter; we need to do something to occupy our minds as well as our bodies. So we did and it helped. We played the alphabet game, and decided that anything that starts with the letter X is a place, song, food, person or animal that is from China.

Mind you the area was more of a flood plain than a river so we had absolutely NIL flow to help us. I had suggested that we make the town of Brainerd. At the top end of the town there is a park, which is shown as having a boat ramp so there is probably other facilities as well, we decide to chain the boats up and find either a hotel or see if the campsite has room for us. There is also the opportunity to find hot cooked food if the other two towns have been anything to go by. It should be, they were small country towns and this is a big place.

With that decided we set off on this wide expanse of flood plain/lake/river and slog our way down to our target. On arrival we meet up with a couple of blokes who work for the Minnesota DNR and chat with them for a while. We ask about camping and they tell us that the site has showers and toilets and is really well looked after.

First disappointment of the day – the 'campsite' is NOT for tents! What a let-down. It's only for RVs and the 'Camp Host' (a volunteer that stays there all season long for free in return for collecting fees and generally looking after the place) tells us that it is a city regulation and "If you do camp there the Police will take your tent down and move you on", Welcome to Brainerd hospitality capital of Minnesota.

Grace takes it bad and so do I, what a let down and nothing like we have experienced up to now. My initial thought is to try and see if any of the houses that fringe the lake will let us camp on their land but the only one I find with someone to ask turns out to be closed up for the summer and he is just looking after the garden for the owner.

I look at the map and suggest trying the other end of town where there is the chance of making it to the State Park and finding a campsite there. After about 3 miles there is a dam to portage around and it is very rough ground. The dam is undergoing construction work and the area is strewn with rubble and potholes. It is also a steep out and a steep back in so we know it won't be easy. Not long after we set off my portage wheels/cart breaks. Her boat comes off the wheels and after a lot of struggling, grunting and swearing we make it to the waters edge and I am thoroughly fed up. Grace rips into me and tells me to stop being defeatist and cheers me up. Seems her skills as a coach have come to the fore! Mind you she does describe what she does as less of technical skills improvement and more like psychological warfare. Sums this trip up nicely.

Back on the river and a couple of miles downstream we find a local park that has been provided by The Kiwanis group in the town. Kiwanis are similar to Rotary except that they do not act internationally, only locally. It is a super little place with swings and sandpits for the young kids, benches with views of the river and a set of bike and walking trails.

I speak to a couple of young mums who are having a picnic with their kids in the playground and ask how far away the town is, they tell me that town is quite a hike away. Cheekily I ask if they can give me a ride to a shop for sandwiches and they agree. They pack everything up into their two cars and I ride with one of them while the other follows us, not that they seemed worried about me but I suppose it's always best to be safe. At the sandwich shop I discover that they have Wi-Fi so have a quick FaceTime with Pauline while sandwiches are made. I also get chance to catch up on some emails and find that the world is still there. The trip has cheered me up; I suppose its just being off the river that was the main part of that although contact with home was nice.

I check the maps and it shows that the campsite is about 8 miles away at Crow Wing State Park. It is shown as being quite big so it is probably well organised with showers and toilet facilities. We set off and are so busy chatting we almost miss the signs indicating the boat ramp to the State Park. We pull up and scope out the area but find that the camp is one for motorised trailers so, no showers. Oh well, the view we have from where we decide to pitch the tents is beautiful and the sun will shine on us at both ends of our stay.

There was a man fishing from the bank near to the ramp and as we are unloading the boats he comes over to talk to us. He is called Scott and is a local who comes down to try and catch a few fish at the end of every day as an 'unwinder', which I suppose it's healthier than going to a local bar. When we tell him what we are doing he is so full of praise it's almost embarrassing. It turns out he was in the US Navy as a submariner for 27 years and has travelled the globe without seeing much of it. He sits and chats with us for awhile, asking about us as individuals, the challenge and the charity, all the while saying how inspirational he thinks we are and what an adventure we are undertaking. After a while he wanders off to do battle with the local aquatic life again.

We set up camp and find that there is not a soul in sight. No train noises, no town noises. Nothing. I decide to have a wash in the river using my 'biodegradable camp soap'. Boy the water was cold, much to Grace's amusement as I gasp when submerging my grimy frame in the river. It may not be the most comfortable 'bathroom' I have ever used but it's nice to be clean.

Scott comes to say farewell and I give him a card with our website details. After yet more praise he goes to his car and then drives down the car park and pulls up by the tents. He asks if there is anything we need and offers to take us shopping. All we need is bagels for breakfast so he runs me to the petrol station convenience store, which is about 10 minutes away. Three minutes out of the car park we hit a 4-lane highway that is busy. Well busy for this part of the world. Civilisation on our doorstep and we couldn't see it.

Scott is such a nice man and constantly praises us, to the point where we do find it embarrassing. We say our goodbyes and thank you's and he sets off for home. Only to turn round again and come back to ask how much we will be charged for camping in the park. We tell him not to worry as we time our arrival after the staff have gone home and leave before they start again (with apologies to the Minnesota DNR) to which he tells us that he will seek out the staff and pay whatever fee they require as a contribution to our fund raising. What a nice guy. He's another one that has so much faith in us and our expedition. I do hope we don't let him down.

We plan another big mileage day tomorrow and have cause for celebration as we have done 354.9 miles as of today and we now have less than 2000 to go!

21/8/14
About 04:00 a huge thunderstorm broke out, lightning that was so intense it turned the night into day. A spectacular show accompanied by lashing rain. I discovered that the cover over the porch ventilation flap was off on the outside of the tent and water was pouring in. Great. I manage to stop any ingress of water to the living area but in the morning the porch, and the bags out there, are wet through.

About 06:00 I hear Grace stir. I get up and check the boats (damn, still there!) as the river will have risen. When I get back into my tent I suggest we have a lie in to ride the storm out as it is still quite intense but seems to be slacking. She agrees. I text home so that Pauline can post that we are not moving because of the storm and Grace updates Facebook. Her mobile phone service is a company called '3' and, unlike me, she can use her UK allowance to access calls, text and Internet in the USA at no extra cost. O2 charge me a fortune so I will definitely be looking into them. Communications is a vital part of any expedition and without sponsorship also an expensive one.

The rain stops and we stir about 7:30 and decide to try and make a campground about 12 miles down the river as the forecast is not good, again using the principle that a short day is not a wasted day. The weather turns out to be OK so we keep going. At one point the river flow is so good we hit 7.6mph for quite a way. Wow we are nearly making a wake!

We reach the town of Little Falls about 16:00, not bad as we only set off at 10:15. There is a portage round a power dam to negotiate and as usual there is construction work going on. I suppose with the severe winters in these parts they take every opportunity they can to upgrade and repair during summer.

One of the workers tells us about a café just at the other side of the bridge and offers to keep an eye on our boats and equipment, as he will be on site for about another hour doing paperwork.

"Donnas Big Joe Diner" is not far and offers homemade, home cooked food. As we enter we find it is a small 'mom and pop' place and that 'mom' is asleep at one of the tables! We ring the doorbell and cough and she wakes up full of apologies.

The coffee pot comes out first followed by hand made burgers with a mountain of chips (fries). We get chatting to Donna and tell her what we are doing and she offers to let us sleep on her floor that night. I think she is joking but don't say so. After settling the bill I leave grace finishing her meal and go back to the boats to make sure everything is OK. It was and the guy from the construction site had actually finished his work and was just waiting for us to come back.

It turns out, when I had gone to look at the kayaks, Donna had made the offer to Grace again. She offered to get someone with a truck to bring the boats to her yard, let us have a key to lock up with if we wanted to go into town after she had gone home, even tell the local Police about us to make sure the gear would be OK. Between her and the building guy it's another fantastic example of Minnesota Nice.

Trouble was Grace didn't tell me until we had started to struggle with the portage or I would have taken her up on it. It takes almost an hour to negotiate the portage but only 45 minutes to reach the campsite.

Our destination was the Charles Lindbergh State Park and access to the campsite was up a small tributary river. We found a camping area that had individual pitches marked out; so we set up on one of them. A quick check round showed that the facilities were over 2 miles away and that payment was required at an office nearly three miles away. I need to apologise to the Minnesota DNR again, it was getting dark and I didn't want to get lost on the miles of hiking trails. Well that's my excuse. With no need to cook we chatted for a while and then turned in for the night. Not the best or softest piece of ground, but home for the night.

Week 3
Little Falls to Lake City, Minnesota

22/8/14
Slept well last night and as an added bonus it didn't rain so the tents were fairly dry when we put them away, that really does make things much more pleasant as handling wet nylon is not a pleasant experience. We had got up about 6:30 and on the water for 8:35, not the quickest start to the day but that's how it goes.

We negotiated the side channel away from Charles Lindbergh State Park back to the main Mississippi River and found that the flow was zero. Again! We were straight into another flood defence area controlled by a dam. It was only 10 miles to Blanchard dam itself but it was hard work every inch of the way; not exactly the best way to start the day but as we had started to say on many occasions "It is what it is" and had to put up with it.

Jim Lewis, and everyone else I had spoken to or read accounts of, described the portage at Blanchard dam as being the worst on the river. Now that is a claim to live up to. On arrival at the dam I found that the claim was completely justified. The portage was horrible, just as described. First there was the mud and reeds to negotiate just to get off the water, then came the steep bank to climb to get to the first level part. This was followed by a climb up, across and down an old railway embankment, then up across and down a second one, then a climb up into a wooded area, then a trek along a winding path before a drop down a steep bank to the river again. A distance of about 1½ miles in total and all of it purgatory.

When I came through on August 3rd with Jim he had shown me a local canoe outfitters called 'Shirley Mae's' and told me to make a note of the telephone number as John, the owner, would help out with transport around this area if he was available. As part of his business he rents canoes to individuals and groups and as a result has a small bus and trailer that he makes available to help Mississippi Paddlers. Another of the Angels. All I had to do was call as I approached the dam and if he was around he would come and help. I did, and much to my dismay had only got his answer machine. I left a message and hoped he would be around.

Working on the principle that he would not be around, if not for bad luck I wouldn't have any at all, as they say, I went and scouted the route, hence the description above.

As I neared the river I saw a man with a fishing rod in his hand walking towards me and said "If I meet a man fishing then the river must be here somewhere then", "Yes" he replies "Just up ahead, a couple of blocks" and we both continue on our respective journeys. As I walk on I wonder how far a 'block' is in the woods.

I had barely gone another 25 yards when I hear him running back along the trail towards me (my first thought was 'OMG mad axe murderer! Where do I run to?') and he calls out "With an English accent like that can you answer a question?" I said "Yes, Halifax, in the North of England" "No, not that question" he replies, "Do you know Jim Lewis?" Slightly taken aback I say, "Yes I do and what a great guy he is".

The man introduces himself as Bob White and then tells me how he met Jim about a month ago while he was on a trip taking photographs in the Grand Rapids area and that he had told him about me and Grace, and how he was helping us with the start of our expedition. What a Small world.

We start to walk back to where the boats are and he offers to help with the portage if we can't get a lift. We chat as we walk and when I arrive Grace tells me the phone had been ringing but she couldn't get to it. I call the number back and it's John from Shirley Mae's. The good news is that he has time to help us and he offers to meet us in 30 minutes. He even tells us that if we go back up the river by about half a mile there is a boat ramp we can use, it is at an angle as you approach from upstream and not easy to see, where he will meet us.

On the dot he turns up with his trailer and bus, and a strapping teenage nephew to help lift stuff. Does today get any better? Well yes it does! As well as offering help with the portage he offers to run us to the shops, so that we can resupply.

Just before we leave Bob turns up at the boat ramp and gives me his business card. He tells us that if he worked it out right we will be near where he lives, just outside Minneapolis, at a time when he will not be working and if this is so, we would be welcome to have a day off and stay with him and his wife. A chance of a bed and a shower and shopping again is too good to turn down so we promise to get in touch and see if we can make it happen.

John takes us to a Walmart that is just up the road, probably the one that Scott had offered the night before, and we are able to stock up on food for when we are camping, I can buy another 2 hats and a camera to replace the ones I have lost AND there is a Subway store in the supermarket so we get a foot long Philly Cheese steak each for lunch! On the way back he tells us that we need to be careful further down the river, as he has heard of people accepting help only to find that they get abandoned at Walmart and have their equipment stolen. It seems the country folk are full of cautionary tales about the city people. I wonder what they say in return?

John takes us back to the boats, we load up and he puts us in at a portage about 4 miles down the river, which is easier than the portage round the dam. A lot easier. I give him $10 for fuel and he is delighted. Perhaps I should have given more but when I offered he said, "You don't have to but I won't refuse", so I just picked out the first note I got to. He didn't look at it, just shoved it in his pocket. Handshakes and good wishes and he is gone. A really nice guy and a true enthusiast about river travel he is just so glad to help and share part of our adventure.

We cover another 12 miles and make it to Stearns County Park, which is shown as having a boat ramp, water and picnic facilities, but not camping. This is shown as being about 500 yards further on without access, water or facilities. We decide to check out the first stop and see if we can find a pitch to make use of the facilities. Only to find a big notice declaring 'No Camping'. And an officer from the Wildlife, Fisheries and Game Police on the ramp. Who is armed to the teeth. But then most of the people he will be dealing with are carrying firearms as well so it makes sense.

He tells us that the park is in the domain of the Local Police who have been known to move campers on as it helps deter the night time activities of the local teenagers. We move a little further down and pitch on the designated site. There is a difference between an out of the way boat ramp or a sneak in and out of the edge of a State Park and actually courting confrontation. The site has a great view of the river and we settle in for the night.

We actually covered 23 river miles today but it seemed like a lot of hard work for not a lot of distance covered. Grace comments that we actually did more than we think when we consider that the river was still at the start of the day, we had the hold up scouting out the portage and got some shopping done courtesy of John.

We have now covered over 400 miles on the river which means that for the first time we are below the 2000 mile left to cover point. Not that much if you say it quickly. And we still haven't got out of Minnesota.

23/8/14
The only problem with the site we had chosen for the night was the train marshalling yard at the other side of the river. The clanging of carriages is one thing but why on earth do they need to sound those horns long and loud all night? And it's not just a simple 'nee-haw' that trains in the UK emit, it's a full bodied "Whooo-Hoo" that is repeated a minimum of 4 times at whatever hazard, real or imagined, the train driver is encountering. That said it is amazing what you can put up with when you are tired enough.

I awake and feel really good in the circumstances, the circumstances being that the trains have got more in number, more in the intensity of their "Whooo-Hoo ing" and have been joined by a steady stream of cars all blowing their horns at each other as they start the early morning rush hour. We have obviously left the countryside for now.

It is dry and overcast but warm with little wind and the weather forecast for the rest of the day is not bad. I check the map and see that we have 2 portages today, the first at the town of Sartell the next about 25 miles down river just below St Cloud.

Between these is the Town of Sauk Rapids, where there are a set of rapids on the river. The maps carry a warning that travellers should consider portaging or at least stopping and viewing them prior to passing through. I confess to Grace that I am a little worried by them but she is looking forward to the challenge and tells me to just go for it and enjoy. We will see.

We get going but soon hit the slack water caused by the dams. Again. The ones here are for flood control and hydroelectric power generation and as a result they stifle flow even more. The first one we come to is in Sartell and is a redundant power generation station that is being demolished.

The portage out is onto a road and is a nice easy lift. The map indicates that the put in is some 300 yards down stream so it looks like it might be an easy route. NO! I walk along the road and find that for nearly a half a mile the banks have been changed because of the demolition work and that the 'in' has gone.

We have to drag the boats, fully loaded with water; food and equipment, along the roadside for almost a mile and still do not find an official site. This is real hard work and is torture for me with my bad leg. Its not much better for Grace either. We have to stop frequently and I confess to using a lot of colourful language, mostly blue, as a means of venting my anger at my own inability to do something as simple as go round a blockage in a river.

We pass a small office building which is next door to some houses that overlook the river and I can see that at the bottom of their gardens is a spot that will possibly allow us get back on the water, so I call a halt and go and check it out. Its perfect and what is more there is no one in either the offices or the house so we can slide the kayaks down the grass.

After a bit of heaving we get to the waters edge and have a rest and a snack before setting off. Overall the portage took us almost 2 hours and a lot of effort and is not something I want to do again in a rush.

We arrive at Sauk Rapids, another example of the inventive naming of places in America! Mind you when you look at the maps and the history of the original immigrants the first European settlers obviously chose names that were familiar to them or, if they could pronounce it, used names given by the indigenous population. Either that or they chose names from landmarks unaware of the fact that another group of settlers were only 100 miles away using the same familiar names or landmark descriptions. They still manage to be a bit unoriginal though.

As we approach the town, which we can't see but is obviously there as there is a road bridge we have to pass under, the flow starts to speed up and the water gets quite choppy. Nothing we can't handle though. It's remarkable how stable the boats are as we swing about through the peaks and troughs of the waves, some of which are starting to have white caps on them. Grace is about 25 yards in front of me and I see her move to the left. I see the top of a wave that looks quite high to her right and realise that she has manoeuvred to avoid it and start to follow her line. I find that I can't make enough of a turn to avoid the deep trough that I can now see as the river flows over a stone or sand bank that is acting like a weir, it is now right in my path and I can't avoid it. The only thing to do is to line up to go straight at it and ride over it putting my trust in the stability of the boat. Suddenly the back of the boat swings left and in very short order I am pulled sideways and am swept into the trough, I stay upright for that and roll over the cresting wave and stay upright for that as well. So far so good! Then the backside of the wave has one last push at the side of the boat and I capsize.

The training we did in the pool in Devon kicks in. Feel for the sides of the cockpit with both hands, hold on with the left and run the right hand round to the front of the spray skirt, grasp the release tongue and pull. A push with the left hand and let gravity and water flow take over. In a matter of seconds I am out of the boat, which has righted itself, and clip my safety line onto one of the deck lines. It all came quite natural and without any real conscious thought. I hear Grace shouting and locate her as she paddles back upstream towards me, clipping her safety line onto the other side of the boat.

The water is still quite choppy, but not as much as above the weir. The water is too deep for me to stand up so we make for the shore with her pulling and me swimming. We are near enough not to have to try the techniques of emptying the boat and climbing in, thank goodness, as that is hard work. We start to laugh at the situation, probably more from nervous tension release than anything else. OLLI is about ¾ full of water but still floats and has all the deck storage attached. A big 'Thank You' to Pete Richardson for his training and advice. Lets hope we don't need to use it again.

At the bank I start to bale out, as I am a bit concerned about tilting the boat and causing damage to the hull. I use my portable toilet to get most of it out before resorting to the sponge to get the rest out. When I check the equipment I discover that not one piece of kit has been lost. As Grace says "not even a hat". Which is a dig at the fact that I had managed to lose two so far.

After baling out and tidying up we are off again. We are still laughing about what would have been a serious situation but one which we knew might happen and had trained for. We also knew that the area might present that sort of difficulty so had the right mental attitude as we approached. Yes, I was apprehensive; yes, I knew it might happen; yes, I had faith in my training and personal ability. Its all part of setting oneself up for whatever challenge will present itself.

The next challenge duly presented itself in another 10 miles, another portage. Not just as far as the last one but just as hard in its own way. Getting off the river, no problem, just pull the boats up a short ramp at the designated point. Then pull the kayaks ¾ mile along a gravel path, up a short, but steep slope, through a car park and then along a grassed area to the top of the put in point. I say 'top' because the river is now, of course, much lower than the take out point. There are 75 steps down to the river bank. And they have 2 bends in them. Who the hell designs these things? Obviously not someone who has to use them.

The portage is actually situated in a very nice little park with some beautiful gardens. There are two wedding parties using some of them as backdrops for their photos (at this point I realise that it is a Saturday, not that it matters to us) and lots of families strolling about in the sunshine. There is also the chance to fill up on fresh water; the only bad news is that we have to carry it to the put in point, which makes the kayaks even heavier.

At the out point we were helped by a chap who introduced himself as Patrick. Grace had gone to scout out the portage route so I stood and chatted to him for a while. It turned out he was from Tennessee and delivered cars around the US. Literally all round the US as he tells me of some of the places he has been to, which includes quite a way into Canada. He sort of offers me a job doing it as well but that wouldn't be an option as I am not a citizen, which is a shame really as it would be a good way to see parts of the country that have changing scenery. Unlike the bits we have been in up to now!

As we cross the car park a chap pulls alongside us in his car, rolls the window down and says, "Are you portaging round the dam?" He looks a little miffed when I ask him "Do you have a degree in stating the bloody obvious?"

At the put in point we chat to a family who are just looking at the river and unfortunately turned up just too late to help. Unfortunate for us that is. I continue to be amazed at the reactions we get when we tell people what we are doing and where we are from. I had thought that people who live by the river would be a bit more used to people like us passing through.

We do another 3 miles before calling it a day at a campsite that is provided by the Minnesota DNR called Putnam's Pasture. A nice little site, which has a 'beach' area where we can pull the boats up while the tent area is quite high above the water and is flat. It has the usual picnic table and toilet, which is just a pit latrine but at least it has a seat and is away from the camp area. Quite laughable is the plastic coffee container that has a toilet roll in it, not the first we have seen but still amusing. The only downside is that people who have visited before have thrown plastic bottles and aluminium beer cans into it, which will impede the natural decomposition of the waste. Idiots.

Once the tents are pitched and we have eaten we look at the videos of the capsize. They show that the situation I was in was dramatic but not quite as serious as might be imagined. Or is that I don't think it's dramatic because it went OK? It could have been a lot worse. The water flow could have kept me upside down or trapped in the swirl, I could have hit my head on rocks and been injured or knocked unconscious; Grace could have been capsized as well and not been able to help me. Any one of thousands of permutations could have occurred but they didn't and it's all part of the journey.

At the end of the day we have worked hard, had a mishap and laughed a lot but overall – it's been a good day.

24/8/14
Well apart from the insect chorus that went on all night and the flash of lightning a couple of times, it was a quiet night. It is a bit of a slow start to the day for me mentally and I feel down for some reason. I

turn the phone on and find that I have a signal so ring home, only to get no answer, which doesn't help. Pauline is actually in Sweden so I shouldn't have been surprised that she would be out and about with our friends George and Monica. Probably Monica and shopping if I know those two! That and her probably not having her phone switched on.

Some text messages come through from friends wishing me well and I reply to them and even get a 'conversation' going with one of them. Pauline rings back a few minutes later and hearing her voice cheers me up.

Sharon Cyr, who works for Rotary International as the Programmes Manager in the Head Office, is also visiting George and Monica as well so I get to chat with her. She offers to come and meet us when we get down towards the bottom of Illinois in a place called Rock Island. This is a place where Guy Hoagland had shown as a campsite so I agree to contact her when we get closer and arrange a picnic. From feeling down when I got up I had turned things round to what was a good start to the day.

How wrong could I be?

As we got going the flow was good, but with a headwind which makes it hard work to make progress. Despite this we do make pretty good progress. Grace starts to pull away from me as my concentration goes, my mood changes and I start to retreat into a slightly darker place. Bad thoughts, doubts, emotions and thinking about quitting the expedition being uppermost. I notice that she has pulled quite a distance away from me so I set myself the task of catching Grace and getting her to talk to me.

Once I have I caught up, I tell her how I feel and we start to talk, playing the alphabet game. For anyone that doesn't know this one it is a good way of distracting, but working, the mind. And it soon has the desired effect, my spirits lift and we are flying. It seems that the mental challenge of this expedition is the hardest part of all and is making me call on reserves I didn't know I had. That and getting help from a friend.

We cover 25 miles, to the town of Monticello, in 4 ½ hours into the teeth of a very strong headwind, which is a fantastic achievement and one I didn't think would be possible when we set off that morning. We are aiming for a public park that is alongside the river and is shown as having a boat ramp. As we get near we see a big boat ramp that gives access to a campsite for RV's, or towns on wheels as we now think of them, and wonder if that is it. Deciding against it we continue a little further and find the park about a mile further on. I walk up the bank and find that we are just on the edge of quite a big town so I set off in search of food while Grace looks after the kayaks.

A car full of teenagers directs me to where I can find the shops and I find Domino's Pizza. I place an order that would feed a family and cheekily ask if they can deliver it, and me, back to the boats. Without missing a beat the guy behind the counter says 'Yes Sir'. It turns out he is just setting out on another delivery so was going out anyway. Again the staff in the shop are amazed at what we are doing. Will I ever get used to this reaction?

Back at the landing Grace sees me pull up in a car with the 'Domino's Pizza' sign on the roof and starts to laugh. She reminds me that someone had said 'Don't forget Domino's deliver but I bet you can't get them to get to you'. We should have had money on that.

Sat in the sunshine, eating tasty, hot food life is suddenly great. Funny how the mind works and how something simple like talking about nothing in particular and then having good food can affect it. We decide to make at least another 10 miles to a campsite at Otsego Country Park so may have some sort of facilities.

We get to the park and find that there is a small beach and then a little climb up a small bank. The park is a wide open and well maintained area with roads for walkers and cyclists, benches at frequent intervals and in the distance we can see a large family group making use of the covered picnic area. This looks like another one that will attract attention from the Local Police if we just pitch on the edge so I go and check upstream while Grace checks downstream. I find a couple of big bushes that we may be able to get behind, but this would leave us with the problem of the boats as we cannot lift them up the bank and the local yobbery would be able to see how far they can push them into the river without us knowing.

Grace returns with news that she has found a small area about half a mile down that is just above a small beach that is flat and sheltered from the park by large bushes. She thinks that it will offer more shelter than the main park and we will be less likely to be moved on, so we go for it.

It is a super little pitch and again has great views so we set up camp and as we are doing so we can hear the beginnings of a storm rumbling towards us.

Fortunately it passes quickly and without being much of a threat but no doubt it will be back by the noise of thunder to the East of us. The sunset looks like it is framing up to be a spectacular show, red sky at night and all that. We had been told earlier in the journey that due to huge forest fires in Canada there had been some fantastic skies as the setting sun had illuminated the smoke clouds being given off. We hadn't even heard about small fires in the forests of Canada never mind huge ones. Another example of selective journalism. If areas the size of small countries being on fire don't make the news what chance have Grace and I got?

As we are eating our cardboardhydrate ration for the evening we hear the sound of a machine sweeping the paths approaching. I look directly at the driver and he merely smiles and waves so I deduce that we are OK in this particular spot. I shall be using this as implied permission should the local Police arrive in the middle of the night.

I check the maps and we are 20 miles or so from Coon Rapids dam and the potential for a side visit to Bob White, the man we met at the Blanchard dam portage. I telephone him and he is off work on Monday and Tuesday, and he tells me to get to Coon Rapids at whatever time you want and then call; I'll come pick you up, take you back to my place for dinner, laundry, shower and boat cleaning. Not necessarily in that order.

He also offers us a tour of the city of Minneapolis on the Tuesday, dinner with his family and then take us to a put in point that will keep us on track for our timescale. WOW! That is totally unexpected and a great piece of news.

I sit and watch the sunset, which is quite spectacular, I reaffirm to myself that things do happen for a reason. Jim Lewis contacts me through a Facebook post to arrange help; Jim meets Bob White while they are sat on the same riverbank and in conversation mentions Grace and I; Bob meets me in the woods while I am scouting a portage, hears my accent, puts two and two together coming up with four and says "Do you know Jim Lewis?" Kismet, Fate, Coincidence, Serendipity, call it what you want. It is some sort of proof of the Universe at work. The force is strong in these parts Obi Wan Kenobi.

25/8/14

Despite not having to go that far today we are still up early, but we take our time about packing up and are on water for 7:50. Flow is quite fast, except the last bit, which is a flood pool for the hydroelectric dam, at Coon Rapids. We make it to the dam in 3 ½ hours, which is fast for 19 miles. I hope it is a sign of things to come.

Bob is already there waiting for us. It turns out he is following us on the Spot3 Maps so knew where we were and roughly what time we would arrive. In no time we have the boats unloaded and on the roof of his car and we are off. He lives about a 45-minute drive away so we arrive just before 13:00.

On arrival Bob shows us to 'our' room, which has a double bed! Grace and I look at each other and laugh and I say to Bob "No problem I will put my mat on the floor and use my sleeping bag". Obviously embarrassed he laughs as well and says that he is sorry but assumed we were a couple, I tell him not to worry and that I should have told him when we met that we are not. It is an easy mistake to make given what we are doing. It is also something of a comment on how society has come to accept that a big age difference in relationships can be tolerated. In our case huge would be a better description. I end up in the spare bed in what doubles as the office and dog kennel room during the day.

Grace had arranged to Skype the youngsters she coaches at the pool in Bradford, but for some reason it won't connect and ends up talking to her boss who can give them an update on how she is doing. I manage to FaceTime Rebecca and Kenneth for the first time in a while, up to now the lack of Internet and the time difference has been against me, so It's good to get a chance to sit and chat for a while just to remind me of normal stuff.

After that has finished the tent goes up to dry out, I hose out and clean my boat including the sides to remove the tree scrape marks. Grace does hers and they both look prettier. With three weeks under our belts they don't look bad, all things considered, but I can't help but wonder how they will look at the end and will I be able to sell them to recoup the outlay I have had to make.

Then it's time for personal kit to be cleaned followed by cleaning me. The White's have a bath, not a very big one, but it's a bath. Which I employ to the full having a glorious soak and scrub, mostly of my feet, which are disgusting. I then spend as much time cleaning the bath as I did my body. Well its been a while since we last had chance to get this clean, up to now we have been 'bathing' with wet wipes and hand cleaner.

I get my clothes out of the washer and dryer and have chance to check emails to sort business stuff out. There is the usual crop of bills to pay, invoices that haven't, queries to answer and instructions to give out. It seems that you can't escape everyday life that easily.

That night we have dinner at the house and their son comes round to join us. Nothing fancy, just burgers and sausage from the grill, salad and bread, simple, easy food in a relaxed family atmosphere. The evening also gave us chance for conversation about, well anything and nothing really. It's just nice to be able to have people around us and for us to be around them. There is a moment of true farce when we are invited back into the kitchen for a second round of food only to find that most of it has gone. And that the dog is sitting on the patio suddenly looking guilty! Funny how an animal that has no real facial expression can manage to pull that one off. Reminds me of my dogs and how they are so much part of the family.

Suddenly I discover that it's 10:30, about 2 ½ hours after I normally turn in, so it's a very late night. But at least there are no trains to disturb us tonight. I hope.

26/8/14
What a night! A comfy bed with no train noises, animals howling or tent

flapping in the wind. Only problem was waking up at 1:00 in the pitch black of night convinced that I was in the tent and was flooded out and floating. I was convinced that my tent was surrounded by water and that I was adrift on my sleeping mat. I actually reached over the edge of the bed to feel for water and then swing my legs out to find I was actually on dry land. It came as a shock because I was so sure that what I was experiencing was real. Before anyone asks, no I hadn't had a weakening of the bladder giving a wet feeling. My mind was playing tricks, a result of being off the ground for a change I suppose.

I manage to roll over waking up at 6:00 and lay dozing until I hear the others in the house moving, which results in me getting up out of bed at 7:45. Somehow it feels strange to be looking forward to a day off the river. I almost feel guilty. Over breakfast we plan a trip out to stock up on various supplies that we will need, including another set of portage wheels for me to use.

Off we go to supermarkets and outdoor shops. One good thing about being in Minnesota is that they have some of the best outdoor equipment stores I have ever seen. OK, so a large part of it is given over to the hunting side of outdoor life the result is that if you need it, they probably have it. And if they don't then the one a bit further down the road will. One feature about stores of this sort is the array of firearms that they have for sale. Again the selection seems to be on the basis of if you want it, we have it. Quite why hunting includes 9mm handguns I'm not sure. Shotguns and rifles I can understand but a Glock 9mm with extended capacity magazine? What are they hunting?

There is one piece of light relief when I spot a camouflage pattern shotgun in the 'ladies' section and manage to pursuede the assistant to let Grace hold it and pose for a photo. Not sure who was most nervous him or Grace!

We return home for a snack lunch and then go on a quick tour of Minneapolis. It is one of the cleanest cities I have ever been to and the buildings have a 'looked after' appearance to them. There is much evidence that thought has gone into incorporating old historic buildings into new developments. There is also much evidence that the local population enjoy the bike and running lanes that have been laid out for them all around the city as there are legions of people jogging and riding about the whole area.

In the centre of the city is one of the biggest locks on the whole river. Even this is incorporated into the cityscape with viewing areas and information centres, bike lanes and jogging tracks. Part of me is annoyed that I won't be going through it and part of me is glad, as it really is intimidating. These mixed feelings are increased when I learn that the lock is due to close in 2015 as a method of preventing an invasive species of fish, the Asian carp, from infesting the lakes north of the city. These fish are causing real problems further down and the authorities are fighting a battle to protect the native species from them and the destruction they cause to the habitat.

Bob has to make a business phone call so we visit an historic fort that overlooks the river. At this point the river is passing through a very deep valley and looks like a ribbon of silver threading its way between the high rocky outcrops. Minneapolis is definitely a place to come back to and look around in detail and perhaps even get back in a kayak and go through the city area. Lets see how I feel about that when I've finished this expedition.

We took Bob and Karen out for dinner, this entailed the usual argument about me paying in return for the hospitality but I won for a change. We had forgotten a few bits earlier on but managed to visit another couple of shops before they closed. Bed tonight was another late night, turning in at 10pm. As I laid waiting for sleep to come I thought about our hosts and what nice people they are. Strangers are friends you haven't met yet is starting to become an anthem, not just a saying on a fridge magnet.

27/8/14
Well, that's almost 3 weeks done and dusted and we are still in Minnesota. Does this state ever end and give up its hold on the Mississippi River? We seem to have been on it forever.

The day starts at 6am with the last bit of packing of everything we have washed, cleaned or bought. I find it strangely comforting to be back in the same shorts and shirt I've had on all the time but, for a change, they don't smell. Well they do but of soap powder not sweat, river water and mud. Some of the people we have met along the way must have been aghast at our apparent lack of hygiene. The ones that let us into their cars, like Bob, must have been cleaning them for weeks!

Last night I had looked at maps with Bob and realised that I had made a serious error in ditching some maps, because I thought they weren't needed, before leaving Jim Lewis. I had the Hastings to Iowa border, area duplicated with a set from the Minnesota DNR and a set from the USACE. I had also got rid of the Minnesota DNR set because they didn't seem as useful as the USACE set. This was a mistake and one that could be costly.

I realised that although the USACE maps gave information about the river in terms of navigation they did not contain the detail of campsites and small towns along the river which the DNR maps did. This information might prove vital if we needed to find a suitable place to stop or re supply. The USACE maps had a lot of information but primarily they are concerned with commercial traffic not pleasure craft so, therefore, do not have the small detail we needed. It would be hard enough further down the river when the DNR area of responsibility ran out; I had just made it harder when I had no need. I comforted myself with the fact that all was not lost as I still had the DNR maps on my MacBook and could check them each night to mark where/what we could find the next day if need be. Extra work and a bit of a nuisance but it is what it is.

After a hearty breakfast, we load the car and off we go to Hastings. We missed out the section that would have taken us through the city, 52 miles in total, but we had a rest, got our supplies and managed to keep to schedule. By one method of reckoning we were actually a little ahead of schedule but only because we hadn't tried to incorporate shopping with moving down the river. As we get in the car I notice that Bob has a suit with him as he is going to a board meeting for Habitat for Humanity, a non-profit housing organisation that he is finance director for, on his return to the city. As we travel he explains how the group works and it sounds like a very philanthropic and sustainable way of providing low cost housing that the tenant has a stake in.

I had left the first of my journal books and the first set of maps we had with Bob for posting down to Louisiana and collection when we finish and when I offered to leave some money to pay the postage he flat refused! Getting him to accept us paying for dinner had been hard enough so after three attempts I gave up asking.

We load up, hug/handshake and off we go with shouts of "Thank you, see you soon". I make a pact with myself that I will visit the area again and this time will manage to pay for dinner without a fight.

We are under way for 10:30 but there is little flow and it is hard work. We are now in the realm of the commercial traffic and the lock and dam system that they use. The dams are actually used to maintain the river at a level that barges can navigate safely rather than for power generation. This means that they still have collecting pools and flood areas, which in turn create huge areas of slack water.

We plod along and suddenly we come to our first lock, No 3 on the river. The first 2 having been in Minneapolis city. I had been told to raise the lock keepers by hailing on channel 16 on the marine radio but after several minutes of getting no answer I began to wonder if it was working. Then a passing boat advises us to use channel 14, which is the lock-hailing channel. Channel 16 is a general channel that is monitored but is not a priority unless being used to signal for help.

Once hailed on 14, they answer more or less straight away and advise a 20-minute wait. This suits us, waiting is easier than carrying! Having said that an examination of the area as we wait doesn't show where we would portage round in any event.

Locking through is a smooth operation, even if when they call and give us permission to go ahead and enter they declare that they can't see us. I tell them of our location and ask them to be gentle with us as it is our first time and they are. The drop is only about 10 feet but the lock is huge, it is 600 feet long and 110 feet wide. It must hold 10's of 1000's of litres of water, which they allow to flow through just for our kayaks. They call us into the lock and direct us to the gates at the downstream end where a member of the team throw us a rope each to hang on to as the water flows out. They have a chat with us, wish us good luck and tell us to move off once the gates have opened and the hooter has sounded. The question I ask 'Is it Ok to just let 2 kayaks through in a lock this size?' Answer? "Yes sir, no problem at all: have a nice day."

The gates open and the hooter sounds. Grace promptly jumps out of her skin in surprise and we laugh about it for the next mile or so as we discuss just how much water was used and the cost that had been incurred for us. I learned later that US Federal Law mandates that any and all traffic using the river, in either direction, has an absolute right to use the lock system and cannot be refused passage at any time of day or night. That applies to everything from a commercial barge to a home made wooden raft.

As we had had a late start and a big breakfast we had decided to snack for lunch and make for the town of Red Wing where we would have a meal and then put a few miles in before finding somewhere to camp for the night. As we move down the river I look at the map and realise that the left bank is the edge of the state of Wisconsin so we have finally found another state. Yippee! This is celebrated by us paddling furiously towards it and running up onto the sand at the edge. It's the little things in life that make it so worthwhile.

A little further down the river there is a 'Resort' marked on the map. When we find this "resort", it turns out to be a campground with a fishing tackle shop, so we stop to enquire about food. Sadly they only have a few sandwiches, and a lot of live fish bait. BUT I do get 2 copies of the Wisconsin DNR maps in A5 size with a spiral binding, just what we needed to replace the ones I had ditched. We also got a tip that in another few miles we would be at Red Wing and to look out for a place called the Harbour Bar.

As we approach we can see that the town is on the right bank as we approach and that there is a boat ramp and what looks like shops and food outlets on the road that runs parallel to the river. We can't see anything obviously signed as to where we are looking for but keep going.

It turns out that The Harbour Bar is also in Wisconsin and therefore on the left bank, a piece of information that had not been divulged. It has several boat docks and is a fairly big place. Perhaps the resort owner being based in Wisconsin didn't think it important to mention this little fact or perhaps she just didn't know what was on the Minnesota side. Or didn't want to support another state's business.

The place is great with superb food and friendly staff. Our waitress, Margaret, talks to us about what we are doing and is interested in our charity efforts and tells us that there is a campsite about 300 yards down stream on the Wisconsin bank. I think I see a pattern developing here and it seems to be almost tribal. She does nothing more than find the site owner, who is enjoying their happy hour, and promptly sends him to see us. She had told him what we were doing and he gifted us a free pitch at the campsite if we want one. I just hope he remembers when happy hour is over.

With the late start and being a bit lethargic from the rest day, we decide to accept his offer and call it a day. The decision is sealed with a dessert before we paddle round to the boat ramp for the campground. It has a bridge carrying a major highway right above and a power plant/railroad marshalling yard on the opposite riverbank so it's not the quietest place on earth but it can't be worse than Elk River with its railroad crossings and trains woo-hoo-ing all night. It is actually another RV campground so the surface is rock hard and not suitable for tents so we find a small patch of grass near the fish cleaning shed and set the tents up. We have access to power outlets on a nearby empty RV pitch so we can top up the charge on our electrical gear.

I am sat writing up my journal when a car containing 2 moms and their kids pulling a caravan pulls up. This is such a novelty for me, as I have never seen such a combination in the USA before so I sit and watch them. After a few minutes it is obvious that the driver does not know how to reverse with a trailer on, and that the gaggle of kids all wanting a million different things is not helping, so I walk across to offer my help. Which is accepted without a pause for breath. Glad to be able to help someone else for a change after all the help we have been given.

Tonight will be the first night we haven't spent in Minnesota since we started, even if it is only 200 yards away. We have now done over 550 miles and an initial assessment shows us to be about on track to finish within the 60 days we have set ourselves.

The river is now much wider but still has broad sweeping bends and meanders. We can take a more direct route round these, if there is no river traffic, and this means that the miles we travel are actually less than the plotted points on the map which follows the centre of the channel. This tends to make the miles planned and covered differ as I am measuring distance using the GPS, fortunately we can compensate as there is now mile marker boards on the banks that tell us what point we are at. There are also more boats. Lots more boats.

I look at the maps again and make a check of the suggested mileage chart we are using and it shows we are about 100 miles/3 days behind. As we are 600 miles from St Louis (14/15 days of travel at current rate) we need to pick up the pace.

One suggestion I make to Grace is that if we don't catch up over the next few days we try and arrange a day off in St Louis, followed by a road transport to make up the losses, plus a buffer to help us along the way. If we don't we face the risk of having to take out well short of the mile zero marker and not being able to do the last section as we will run out of time. As we already have a contact in St Louis, Tom Drennan, who is holding our maps for us, this may be easy to arrange. It's an option not a decision.

It turns out to be a horrible night; well it was for me as Grace said she slept OK. The trains ran more between 23:00 and 4:00 than they had done at any point up to then. One was unloading its cargo of oil for the power station so it pulled up with a screech of brakes, a concertina of thumps from the carriages, banging and crashing of pipes as it was unloaded, the engine then revs loudly and the concertina of thumps rings out again as the carriages are stretched out. This repeated 126 times until the last tanker is empty. Yes, I did count the carriages on the train. Then another train pulls in to take its place. And the road above us must be a truck route judging by the noise coming from the metal plates on the bridge and the sound of exhaust brakes.

Might have been free but it wasn't restful.

28/8/14
The day starts after another train disturbed night, I still wonder how/why people put up with such a situation, but we were in good spirits and get set off before 8:00. Bob, the campsite owner, came to see us off and warned of a possible weather front moving in. Thanks Bob.

As we get going I make my proposal about the potential for a rest day and a bit of make up time in the St Louis area and discuss the transport suggestion. Making up the deficit is agreed but not a huge leapfrog of a make up and only if we feel we need to.

We get going and soon get near to Lake Pepin, which is actually a flood plain/collecting pool for another of the big locks; it's just that it is so big it resembles a lake in every respect. Apart from the fact that it actually has some flow. Couple this with it being relatively shallow, less than 5 feet over everywhere but the dredged channel, and the potential for it to generate waves when it is windy, is a serious issue.

The first 2 hours of our journey were on target at 9 miles or so but then things started to get difficult. No sooner do we get onto the beginning of where the river widens out than a wind gets up. A headwind. A 10mph headwind. With gusts of about double that. We actually went backwards at one point. A swell of 3 to 4 foot built up on the surface but we pressed on.

The plan had been to do 40 miles or so today and stop for a quick lunch at the town of Lake City on the shore of the lake, but the wind and subsequent waves make this look unlikely. Then the rain starts. As we look towards the far end of the lake it starts to disappear in the rain and low cloud. Not without a struggle we cross the lake and head for the town on the right bank and make for an area with a beach in front of some houses. We pull up in front of one of the homes where there is a sign of life and ask the young lady resident, who introduces herself as Kylie, if we can leave the boats there while we go into town. No problem, as always.

As we walk towards the commercial part of town the rain and wind starts to get worse and we find a place that rents the holiday flats, they call them condominiums in America (I have no idea why), so we decide to call in and see how much a room would be if the weather does not improve. The lady on the reception tells us that she has rooms available. She also tells us that a storm is moving in but recommends that we try the hotel across the street, as it's cheaper. We visit the hotel across the road and find that it is part of a chain and that they have rooms available. The warning about the weather is repeated but looking out of the window we see that it is not a warning, it's already arrived. Unless she means that it will get worse.

The first bit of good news is when I enquire about the room rate and she asks if I am in the American Association of Retired People (AARP) as I would qualify for a discount. I wonder just how old I look at this point. I tell her no as I am not a US Citizen, but then in a flash of inspiration ask if being a retired Police Officer would help. Certainly did! I got the government rate of $75, which is a $10 discount, and breakfast included. All I have to do is show her the ID card. I make a mental note to make sure I ask about discounts this way in future and we sign up for the room.

We pick the boats up and paddle them further along the beach to the head of the bay. That was quite a hairy journey as the wind and waves are now raging and making launching and steering difficult. Difficult is an understatement. After a short portage across the road to the hotel we chain them up to the fence at the side of the lawn, empty all the gear out and take refuge in the hotel.

Once we get into the room The Weather Channel has even worse news, heavy thunderstorms all day with a promise that they will get worse. The radar and other graphics show that the storm is quite intense and that it is not only headed our way but that it will get worse and stay in this area for a while. It would simply not have been safe to continue.

There is a Subway sandwich shop just down the road so we brave the elements and walk the short distance to have a meal. By meal I mean a Foot Long Philly Cheesesteak with Fries and coffee but we are in somewhere warm and dry which beats sheltering under a tarpaulin boiling water to make rehydrated mashed potato and pasta which would have been our other option had we not made it to Lake City.

Having spent an hour or so in the Subway we brave the elements again to struggle back to the Hotel and message John Sullivan, who is the originator of the Facebook group, The Mississippi River Paddlers. John lives in La Crosse, Wisconsin and has spent all his life either working on or just travelling the rivers of the northern states. As a water quality and environmental scientist for the Minnesota and Wisconsin DNRs, he is very knowledgeable about river and weather conditions and as a keen kayak and canoe user he is a wealth of information about routes, campsites and wildlife of the areas.

We had planned to be in the La Crosse area in a couple of days and visit John so that we could shop for supplies. He was following us on our Spot 3 page and would know that we had stopped and where we were. He would also know about the weather conditions so the idea behind the message was to assure him that we were safe. I also give him our USA phone number so that he could contact us if he wants. Having looked at the weather forecasts I think it prudent to check if the Hotel has another night available just in case we have to sit out the storms. They have, so that is an option should we need to. Not what we would want to do but safety must always come first.

John Sullivan phones us and tells us that he is pleased that we are safe and sound as he had seen the weather in our area and was concerned for our safety. I tell him of my concerns for the next day and that, if it turns out to be as bad as predicted, we should consider staying another night in the hotel to stay safe. He agreed about the weather and the plan to avoid it but insists that we don't book another night as he will drive up to collect us from Lake City and take us to his house where we can stay the night. He tells me that the weather will be bad and that he is happy to help, telling us that we are about 50 miles or so north of him by road so its not a long journey. We arrange for him to pick us up about 11:00 the next day.

A couple of days ago Grace had got sunburnt on her shoulders and upper arms. At first neither of us thought it was too bad, just a touch red and not overly tender, so we had just put some cream on the affected area and she kept it covered. During the late afternoon while we were resting Graces' arm became blistered with the sunburn and she is in some considerable pain. I didn't realise it was that bad and feel some responsibility for not asking about it earlier, instead I had assumed that it was OK because she didn't say anything. Not having anything in the First Aid Kit I obtain some gauze pads and a bandage from the Hotel and the Petrol station next door to cover them as they are starting to weep.

Dinner that night is another Subway and Fries but the food has lost its appeal for me as I feel very disappointed with myself, our lack of progress and because I have failed to look after my partner.

Week 4
Lake City, Minnesota to Pleasant Valley, Iowa

29/8/14
It is about 7:30, when I wake up. I didn't wake up any earlier today because I didn't have to. Such has been my frame of mind all night. When I look out of the window I see that the skies are leaden and giving off light rain and there is quite a wind out on the lake. Not quite the storm of biblical proportions that the TV had prophesied but looking down the lake the clouds are quite heavy so there is time for it to be fulfilled.

Grace tells me that her arm is now stiff and painful and I can see that more blisters have appeared and burst. I peel off the gauze and it obviously hurts but she grits her teeth and bears it. I still feel responsible for not asking or acting earlier. She has helped me with my dark moods more than once and I couldn't even spot a bit of sunburn until it was too late to prevent it getting worse.

We go for breakfast and I chat with a few people who, as usual, are very complimentary of our efforts. They are also sympathetic about our plight with the weather. They are in town to attend a wedding that they planned to hold in the open air so they have the same fears about it being washed out. As I walk past the reception desk the hotel manager is on duty and asks if I am Ken. When I tell her I am she chats with me for a few minutes about our expedition and how she admires our courage.

Not sure that I agree with her this morning. After a few minutes she gives me an envelope that a guest has left with her simply addressed to "Ken & Grace". In it is a note that says "good luck on your travels – John" and $20. We have absolutely no idea who that was, in fact neither of us can remember talking to anyone in the hotel yesterday other than the lady on reception, so it must have been someone that overheard our conversation. Once again I am amazed at a strangers generosity and how our journey and cause is touching so many people.

As I start to pack I look out of the window and see that the skies are starting to clear and the sun comes out. Boy do I feel a fraud! Suddenly the weather looks great and here we are hiding from it and the river.

I ring Pauline, and find that she is now on the train from the airport to home and tell her as much. I also tell her about Graces' arm and ask if she has any ideas. She recommends visiting a pharmacy and buying some Aloe Vera cream as that will help. She also reminds me that in the USA Pharmacists are used more often than in the UK for medical advice so they may well have other treatments they can recommend.

I confide in her that I am worried that a combination of bad weather and the injury to Grace will hold us back so much that we may end up failing. I also tell her that I have overheard Grace on the telephone to her parents and boyfriend saying that she is struggling and worried as well, and I start to get a bit tearful at the thought of failure. We then get cut off as the train enters a tunnel and even after waiting a while cannot get back in contact with her. If it wasn't for bad luck I wouldn't have any at all.

I try to remind myself that there is no shame in failure only in not trying but don't even convince myself.

I feel like crap! We spent two nights in a house, skipped 52 miles, spent one night in the tents and then gave up after 20 miles and found a hotel. And now I'm waiting for a lift that will take us about 60 miles or so down the river and to spend another night in a bed.

OK so it's about the experience and meeting people as much as the physical challenge but we didn't set out to do it this way. As the sun gets brighter my mood gets darker. I don't even talk to Grace as I feel so bad and such a sense of responsibility for our potential failure.

We sit about in the reception area until John Sullivan arrives and we load up and set off. We stop at a pharmacy on the way, which was just at the other end of town. Why didn't I think to ask about a pharmacy yesterday afternoon? I might have been able to reduce the pain and blisters for Grace. Another failure to notch up. Once the appropriate treatments have been obtained we set off for John's house.

We chat about what we have encountered as we travel and John assures me that this happens often. The sheer unpredictability and force of the weather has more of an effect on river travellers than anything else and that I shouldn't feel so bad. More experienced people than me have been caught out and at least we are safe from the elements. As we talk I realise that in the back of my mind has always been the simple fact that we are constrained by Insurance, Visas and flight bookings so do have a schedule to keep to. USA residents can always pack up and go home for a while and then come back or just pitch camp and wait until things are more in their favour. Not something we can do.

At John's house we have lunch and he and I consult maps and our predicted mileage chart. He proposes to take us a little further down the river tomorrow and put us in where we thought we might be at the end of 30th August. This will enable us to stay on track and within schedule. The actual distance we will miss is around the 80-mile mark in total and when I talk to Grace she agrees. I redress her sunburn a couple of times and apply the cream that we bought. Her shoulders and upper arms are red and she has some very large blisters that seem to be getting bigger rather than responding to the treatment. She sleeps a little while I end up spending an hour writing up an objection to a planning permission application that has been made on the land next to our home. It seems that normality has a way of catching up with me whrever I am.

It's the Internet's fault again so perhaps the Orwellian view and the fears of Winston and Julia about being constantly under surveillance are coming true. Even in the middle of nowhere.

We plan to go out for dinner with John and his wife, Beth, and as we set off the thunder and lightning and rain sets in, so it did come just 10 hours later than advertised. On the way John has to stop for fuel. He refuses to accept any money for it, why am I still surprised at this? It's normal. I don't like it and become determined to pay for the meal. Of course this doesn't happen either as at the restaurant, he grabs the bill before I can pay and will not hand it over.

Back at John's I dress Grace's shoulders again and see that they seem a little less 'angry' which is a good sign. I hope she has a restful night, as she must be in some pain with it all.

Laid in bed I let my mind wander and realise that I desperately need to get back onto the water and in the kayak or the trip will become a tour of hotels, houses and new friends. In my mind the next non-tent stop will be St Louis in 450+ miles. I hope it is and that nothing stops or diverts us.

Tomorrow is day 24 which means over a third of our target days have gone by and we are not quite on target. It would be very easy to stop now, sell the kayaks and use the Greyhound bus to get to Louisiana and our final destination of Marguerite and West Constantine's Farm in Moreauville.

I go to sleep with the sky flashing like a neon sign only barely thankful that I am not in a tent. Not that I am ungrateful for John's assistance but doubt is a huge enemy and he is creeping up on me and being in the tent means I am on the river, being on the river means I am moving, moving means I am attaining my target, attaining my target means I have beaten my enemy.

30/8/14
The day got off to a good start, up early, with clear skies and good weather forecast. The Kayaks had been loaded onto John's car before going to bed last night so I dressed in my paddle gear and started my breakfast. It went downhill from there.

Grace came in and I saw that both her upper arms were covered in some new and very big blisters and that they were obviously very painful. As soon as I saw her I realised that paddling today was out of the question and even if she had wanted to I would have said no. When she started to cry I knew for certain. She's physically tough but this was too much for her. I give her a hug in silence and then tell her that I will do everything I can to make her better.

Over her shoulder I look at John and he silently agrees that we will not be paddling and slips out of the room. I then hear him unloading the boats from the car. I followed Grace to her room and cleaned up the blisters and put some more lotion on them. Even being as gentle as I could it was painful for her. John and I had a quick discussion about what we could do. I suggested he put us in a hotel so that we wouldn't be in his way but he wouldn't hear of it. Another angel at work. Later we found out his son and two grandchildren were coming to stay for the weekend, as it was the Labour Day holiday, I repeated that we could move out and make room but he kept insisting that we stay. Another pharmacy visit for more/different advice, creams, potions and pills, a couple of store visits with Beth and then home for lunch. I hope that these treatments help Grace and reduce the pain.

I talk with Pauline for a while, more about a planning application that affects us than anything else because if I start talking about the expedition my enemy will be back in the room and he might win this time. Beth and John are busy with their stuff so I go to my room to read for a while. I actually fell asleep for about an hour and when I wake John's son has arrived with the grandchildren. The rest of the day is spent feeling like a spare part and a bit down, even a child's laughter could not lift my spirits.

After dinner we went up the hill above La Crosse to see the sunset which is magnificent and more than a little uplifting. We could see the Mississippi River stretching out before us, a huge ribbon of silver winding through the land below us. I just hope that we will be OK to get back on. If Grace is not well in the morning, or my moods get the better of me, I am not sure what we will do.

John tells me of his plans to take us even further down river to a put in point that will help with mileage deficit, but not so far that we could be considered to be doing more than making up for lost time and it being an issue for us. The real issue is Grace's health. I really don't care what people think about the mileage we miss as long as we are safe and I keep my promise to her parents to bring her home safely.

With all this going on in my head I am beginning to wonder how things will pan out. I am wondering if we can have any more bad luck when I recall a message from my son, Kenneth, who on reading of my doubts in an email to him said "one day the pigeon, the next day the statue". He is right of course but when did he become the philosopher in the family?

I am spending the night sleeping on a screened porch on a US Army camp cot tonight, another first for me and as near as I can get to being in the tent.

31/8/14
Apart from going to the bathroom at 4:40 and waking up the dog, and therefore everybody else in the house, it was not a bad night. I may have to invest in one of the cots I used, it was actually quite comfy. Grace looks a little apprehensive when I go to her room and her burns are still blistered but not as bad as they were yesterday. I give her the option and tell her that I do not want her to do anything that will injure her health and that the decision to continue is hers. She affirms that she wants to go on and go on today, so we do.

Once we have eaten and loaded up John takes us down the river to just below the N°10 lock. This is a total of 160 river miles from where he picked us up in Lake City and about 60 miles further than the original plan. At Lake City we were about 100 miles/3 days or so behind our proposed schedule and dropping back because of weather. The original plan proposed by John would have helped make this up, the revised one put us back nearer the target without missing too many miles that we would not have covered under our own power, given good weather.

By road it's quite a way, unusually as road miles are frequently more direct than the river, and while John and I chat, Grace sleeps. I am sure that the physical and psychological pain is wearing her out. John continues to assure me that what we have done is not cheating or failing as we had to face decisions based on safety and health considerations as well as time constraints. He also reminds me that not only have we come a long way but we still have a long way to go and that it will get 'easier' as the river flow will assist us.

At the put in point Grace just gets on with it and grits her teeth, while I keep my mind busy to stop me from dwelling on potential problems. It seems that determination is something neither of us have a short supply of.

I make one final effort to give John some money but fail. As well as hospitality, travel costs, and time from family he has also given us clothing and a new air mat for Grace as we found that hers had sprung a leak and wasn't inflating. What a great guy. I just hope that I can repay him someway one day in the future. He would probably say "Just do someone else a favour"

Once we are underway I tell Grace that distance, pace, rest, everything is her choice, just keep within what she is comfortable with. We started at about 10:45 and by 12:30 had done 8 miles. Not bad given yet another headwind, lots of idiots in boats and plenty of swirling currents that we had not experienced before. The other piece of news we have is that we have now crossed into Iowa and have another state to cross off the list.

We stopped for a rest at a Town called Cassville and had a lunch of burger and fries from the BP fuel station in town. Given the bad press over the Gulf oil spill I am surprised that there is such a thing in the USA. While we sit on the riverbank in a picnic area two chaps come to talk to us and make the, by now, usual exclamations about our journey. One of them gives us $20 as a donation. Nice people again.

The map shows a place called Anthony's Resort, which is marked as having boat ramp facilities about 7 miles down river. We head for it as we will be able to camp and get water at least, possibly even hot food if we are lucky. On this last leg we talk about the missing miles, how we explain them and other stuff that has been experienced on the expedition so far. Once that topic is exhausted we invent a game of writing a short story by telling each other a line at a time and they get more and more ridiculous which makes us laugh. Grace keeps smiling and laughing but I can see she is in pain.

We find the place about 4:30 which is a stoke of luck as it is tucked away behind the railway line that runs parallel to the river and the entrance is under a bridge and at an angle. If it had been dark we may have missed it. It seems to be another RV 'camp' so I make a quick enquiry of someone who tells me he is the owner's brother and we have a campsite sorted.

As we are unloading the boats I strike up a conversation with a family who are just launching their boat for a final cruise of the day before dinner and for some reason one of the topics is injuries, I suppose they may have seen a bandage on Grace's arm or seen me rubbing my back and stretching. They set off and I think nothing more of it. We find a grass area near the boats and the toilets and start to pitch the tents and are approached by more people who have seen us land and are intrigued by us.

One lady, who has a couple of near teenage boys with her talks to us for a while and offers us the use of the showers in her RV and to join her family for dinner. We accept of course, as they knew we would. No sooner have they wandered off to leave us to unpack than another lady pulls up on a golf buggy and introduces herself as the wife of the man that sorted the campsite and she invites us to join them for dinner. We have an embarrassment of offers now.

The first lady to invite us, Tammy Hafeman, sends one of the kids down to tell us that coffee for me and hot chocolate for Grace is ready and would we like to join them for a while. How could we resist? After a coffee I start explaining to the kids how we do things and take them to show them the tents and kayaks. I show them the space we use for storage and all the stuff we carry in and on the kayaks and then the tents. They are absolutely amazed at how small and compact everything is and cannot believe that we are willingly putting up with these conditions. I give them my "Don't let anyone tell you ..." speech and they run back to the RV's to tell the adults how "Cool" we are.

I am just closing up the tent to go and eat with the Hafeman's, the man I had spoken to at the boat launch comes to me and introduces himself as Greg and his wife Diane. First of all he hands me some rubbing liniment to help with our aching muscles, then tells me that he has just seen the weather forecast and it shows a storm with heavy chance of hail is headed this way. He goes on to tell me that there are some cabins on the edge of the campground and that he owns two of them and that he would "Be real comfortable" if Grace and I would stay in his spare cabin to be sure that we will be safe. I really don't know what to say, and say so! So his wife says "That's a yes then". I explain that the Hafeman's have just cooked dinner for us and he says, "Not a problem, I'll be back in 45 minutes with a golf cart to take your stuff up for you".

I get back to Grace and she has had the same warning about the weather and a similar offer of shelter! The other family that invited us to dinner turn up, it turns out they are next door, and everybody says join them as well and have more food. Where do all these nice people come from?

After dinner, Greg, Diane and their daughter come to take us to the cabin, which has everything we could need, air conditioning, showers, fresh water and two bedrooms. They leave us a golf cart so we can a) go and say goodnight to our dinner hosts and b) carry all the stuff back to the boats in the morning in comfort. We never expected this and I am running out of ways to say thank you. We go back to the RV's, to say goodnight to everyone, and to ride on the golf cart, and Tammy offers, no insists on feeding us breakfast in the morning and will be up at 6:30 looking for us so don't we dare try and sneak off.

Yet another example of 'Strangers are friends you just haven't met yet'.

Not the longest day we have done but probably one that will last in my memory for a long time as being one that started out in something of a state of despair and ended in laughter and friendship.

1/9/14
True to her word Tammy is up and cooking breakfast as we pack the boats and waves to us across the campsite. She has made pancakes with maple or blueberry syrup, and cooked bacon for us as well. She obviously got up especially early as no one else from the family has stirred. This is true hospitality and friendship being offered to strangers and once again we are struggling how to say thank you.

With breakfast over and our goodbyes said we start to put the last few items in the boats and get ready to launch them when a woman turns up on a golf cart and announces herself as the site owner and asks where did we camp last night as she hadn't seen the tents. I explained that we had stayed in a cabin at the invitation of the owner, Greg, who also had another cabin on the site so we hadn't actually pitched and stayed in the tents. She simply said "Well, as you didn't need to pay for the tent site that will be $5 per boat for using the launch ramp". Determined not to let this little episode take the shine off our stay I simply paid up, smiled and walked away. I did wonder if she was offended because we hadn't taken her family up on the offer of food.

As we pull out of the marina and pass under the bridge into the main channel it is a real WOW moment. The skies are clearing and are a glorious blue, the water is still and wide and the view simply stunning. Its almost like we haven't seen the river and its tree lined majesty before. For some reason this is a view that takes both of us by surprise and we both sit for a moment just taking it in. For long enough there is only us on the water, no other craft at all and only the soft wake from our movement creates a disturbance in the mirror smooth surface of the river.

It is along this stretch that we meet our first set of barges and to be fair the wake they create is not half as bad as some from smaller, but faster boats. They are very big, as individual units but when there are three of them abreast and three deep with the power plant at the rear pushing them along, they resemble a slow moving grey-sided sports field. We keep them at a respectable distance and I wonder what all the fuss is about when people tell you that they are the most dangerous things on the river. They are easy to spot and hear, are in the marked channel and do not create the monster bow waves that I had been told about. Perhaps it's just this one and the worst is yet to come.

We continue to bumble along at a steady pace only to find that the collecting pool before the next lock has a considerable crosswind that makes heading in the direction I want to go difficult to say the least. Little OLLI is designed to turn into the wind as an aid to increasing stability but this does nothing for me, as heading into the wind is not taking me where I want to go. I have a rant at the wind, the kayak, the designers and external forces in general but it has no effect and I just have to put up with it. Eventually we arrive at the lock and pass through without any hold up. Again it is a huge thing that uses vast quantities of water. At least they don't have to worry about pumping it in from downstream as there is plenty more water coming down behind us.

Just past this is the town of Dubuque, Iowa, which has a marina not far up a side channel that leads into the town. We moor up and find that the marina bar is only two days away from closing for the season and as a result has a limited menu. As in have a pulled pork sandwich or nothing. We stop for an hour and are on our way again. Grace's arm is holding up, and it seems the medication is helping. Either that or she just grits through it. Probably both.

Once back into the main channel we start to pick up a bit of pace and then once again we hit a wide channel with a headwind! The crosswind on the approach to the last dam was driving me nuts with directional problems but this is just insane hard work. We persevere, not that we have a choice.

The map shows a campground/marina that is up a side channel called Massey Marina so we decide to head for it. It turns out that it is a nice little park, mostly for RVs again, but it has a restaurant and shower facilities. Not only that, but it has WIFI, so we can get in touch with the world and tell them how we are.

The people are really nice and do not rush us as we sit and use their WIFI for quite some time before we order a meal and as we are talking to them they ask for a photo to be taken so that we can go onto their 'Wall of Fame' which is located right outside the toilets. Fame indeed.

Another 'real food meal', the second in the same day. I also weaken somewhat and have a couple of small beers. After a chat with Pauline on FaceTime it is time for bed. This will be our first time in the tents for 4 days.

2/9/14
Not the best night I have had so far, but not the worst. Perhaps I had just got out of the habit of being in a tent? Last night we had decided to get up at 5:30/6:00, get sorted and off to take advantage of the still morning weather as we had found that in the very early hours of daylight the winds did not get as strong. Our idea was that if we could avoid wind for long enough we would be able to make better progress.

We had just set off and it was still ok but it also started to rain. We had not gone far when the thunder and lightning came back along with rain like stair rods. We had to shelter for a while under some overhanging trees on the bank before it was safe enough for us to continue. Fortunately it was not more than half an hour but it was a delay we could have done without.

After 17 miles of wide open river and utterly unremarkable scenery we got to lock 12 and the keepers announced that we had a 2-hour wait while they sent a 15-barge set up south before us. If we had not had to stop for the rain we could have been in front of that barge. It is not that much of a problem and would not have made much difference as we had planned about 45 minutes for lunch just below the lock. There is a small boat dock that belongs to a private house just upstream from the lock so we beach alongside and sit and have a 'Jetboil' for lunch.

Almost to the minute we are called up on the radio and pass through the lock without incident. The sun has started to shine and it gets hotter as the day goes on so we decide to call it a day and look for a place to camp.

We decide to camp on 'Island 259', I have no idea why it is distinguished by a number in its title as it looks no different from any one of a thousand other islands we have seen, but it does have a nice wide and inviting sandy beach that we can pull up onto. It's peaceful and almost Caribbean in its outlook but more remarkable is that we are now camping in our 4th state along the route, Illinois.

On quite a few occasions along the way, although not recently, we have both had the feeling that we are the last two people on the planet. This evening as the suns sets and as the night starts to grow I get that feeling again.

3/9/14
Today is the last day of week four we are now very close to the 30-day mark and the halfway point of the time we had set. Sadly we are not anywhere near the halfway in distance.

We had decided on another early start this morning and when we got up there was heavy fog, a sure sign of a hot, sunny day to come. As we set out on the river at 7:10 the fog was lifting and making the place look almost magical.

We had the almost customary good going for the first few hours followed by a slog across another dam and lock pool. Officially still the river, although again it looks more like a lake than some of the ones I have visited in the UK. Of course the flow is negligible and when the headwind starts, as it always does, the waves just get bigger and bigger. A swell of 2 to 3 feet is not unusual. The lock is 20 miles downstream and we make it in a shade over 5 hours. Not bad given the wind, no it's actually very good given the conditions.

As we pass through the lock we ask the Lockmaster if he knows of anywhere we can eat as we have seen that the town of Clinton, Iowa is downstream from the lock. He recommends the "Candlelight" restaurant, which he tells us, has a marina out front and is a nice place and is 'not far'. It is almost 4 miles with the headwind slog, obviously a 'country' not far. When we get there it is a proper restaurant complete with real cutlery and cloth napkins. It also has a 'no shirt, no shoes, no service' sign on the door but I obviously pass inspection in my stained shorts and tee shirt and rubber shoes with the strap hanging off. The food is excellent with big portions and, best of all, strawberry cheesecake! One slice of which would be enough to sell your soul for. A quick chat with three ladies on the next table, who make more exclamations about our trip, one of whom is also a retired Police Officer and then we are under way again.

We have been so fortified by the lunch that we fair steam ahead, Grace christens our new found turn of speed 'Pudding Power' and we fantasise about what sorts of food we would have to eat to make our progress even faster.

As we leave we take a back channel to avoid the wind and it is about a mile shorter, one of several short cuts we try out. It is effectively a canal called a slough (pronounced slew in USA) that takes us past the industrial area of the town. This is really our first introduction to the commercial side of the river and how the industry that grew up around it over the hundred years or so has continued to develop. Not very pretty and, although heavily built up, strangely deserted.

I propose that we try to reach the town of Cordova, which will mean we have covered quite some distance today and Grace agrees. Just north of the town is a site that is designated on the map as being a power plant and as we get to it find that it is actually a nuclear power generating station. The land alongside the river is festooned with signs declaring that landing is forbidden and subject to various state and federal laws and there are booms in the water preventing an approach. Not that we want to thanks.

We are about a mile north of the power plant when I see a man in a small motor boat approaching from behind and to my right. He pulls alongside and asks where we are from and where we are going. Not unlike many others, but his reaction is not just the same as the others, he is more "Oh, OK".

He tells me he has bought his boat in Minneapolis and is sailing it down to St Louis. We exchange pleasantries and wishes of safety and just before he sets off he raises his iPad and photographs me.

As he disappears into the distance I realise that his boat was spotless, he was clean and so were his clothes, yet he had told me he had been camping for the last two nights and I had not seen evidence of any equipment stored on the deck. Have I just been interviewed by Homeland Security?

Just after we pass the bottom side of the power plant area we see a boat just ahead of us with three people in it, apparently fishing. As we get closer they stare and then wave. Manned by two men in their 20's and a woman of similar age I can't help but wonder if they actually are 'fishing' or are there to have a look at us as we pass by as we have obviously been observed on the upstream approach by one of the cameras on a tower that I saw. Homeland Security again I suspect.

We spot a nice looking beach about a mile above the town that is below some houses. We pull up and I go up to the house to ask permission to stay. There is a young woman in the house and when I tell her of my request she says that it is fine by her but she will have to ask her dad. Expecting the next line to be, and he isn't here right now, I get set for a disappointment. But no, he is in the garage with his friend tinkering with his boat so we go and meet him.

I ask him for permission and tell him that we won't be lighting any fires or playing loud music and he says 'Help yourself and feel free to burn anything but the house'. I walk back down to the beach to give Grace the good news. We have just finished pitching the tents when our host, Eric, and his daughter, Ashley, come down to the river with fishing rods and a six pack of beer. 'Just heading out for some father-daughter time' she declares, while Eric offers us a beer. I decline and say that I may take him up on his offer when he returns so that we can swap lies; his about fish and mine about kayaks. They laugh and push off out into the river.

They return in less than an hour, obviously nothing is biting, and immediately ask if we would like to join them at the house for a beer, a shower and dinner. Needless to say we accept. Eric explains that his mother and her husband are staying with them otherwise they would have offered us their spare room for the night. I just cannot believe the hospitality we are being shown, it just keeps happening.

We gather our 'clean clothes' and go up to the house where we meet not just his mother and her husband but also the next-door neighbours as well. We take it in turns to entertain them while we shower before dinner. Another day of two hot cooked meals, we are getting spoilt. Eric and Ashley are two fascinating people. He is a former member of the US Coast Guard where he was an electrician and now works at the nuclear power plant up the road plying the same trade. It turns out Ashley is also an apprentice electrician, but with a commercial company, having previously been in the US Coast Guard as well. They had even both been posted to the same station in Alaska, although at different times. She has also spent a year working in a fishing yard in Alaska. Without being asked she tells me that, yes it is a strange occupation for a woman but if someone tells her she can't do something her first reaction is "Challenge Accepted". Sounds like another young woman sat at the same table.

We retire to our tents for the night, having had a good meal and settle down for the night. Unfortunately we are woken at about 2 am when a thunderstorm starts with such huge flashes of lightning and loud crashes of thunder that I begin to think that the nuclear power plant has blown up. I did actually wonder what would happen if it was struck and would we hear/feel anything if it did explode?

The storm continued and I slept fitfully and dreamt that my dog Bess, who had died over two years ago, was in the tent with me. She was always frightened of thunderstorms and would cower and cuddle up to me when they happened. The dream was so real that I was convinced that she was real and there in the tent with me. I could even feel her when I put my hand out to comfort her. I'm still not sure that I was fully asleep and have to accept that my mind was playing tricks. But I swear she was there and, perhaps, wanted to believe it. Perhaps I still do.

At the end of today we have covered almost 40 miles on the river for a paddled distance of 36 miles. The ability to cut corners and take side channels is paying off.

4/9/14
When we wake up the storm is still raging so we decide to sit it out for a while, as there is no sense in putting ourselves at risk. Eric comes down about 8 am to see if we are OK and tells us that he is off to the airport with his mother and that he will be back later in the day if we decide to stay due to the weather. Looking out of the tent it's a tempting offer. However 10 am sees the weather improve, a relative term in truth, and we set off.

Before we get going and while I am alone I recall the dream about Bess and this gives me a very weak and weepy moment. I still miss her so much. She had been an almost constant companion for 14 years and we had had some good times together. I thought I would be OK once we got under way but about half an hour after we set off I was struck with a full blown sobbing session. I suppose it could be put down to a combination of bad memories, lingering grief and a lot of self-doubt about the expedition at this point, as today the winds are truly horrible.

Grace pulls alongside me and I was ashamed to admit to her that I was a wreck and why. She takes it in silence for a few moments then says 'Its Ok I understand' and paddles alongside me in silence. After a while I ask her to talk to me about anything to take my mind off it. She does and it works.

It takes almost 3 hours to cover 11 miles and it is all hard slog. This probably the worst wind we have had so far and for 2 pins I could give up right now. That is how I feel. We keep going and stop for food on the waters edge just north of dam 14. It was a sombre affair.

My mood is not improved by having a 2-hour wait to lock through as a commercial barge beat us to the lock, again. As if the wait wasn't bad enough then the exit would prove to be a nightmare. As we passed through we asked the lockmaster if he knew of any campsites and he told us that camping was almost non-existent till the next lock, which was in 10 miles. Given the late start and the winds we couldn't face that so decided to start looking for property that we can pull up to and camp on.

As we exited the lock there was a barge about 15 yards away from the gates and it was causing a wind tunnel effect by funnelling the already high winds between its bows and the lock system walls. The already large waves that were being created by the wind blowing across the river, which was very wide, almost like a collecting pool, were being funnelled as well. This made for some bigger waves, which not only came towards us but also were bouncing off the walls of the lock and the sides of the barge creating crests on waves that were coming from all angles. To say that it was scary is an understatement. These were the biggest waves we had encountered so far and in an area that had the added difficulty of a huge barge sat with its engine idling and, probably, its propeller turning to keep it on station.

My heart was in my mouth as I heard the lock master hail the barge captain and ask him to report when we had cleared him and not to engage his drive until we were well clear. I am sure he didn't need telling but I am glad he was. When we got past and managed to get together to check on each other Grace told me that she almost went over. I am so glad that neither of us did.

About a mile below the lock was a row of houses that had gardens that swept down to the rivers edge and at some, but not all, we could see boat ramps or jetties. We were keeping close in to the bank and looking for signs of life when right on cue we are hailed by a couple in their garden. Well actually he is up a ladder nailing a tile to the roof and she is holding it steady for him. She waves and calls to us asking if we would like to come ashore. We do not need a second invitation and before I can get to the boat ramp Grace is ashore.

They introduce themselves as Tom and Arlene and they are really nice people. Almost at the same time as we meet them the sun starts to shine which is a true omen of good fortune. They offer to let us use their lawn to camp on and show us to one of their garages where there are washing and toilet facilities we can use. As we are talking to them he shows us a contraption he has that can be fastened to a kayak. It is pedal powered and has paddles that mimic the action of, wait for it, Penguin feet! Do I need to tell you that it was invented in California? We want some but as they only have one set and we don't really want to carve holes in the boats, we settle for jealousy.

The surprise continues as Tom asks if I like cars and tells me of his little collection. Little! He has an MGA, a Corvette, an Oldsmobile 88, a Cadillac Deville, a Jeep, and an RV. The MG is in concourse condition and is probably better than the day it was made, the Corvette is the same. The Cadillac is the shopping car and the Jeep is towed behind the RV when they travel. This man is serious about his cars and Arlene tells me that they only bought the house for two reasons, six spaces in the garage and the river view. I notice the order she puts them in.

I ask if they would be kind enough to take us to a Walmart, or similar, in the area so that we can get some supplies and offer to give him money for fuel. Immediately Tom says that he will gladly take us to the shops and will not entertain taking money from us and in the same breath tells us that he will not enter Walmart as he does not agree with their business practises. He then starts to tell us of all the evils that they perform and how they cheat suppliers and staff alike. Arlene rolls her eyes and smiles sweetly before inviting us to have dinner with them. I get the feeling that not only does she want us to have dinner with them but that the timely invitation was a way of getting Tom off the subject.

We put the tents up and the sun is now shining brightly and the wind has dropped so they will dry nicely. We get washed and changed and set off for the shops. Somehow Arlene, Grace and I get split up in Walmart, the biggest one in the area of course, and I end up asking the staff to use the public address system to hail Grace. Arlene has had the same idea and we meet at the customer service desk. For some reason they call Grace's name and tell her to go to the tyre sales section. Is my English that bad?

Eventually we are reunited and head back to the house. On the way they give us a tour of the area and we learn that they had owned a company that makes and services industrial cranes. They are proud of the fact that it was a small company started by Tom's father and that their son, and now their grandson, had followed them into the business. They also show us the Alcan factory in town, which is a one-mile long shed and is the place where they roll the aluminium wings used by Boeing, the only place in the world big enough to do it. And they have the contract to service the cranes. Nice pension plan.

Back home we have a super meal, fantastic conversation and a lot of laughs. Grace has a theory that they were high school sweethearts and best friends who never really forgot that life is all about fun and married each other to prove it. They certainly are super people and amongst the nicest that I have ever met. Anywhere.

The weather is shown as improving tomorrow and for the next few days so, hopefully, it's correct and we can start to make progress again as today was about the shortest we have done.

Week 5
Pleasant Valley Iowa, to St Louis, Missouri

5/9/14
Halfway! But only in the number of days we have set ourselves.

It was a really good night with (almost) no train noises and no wind or rain. We are also up early enough and packed before the dew settled on the tents. What a bonus; packing away dry tents for a change!

Arlene has also got up and has made us a breakfast of apple slices and warm sweet rolls with a big pot of coffee for me and orange juice for Grace. I told you they were nice people. She comes to the rivers edge as we launch the boats and waves us off. She looks to have a tear in her eye as we leave and certainly lingers for a while as we start down the river. I do hope that I will get to meet them again one day. We have set off at exactly 7 am, possibly the earliest start we have had to date.

The river is much calmer than yesterday and has a good flow that is helping us, so we set quite a steady pace. What a difference a day makes, certainly to me. I am much clearer in the head and feel good. A bit sad to leave Tom and Arlene but that's just river life for them. I suppose its also becoming river life for me as well. We make good time; hit a lock that is empty and has no one waiting for a change, go straight through and bat onto the town of Andalusia for lunch, arriving at 11:30 with 19 miles covered.

Andalusia is up a small side channel that looks like it might be a small river but is actually a dead end that has been made into a small marina. We moor up and walk into the town. It would be a fair description of Andalusia to say that it is a 2-horse town. But one of them has died. Mind you, the little 'mom and pop' restaurant located right in the centre of the town served great food in big portions.

I make contact with Sharon from Rotary International HQ in Evanston, Chicago and she repeats her offer to come and meet us and bring a picnic so we arrange to meet her, and her husband, further down the river at Lock 16 at about 5 pm. I only found out later that this would represent a 3½ drive for them. It will be good to see them and to have a chat about further promotion of our expedition through Rotary International channels.

Things are going well, we stay in a side channel that offers us flow whilst away from the barges in the main channel and has the bonus of being slightly shorter than the 'map miles'. Then our troubles start as at about 4 pm the skies start to darken ahead of us and we can hear thunder. I look at the clouds and see that they are moving left to right across our path and declare, "We'll be OK it will miss us". The clouds start to thicken and head for us, as does the lightning. It is striking something directly up ahead, hopefully trees or power lines, and suddenly we are about to get caught up in a lightning storm. We are not in a good place; the middle of the river waving carbon fibre poles over our heads. Then the approaching rain starts to hit us. Not just rain but a torrent of water that hits us with the force of small ball bearings.

The only thing to do is make for the shore. And that is not an easy task either as the riverbanks have trees and shrubbery right up to the waters edge and the ground is just thick mud. We pull up as far as we can and sit under a bush with the tarpaulin over our heads. If we thought the rain was heavy when it first hit us we had underestimated it. The heavens opened and the rain was more like a waterfall, visibility is almost zero and the temperature has dropped dramatically. We end up under the tarpaulin shivering and sheltering for half an hour before it passes and we are able to continue. As we set off again Grace looks at me and says, "You are now officially banned from commenting on the weather as it ALWAYS does the opposite of what you say". I wonder if I can make it work in reverse but she vetoes that idea as well.

When we arrive at the lock we ask about a campsite either above or below their location. The lockmaster tell us that there is nothing below the lock but that there is an old boat launch area that "the kids use for parties" about 1000 feet upstream, just before the lock wall starts. So we head for it. The bottom of the ramp is a mud lined stone floored, insect-ridden hole. Those are its good points. I walk up and onto the farm service road only to find that there is no flat soft ground that we can camp on. There is a farm building a bit further on but the lack of people and the big 'No Trespassing' sign rules it out. We find an area about 25 yards up from the river that has a flat(ish) ground and some shelter from trees. The ground is dry and quite hard but we manage to pitch the tents.

Sharon, and her husband Brian, arrive and we sit in the public viewing area of the lock to eat the picnic they have brought. I look around at the level lawns, picnic tables and toilets and wonder if it would be possible to camp in this area. It would be easy enough to move the tents and leave the boats hidden in the bushes. I ask a member of the lock staff and he tells me no, as the federal rules prohibit any such activity. He did offer to let us use the staff showers though, which was good of him, although we didn't take him up on his offer.

It is good to see Sharon again as it has been quite some time since we last worked together on a Rotary Project although we have had several email and telephone conversations over the years. It's also nice to meet her husband, Brian, after all these years. He is an ordained Minister and has taken a sabbatical at the end of his most recent assignment as they are expecting their first child in the near future and he will be a stay at home dad for awhile. Rather him than me.

Sharon tells me about an online 'blog' that is managed by RI staff called Rotary Voices that is a showcase for programmes, projects and activities that individual Rotarians or clubs can share with the world through their website and encourages me to write a piece about the expedition for it. As I am never sure when we will next get an internet connection she promises to have a word with the staff member who moderates it so that he can be on the look out and perhaps give it a bit of priority or even edit it for us if necessary.

It is really good to see someone I know and can call a friend rather than starting from scratch at every encounter. I realise it must be hard for Grace as she only has starting from scratch to look forward to at every encounter. All too soon they are setting off back on the long drive to Chicago and we are headed for our less than ideal campsite.

As we walk, and I don't know why, the conversation turned to our toilet habits, specifically how often we were 'going' and what it was like. Without going into graphic details we both found that overall we passed smaller bowel movements than normal. We put this down to the type of food we were eating, which was mostly dehydrated packet stuff, and the fact that our bodies were obviously stripping every scrap of nourishment and energy they could leaving behind, literally, the indigestible parts.

The production of urine was also not that much of a surprise as our bodies would be using the water we consumed to process food and produce sweat to cool us down, hence we had a lesser need to pass excess water. The remarkable thing was that we both found that when we had eaten in restaurants and had 'proper' cooked food we did not produce any more solid waste but that we did pass a lot more water. We put this down to the fact that the processed foods we had consumed contained a high water content, possibly as a factor in their production and preparation. We do have some strange conversations.

6/9/14

The campsite turned out to be horrible. Half of my tent collapsed during the night because the pegs had pulled out of the ground and the sleeping mat did nothing to alleviate the feeling of laying on ball bearings all night. In the small hours I heard a barge came so close to the landing as he manoeuvred into the lock that I could hear the wash from his propeller hitting the kayaks and had to go out and pull them a bit further up to stop them getting swept out into the river.

I had arranged to do a live radio interview with a friend of mine at North Highland Radio in Scotland so had set an alarm to wake me at 5 am. I didn't need it. I was awake anyway. I had been disturbed by someone in a pickup truck with a boat on a trailer who was making a complete hash of reversing the rig to the waters edge for launching. I went and looked and it seemed like he had managed so started the interview.

Only 5 minutes in I could hear the truck engine roaring and the trailer clanging as he was trying to extricate himself from the mud. I went out to the ramp and looked and saw that he was swinging wildly and was close to our kayaks. There was a danger that he would actually run over and destroy them at one point so I passed the phone to Grace in mid sentence and ran down to confront him. I got him to stop while I manhandled the boats out of his way and he managed to pull onto more solid ground and away. At least he had the decency to apologise. I was covered in mud up to my knees and feeling like today would be better forgotten and it had only just started.

I heard on the radio that a barge was finishing off its transit of the lock and we would be good to use it in about an hour so we ate breakfast and started to pack up. We were about halfway through when a downstream barge moored up right across the boat ramp to wait to use the lock. I had a short radio conversation with the Lockmaster who told me that as the commercial traffic had priority we would have to wait. It got worse. He told me that there was another barge about to arrive that would also have priority over us and that we would have to portage or wait nearly all morning.

We started to look at hauling the boats up the ramp but it was all but impossible due to the mud that the redneck fisherman had churned up. I called him a few choice names and not under my breath either. Fortunately the captain of the barge alongside us had seen us struggle and asked the lockmaster to let us pass through before him, as we would not be able to get out by portage. The lockmaster agreed and we were given friendly waves and good wishes from everyone on the barge and in the lock as we passed through.

We had not got going till 8:30, 3 ½ hours wasted after getting out of bed, but at least it was calm and sunny, if anything a bit too sunny as it was quite hot as we paddled along. The barge that let us through passes us, and then we catch him up at the next lock along the way, only this time he was almost through when we arrived. A steady paddle and a stop on a deserted boat ramp for lunch is about the only comment to make about the day. It's almost turning into 'Groundhog Day' for the paddling, only the nighttime stops differ, and some of them by not much.

Our stop for the night was in the town of Keithsburg. A great little campsite, one that actually has tent areas and not just sites for RVs, and we are able to wash kit and shower, yes at the same time. Why take it off to wash it when you can do it while wearing it? The camp host gives us our pitch for free as a donation to our charity and wishes us well. We walk into the town and have a meal in the only bar. Not the only one that is open but the only one there is. It's a bit of a strange place as we see people driving round town in golf carts and notice that many of the properties are closed up. The only thriving place is the campsite. Grace goes back to camp to talk to her parents and boyfriend as we had a signal there but nowhere else and I finish off my coffee. I realise I am tired when I cut a conversation short with some young ladies. They were interested in the expedition, having seen the logos on our clothes, but I was just not up to talking to them about it. Sorry ladies. An early night is called for I think.

As I approach the tent the occupants of an RV near to us invite me for a coffee and as they are offering food for breakfast in the morning I accept. The man of the 'house' is wearing a cap that proclaims that he works as a driver for Walmart and has completed 1 Million accident free miles. He is full of praise for the company, which is a complete contrast to Tom a few days ago.

As I lie in my tent I start to think about our progress and the big problem for me is that we are about 30 miles, or 1 day, behind schedule with no real prospect of making it up anytime soon. It is starting to haunt me that we are still some 400 miles from St Louis, where we will meet up with the bottom set of maps and the days are running out. In an email some days ago I had asked Tom Drennan in St Louis about the possibility of a day off and a short road transport to make up the deficit, but have not yet had an answer. So far we have had just five days off in the 31 we have been travelling and as we undertook some activity on each of them, they were not real rest days.

We need rest, not just for our bodies but minds too. I just hope Tom can come through for us. We need a good night's rest and then a big day tomorrow to help with the mileage we need to cover.

7/9/14
What a superb campsite. No trains! Which makes it worthy of five Stars in my book.

The weather was good today, with clear blue skies, no wind and a smooth river. The flow has picked up as well so we manage 5mph or better for most of the time. This is quite a change from what we have been used to as we do not have to put up with any slack areas or collecting pools around locks and dams. Well not for a while anyway.

I felt very tired, physically and mentally, from the outset and it was obvious that Grace was as well. We just keep going. The paddling has become an automatic action and we simply follow the channel markers as a means of navigating, cutting across corners to save miles where possible.

There was not much conversation but when we did we usually managed to laugh about something. One of the things we have constantly laughed about is the books we are writing and how one chapter will start *"We paddled along a wide ribbon of gleaming water under a clear blue sky with tall trees lining the banks standing like silent sentries as we glide past"*

The next chapter will start *"We did it again today"*

And the next one. And the next one. I think that that time and descriptive narration has arrived.

The stunning views are still boring, only the width of the river has changed now it is VERY WIDE. We set off just after 8:00 and make the next lock at 17 miles in 3 ¼ hours. Even the collecting pool was easy to cross today, or perhaps we are getting used to it. The bad news is that we had an hours wait lock through. A rest of sorts but not a complete one.

A check of the maps shows a big town called Burlington about 5 miles downstream where we can get lunch and a further check shows a town called Dallas City another 14 or so miles further on. We elect to push on to both of these, as there is a chance of real food, which is always a bonus, and twice which is an even bigger bonus.

Our first call is at the Marina in Burlington, which is full of very expensive looking powerboats but does not appear to have much in the way of a restaurant. A check with a couple just going out reveals that there is not much for non-members at the marina but just a little further down there is a place in the old railway station that has a boat dock outside. They also tell us it is a nice place so we set off for it.

As described it has a boat dock. Designed for rather large boats it seems as the deck is about 3 foot above the water and the sides are sheer. With a bit of acrobatics we manage to climb out and stroll across to the restaurant. In doing so we have to cross an old narrow gauge railway that looks like it might be used about once a day for tourists and I make a big thing out of listening for the clanging bell and the train horn before crossing it. Anybody watching must have thought we were mad.

The rest of the diners all seem rather better dressed than us. Not hard really as we have been in the same clothes since the start, but this time they really are quite smart. Then I realise that it is Sunday and they are out for Sunday lunch. Never mind, my money is good and that is all the staff worry about. We have missed the buffet, which included an array of desserts, and have to settle for burgers and fries. Again. Our waitress tells us not to bother buying a dessert just go and help yourself to the ones left for clearing up. I modestly take a couple of small profiteroles but she then wanders across with a plateful for us. We must look like we need feeding.

Back at the boat dock we have to struggle to climb down to the kayaks and it looks much more daunting going down than it did going up. Not helped by the waves being created by passing boats either. We have to lie on the floor to load wallets and cameras back into the deck bags and then carefully untie the tether lines so that we can then cast off using slack lines. I have just got my handling lines ready when I see that Grace has accidentally left her dry bag with money, passport and other important documents on the deck and it is caught around her handling line being slowly dragged to the edge. I shout to her and try to fasten my boat up quickly so that I can run to it but I am about a yard short when it drops into the water.

Fortunately it was sealed and had some air in it so it floated, unlike my camera several weeks ago, which was a stroke of luck. Much relieved I climb into my boat and we set off again. Laughing with relief at what could have been a serious situation.

It's a slog down to Dallas City but we get there at 5:30 pm and start asking along the bank about a campsite. Someone says "Go to Ike's, he'll sort you out". It turns out that 'Ike's' is a bar with an outdoor live band and crowds of rednecks steadily drinking the bar stocks dry. I go to the bar to ask a member of the staff for Ike and I am introduced to him. Grace has stayed with the boats chatting to a couple that are just leaving the boat dock. I say chatting as they are both well past the point of feeling no pain and constantly ask Grace to tell them again about what we are doing, so its more like an interview.

He tells me that he doesn't have a campground himself but points us towards the lawn of the house next door saying, "Go ahead, I'll square it up". And he does. As does the lawn owners daughter who comes down to see us while we are unloading our gear, a friend of the lawn owners who has stopped to see us unload on her way to meet her friends on a boat that has just pulled in and some guy who was stood next to and agreed with Ike. They all ring Dorothy, the lawn owner to tell her about us, who promptly comes to meet us just as we have finished putting the tents up.

She makes us most welcome and is delighted to offer us her lawn. All she asks that we come up to the house, but by a specific route across the lawn that she points out, to meet 'Buddy'.

Buddy is her dog. A Rottweiler. A bloody huge Rottweiler! And as we get closer he gets bigger and Grace decides now is the time to tell me that dogs this size scare her. They scare her? Buddy is not doing much for me either as he bounces off his chain that looks barely big enough to hold him back.

After a few tense moments of standing back we get invited to sit on the porch, which places me within the chain's radius, and Buddy promptly walks up to me and licks my face. That's close enough to those jaws, thank you!

We sit for awhile so that 'Buddy can get used to you and not come visit you in the night' and then go to the bar for a Pizza. Various people chat to us before we return to the tents and sit and listen to the band from a distance. The really amusing part of it all is that there is a railway line right alongside the bar and the 100+ carriage goods trains all sound their horns at three different spots on their approach and the band will start a new number just as the train starts to pass by. Perhaps it's true that the locals don't hear the trains after a while. Don't know how they can miss them.

Tom Drennan rings me to tell me of his plans. To cut a long story short we are to meet him in another 2 days at a pick up site to be determined nearer the time. He finishes work at 1 pm and the road runs almost parallel to the river so finding us is not a big problem. We will then have a chance of a rest day with him. That will be most welcome and once again thank you will not be a big enough phrase.

At lunch today I had overheard Grace talking to Phil and somehow the topic of quitting was mentioned. I mentioned that I had heard this and just said 'don't give me an excuse'. So did Grace. Commitment obviously wains when tiredness sets in and we are seriously tired.

I am giving serious consideration to missing a huge chunk somehow and putting in again around Arkansas so we miss out the long lonely stretch that is below Memphis. That is a really tempting thought but one I manage to dismiss. By Tuesday we will have done 1000 miles, one way and another. Quite an achievement but not as far as I wanted to be and things will only get worse for us in terms of tiredness, mental strain and difficulty in finding campsites. I set myself a target of getting to Memphis and seeing how I feel about continuing. Serious conversation time at some point over the next 2 days I think.

As we lay in our tents writing journals or just chilling the band strikes up for its last set. They start to play 'Sweet Home Alabama' and Grace declares that it is one of her favourites. After the first two bars the singer has clearly enjoyed a little too much throat oil during the interval and commences to murder the rest of the song. 'Well it was' she declares. He goes on to massacre several other tunes we both like and at one point is joined in the assault by a woman from the audience. Thank goodness they stopped at 9 pm.

Unfortunately the trains didn't and every 15 minutes one woo-hoo-hoo'd its way through town carrying oil or coal to the power station up the track or taking the empties back for a refill. During the day I had spoken to a barge captain on the radio and asked about the weight of his barge units. He told me that each one carried 1600 tones and they frequently had 9 as a travelling set. That's some 14,400 tons of freight. We had looked at trains that were parked up earlier in the trip and saw that their carriages held 100 tons each so they carried about 50% less. Grace and I vote for the increased use of barges, as they are much quieter.

8/9/14
The previous night had been horrible. I had hardly any sleep because of the trains and the first time since we set off I felt cold which also kept me awake. This does not put me in a good place for the start of the day.

After breakfast we set off and it was not a bad start as the wind was present but low and the water was fairly calm. I had banked on reaching the town of Keokuk for the lock about 1 pm as there was a marina shown just upstream where we hoped we could have lunch.

That was the plan but the wind had other ideas.

We were not making any headway at all and just getting more and more tired. To make things worse we had reached a point where there was nowhere to stop and get food and nowhere that was suitable for us to pull up and make ourselves a meal from the supplies. We were keeping going on snack bars and nibbles but, clearly, it was not enough

We were both fading fast and needed to eat far more than snacks but still there was nowhere to stop and it was now past 2 pm. We were at a point where we could see the Keokuk Yacht club and made one last effort to battle across the lake sized river, battling high winds and a large swell before we finally pulled up on a boat ramp at the side. I went to see if there was anyone at the marina and walked to their clubhouse. Another place with floating gin palaces but, as I entered, the girl behind the counter broke into a huge smile and said "You made it, great. We've been watching you come across the lake and hoping you'd be safe". I ask if we can stay anywhere in the marina for the night and they are most welcoming.

They point us to a grassed area on the side of the marina for the tents, tell us that we can use the facilities to shower and wash clothes and, best of all, we can bring our boats into the marina proper where they have an electric hoist to lift the kayaks out. This is the best news I have had all day (possibly week) and I cannot wait to tell Grace.

We paddle round and use the hoist deciding immediately that these should be standard issue at all stopping points. After pitching the tents we get a pizza from behind the bar and then shower and clean up. The marina manager tells us to make ourselves at home and set up in a corner so we can use the WIFI and charge our batteries. I ask if there is a charge and he says that he will sort it out with the chap who decides these things when he comes in later.

I manage a call home on FaceTime and get them up to date on what is happening. Kenneth and Helen have obviously been following our progress and the Facebook posts. I tell them about how tired I am and how doubt is creeping in about being able to continue, especially after today, Helen tells me how proud they are of what I am doing. She also tells me that Thomas has started to tell everyone at playgroup, and anywhere else that has an audience that 'My pops is in America,

Kayaking the River" when asked what river he says "The Mississippi River for the poorly children". How Dare I give up now?

We are happily downloading pictures and videos, uploading and videos to YouTube (well Grace is) charging batteries and other techie stuff when I am approached by a couple of club members who have seen the Rotary roundel on my shirt and introduce themselves as Past Presidents of the local Rotary club. Strangely both are called Mike, as is another Rotarian who I meet later in the evening, so it seems place names are not the only thing frequently repeated in the USA.

They tell me that they are an investment club and they have a meal, usually a BBQ, followed by loads of beer and then spend 5 minutes on the investment stuff. In return we tell them about the expedition and our fund raising efforts and swap cards. This introduction is followed up about 5 minutes later by one of the Mikes inviting us to join them for dinner. Not only is it a BBQ but the steaks are the biggest things I've seen without still being attached to the cow and walking about! We accept of course and for once cannot actually eat everything that is put in front of us. I must be tired. As I am eating the marina manager comes to me and tells me that there will be no charge for the using campsite and facilities. I suspect someone has paid it for us but don't delve and ask him to pass our thanks on.

Before we leave for the tents we get given $40 in donations and an invite to visit them again if we are ever in the area. That is something I would gladly do, as they are, once again, nice people.

We are short of how far we thought we would get today so I message Tom and tell him that I will have to review where we will meet. No problem for him, he says, just let him know and he will meet us.

9/9/14
There were only 3 trains last night and those were in the distance. I could still hear the damn things though. It is 6 am as we start to wake up and move about and as we do the thunder and lightning starts, the wind starts to increase and we see a barge going past that will, hopefully, be gone by the time we are set up and ready for the off. The club maintenance man is about as I start to take stuff to the boat and he offers to put a table and chairs in the bar lobby for us to use as a

breakfast room, which I accept.

I am all packed away and Grace joins me for breakfast. We have decided to wait and see how the weather pans out for an hour or so rather than risk getting on the water and being caught out. I am talking to Pauline on FaceTime when suddenly the wind gets much stronger and the rain really starts to pour down. We haven't got the tents down yet so we have to dash out and drag everything into the club boat shed. Unfortunately Grace's tent collapses before she can get her sleeping bag put away and it gets wet through. Thank goodness for the driers that the marina have let us have use of. The weather gets worse and is truly horrible and is going to hold us up quite a lot, if not stop us completely.

The rain starts to ease and the thunder and lightning stops so I ring the lock using a courtesy phone in the lobby area. They tell me to be there at about 11:30 and we can lock through, as they will book us a slot between two barge units going in opposite directions. I hope that the downstream one has gone and that we do not have a repeat of our previous experience. Fortunately it had. The wind is still strong when we set off but we go for it. The lock we pass through is the largest drop on the river and a huge piece of civil engineering. It is 1200 feet long, 110 feet wide and we drop 40 feet. I later worked out that this represents 5,280,000 cubic feet of water, which is 34,320,000 gallons or 154,440,000 litres. For two kayaks. 'You're welcome. Have a safe trip' being the only comment made to us as we pass through.

As we have set off so late in the day I have spoken to Tom Drennan and arranged to meet him at a town called Clanton which is just over 20 miles away and another lock further on. My mind is so numb and tired that at the end of the day I don't recall any of the journey other than the locks or even if we stopped on the way. That is a dangerous state to be in and one that can have serious effects on our safety as lack of concentration and allowing complacency to set in is an ever-present threat.

The only high spot of the day was that on this leg we passed the 1000 miles travelled mark and made a short video about it for posting on YouTube. In a moment of silliness a mile further on I ask if Grace is still filming and as she is ask her to stop paddling and I glide past her singing "1001 cleans a big big carpet, for less than half a crown". She has no idea what I am going on about, probably something shared by a lot of readers of this book, but puts it in the video anyway.

The only good news was that once through the lock the wind has dropped and the flow has picked up, at one point we are doing 7.2mph for quite a distance without paddling too hard. We have a deadline of 4 pm to meet Tom, well OK not a deadline but an arrangement and we get there exactly 10 minutes before him. The lock at Clanton was empty when we arrived which helped, as did our passage through it. I had radioed the lockmaster as normal and the gates had only partly opened to let us through before closing again, then no one came to throw ropes for us to steady ourselves on, which was strange. We heard a rush of water and the bottom gate started to swing open. As it was half way open the hooter sounded and we were able to set off. We had dropped exactly one foot. What a contrast from the previous lock.

Tom Drennan picks us up in his brother-in-laws Jeep and we set off, via a petrol station for a burger. Arrangements seem a bit loose and on the hoof but Tom has ideas, which he starts to put to us. As we start down the road a storm really kicks up. One that may well have done serious damage to us in tents had we been out in it. The weather is not just bad, it's dangerous. Lightning continually, sheets of water and very high winds. The conversation stops as Tom concentrates on driving, how he can see where he is going is a mystery, it is that bad. I get really despondent looking at this but at the same time really glad that Tom has picked us up. I hate to think what would have been the outcome otherwise.

He has arranged a hotel for us and confirms the booking while we travel. Obviously he had erred on the side of caution should we not make it, but we did.

One option that was proposed was that when he finished work at 1 pm tomorrow he would collect us and move us to a campsite down river so that we can set off the day after, which would be a Thursday. Tom tells us that he has to work all day Thursday and that if we wanted to have a day off he would collect us at lunchtime on Friday to move us a little further down the river. The weather forecast is for another series of storms tomorrow and heavy rain on Thursday so I tell him that in view of the weather, and the fact we are very tired, that this might be a viable option but that we would have to discuss it.

We do and I propose that we take the option to have a proper rest day. OK, so we miss a chunk but we will recover and be out of the weather, which does look bad. I don't mind admitting to Grace that I would rather rest and miss miles now than get tired and make mistakes later. Mistakes on the next bit could be dangerous, as the boats get bigger and more frequent. I also tell her that I am absolutely beat and really would appreciate the rest. She will never know how grateful I am that she agreed.

The weather report that night showed that 7 inches of rain had fallen in 5 hours in the area around Clanton and that the devastation caused to buildings was immense. It does not bear thinking about what it would have done to our tents.

We did a quick check in at the hotel, drop our gear, have a wash, change and go out to meet Joy, his wife, for dinner. Which, despite our protests, he pays for. The conversation is a little stilted, as we are both so tired. The only thing that stuck in my mind, other than how nice they both are, was the 7 foot 2 inch waiter that served us and that is NOT an exaggeration or the result of a hallucination caused by tiredness.

10/9/14
Boy did I need the rest! I slept like a log all night. Not waking up once, not even for a toilet visit courtesy of the 'real food syndrome'. We had breakfast and then lounged about during the morning. The most strenuous thing I did was have a bath and clean my feet! I hadn't realised how ingrained the dirt had become till I had scrubbed and sweated in the bath. I have no doubt that they will get filthy again, not to mention garnering more cuts, broken toenails and bruises from walking about at campsites with no shoes on. The Crocs have just about died and are only useful on really harsh surfaces. Like broken glass. Everything else I can cope with now.

We ate lunch at a nearby burger place, where else did you expect? Then at about 2:30 Tom picked us up to do a brief tour of the city, take some photos at the "Gateway to the West" arch, do a bit of shopping for supplies and then have dinner before going to bed.

St Louis is a fascinating city with some historic buildings, museums and parks and the arch is a stunning sight. Apparently visitors can travel inside it to view the area from the top but we passed on that. The river runs right through the centre of the city, just like Minneapolis. Unlike that city it is a commercial port and not very scenic and Tom tells us that it also passes through some of the most dangerous parts of the city where crime is rife and gangs battle for territory. Sounds like a nice place to have to camp.

We stop off for a beer at a microbrewery and as we are leaving the rain starts again. It's been on and off all day but nothing like we had seen on the forecast, which does nothing for my mood and the decision to avoid travelling in it. This time it really belts down and is like the storm we had experienced the day before. The streets of the city are flooded and the Jeep resembles a boat as it carves through the small lakes that the roads have become. Once again I am glad that we have avoided it.

We have dinner and it is another late night as I get into bed at 9 pm. It has become the norm for us to be settled at about 8 pm when in the tents.

11/9/14
Thursday was just us, no sightseeing, no shopping, nothing. We had another lie in, a lazy breakfast; I had another bath followed by a nap. We went out for the, by now, obligatory, burger and fries lunch and then I had another nap. Yes I was tired. Very tired.

We did manage to get some washing done and Grace took her tent outside to air and dry off, we managed some calls to home and I called some of my friends in Louisiana. I had composed a write up for Rotary Voices and managed to send it to the moderator yesterday morning and he had sent a request for photographs as he wanted to publish it at the beginning of next week. Worldwide publicity at last!

I had a close look at the maps for the bottom half of the river as it leads to the Gulf of Mexico and saw that the pages are approximately 10 miles per page, some more, some less, so I did some calculations on our potential progress. I tried to bank on 40 miles per day so that would put us in the Gulf on 4 October. This would be a Saturday and would allow our friends in Louisiana, who were offering to collect us, the opportunity of doing so without it disturbing their working week. Later in conversation with Tom, who used to work the river, he tells us we can expect better than that. I hope he's right as this will give us a margin for error should we encounter weather or injury problems.

That evening I put this to Grace over a pleasant meal in a small, but expensive, Italian Restaurant and we decide to see if we can do it. I am still not certain that I can complete the trip but am feeling better for the rest. As we walk back we come across a Policeman and I persuade him to let me take Grace's picture with him to replace the one at the bottom of the river. Suddenly that memory seems like a lifetime ago.

And then another late night 9:30 pm no less!

Week 6
St Louis, Missouri to Memphis, Tennessee

12/9/14
I had arranged to get up early and go into the city with Tom this morning to visit a publishing house to pick up a specialist river guide that they produce which gives details of food and supply points along the river. An interesting place, even at 7:30 am, with some nice people who take details of our trip and promise to see if they can use it as a filler in one of their magazines.

The good news about the publication is that it's comprehensive. The bad news? There are not a lot of places shown on our route. We will manage I have no doubt. It will be hard, but what's new?

I just want to get underway now, I really did need to rest and have no problem with losing river miles. I can justify the 'missing miles' and have said that I'm not going to get fried in a thunderstorm or die of exhaustion just to travel a river. If some people don't like it that's their problem.

Mind you we would get some serious media coverage if we did, such is the parlous state of affairs that is ordinary people doing extraordinary things.

After lunch (can you guess what we had?) Tom drove us down to the "Trail of Tears" State Park and camped overnight with us rather than drive back again that night. This would put us at river mile 66.5 so we have missed over 250 river miles. As I write this at a later date I feel ashamed at missing so much but at the time was convinced that it was the right decision. Hindsight is always a perfect tool for planning and having reviewed my actions many times since completing the expedition, I still do not think that I would, or could, have made any other choice. I leave to my reader to make their own judgement on my actions.

I specifically say 'my' as in many respects I think Grace followed my needs and accepted what I was proposing. Not without some discussion, I admit, but perhaps I was a little forceful.
The good news of the day was that at least it gave us chance to fill the

car with fuel and buy him dinner in the nearby town of Cape Girardeau. That was a first as no one else has, not even Tom up to that point.

13/9/14
Having woken at the customary 6 am we are actually on the river and get moving at 8:15 am. In a matter of minutes we found that our speed was around 8mph, has someone attached a motor to the boats? As the day went on this varied, but never dropped below 5 mph as long as we were paddling. We didn't seem to be paddling any faster or harder than we have done previously but we certainly were moving faster than we had been.

After a couple of hours, and as we had arranged, Tom met us for a brief stop to give us some sandwiches at Cape Girardeau and we met our first really big barge. This one had 25 cargo units and one power plant, the previous biggest we had seen had been a 9-cargo unit. It was making its way upstream and was over to the right bank, the side that we was on, as this is where the town boat ramp was. The front wake that it creates is not much bigger than those of the smaller barges but the wash from the propeller is huge and forms repeat patterns, in a sort of Loch Ness Monster series of humps, for several hundred yards at the stern.

We are pretty close, mostly because of the lack of room between it and the bank, but manage to ride the waves it creates without any real problem. As long as we give them as much room as we have done things should OK.

The weather is kind, there is a headwind but not as bad as previous days, and we continue to zip along. We stop for lunch, and a rest, on a sandbar and off we go again. About 3:30 pm we hit the 40 mile mark, which is something of a quick pace and a record for us, and start to look for a place to camp for the night, as we are nowhere near any towns or marked boat ramps.

As we look down a side channel we see a beach on an island that looks inviting and decide to check it out. When we get to it we find that the island has actually been split in two by the river and the beach has a channel cutting it in half. As it is easier to get to, we don't have to head upstream that is, and is nice and big we decide to take the lower half. We pull the kayaks up onto the sand and start to unload and erect the tents.

Problem number one; Suddenly a wind has got up and the tents develop a mind of their own about being pegged down. Problem number two; I look around and see that not 10 yards from where I have put my tent the water is starting to creep up the beach. My first thought is to move everything higher up the beach to avoid this and go further up the beach to check it out. When I return Grace has started to pack her tent away as the water has risen quite a lot and she proposes that we move across the channel to the other side which actually looks higher and seems to be unaffected.

It is hard work getting across the narrow strip of water as it is flowing quite fast and there is the wind to contend with, but we make it and set up camp. Being cautious about the rising waters I suggest that we make sure we are about 20 yards up where the beach is higher, as evidenced by a wall that drops down to the river on one side. Grace tells me I am being overcautious but I insist and we set up camp. I'm still wary so pull the boats nearer to the tents and clip them to the frames and declare – "If the water rises the only things that matter are the boats, passports and money".

Within minutes of pitching the tents the water on the other side has risen so much that the area we had chosen to stop on was underwater. The water rises at an alarming rate and will need watching. I realised later that we are now well below the locks and dams that act to maintain the river at an even depth and that the river would rise and fall under different influence, not least rainfall in other areas, remote from our immediate vicinity, being brought in by tributaries to the Mississippi.

There is a magnificent sunset and we pause to enjoy it and take photographs. Grace does handstands, with the sun and a bright orange sky as a background we could literally be anywhere but in the middle of one of the busiest commercial waterways in the world. On the other half of the island we see a small herd of deer come out of the trees and drink from the river before disappearing again. I wonder how they got there and then realise that, in winter, the island may well be joined to the banks and that the deer have been cut off by the rising waters after walking across to feed on the trees and bushes.
After our evening meal, I hesitate to call dehydrated potato and pasta

with tinned chicken 'Dinner' we sit and talk for a while. One of the big questions is "What are the arrangements for getting back from mile zero?" Answer "Not a clue, but my friends in Louisiana are working on it". And that is the absolute truth of the matter. I know it will involve the use of a boat, to bring us off the water and a vehicle and trailer, to transport the kayaks the 5-hour drive to where we will be staying. I also tell her that my friends are planning on finding accommodation for her and Phil in New Orleans for a couple for days so they can visit the city, but that is all I know. They have also asked if it would be possible for us to aim for a finish on Saturday 4th August as this would mean that they do not have to break the working week to collect us. It also gives us a target that has some leeway as the first of the flights home is on the 10th for Grace and Phil. And that is as far as my plans go.

This led to me suggesting that we cover in the region of 50 miles a day, if possible, to meet these targets. Grace has a small rant about us finishing early, how Phil won't be able to be at the finish to meet us and how it was OK for me as Pauline comes out soon and she will be able to meet me. I get a bit cross and tell her that I don't care about anybody else being there, just us finishing safely, in time to have some rest before flying home and being able to have definite arrangements so we are not still wondering what we will do as we approach the end. She seems to be hung up on Phil walking out of the airport and joining us on the river for the last few days. That would be nice I agree, but we don't know if we could source another kayak, where he could meet us, and how he would get to us even if we did know.

I try to explain to her the logistics of it all and how we are dependent on others for everything and perhaps even need to build some distance to allow a day off further down the river, I am sure we will need one. Another 21 days of solid exercise is in front of us, minimum, is what faces us. I fully agree with one point she made and that is that missing out another big lump of mileage is not an option as, if we do, we might as well give up now. I hope we are fit enough to make it to the end.

This is the first time we have had what might be called an argument. As tired and frustrated as we are and have been, I am surprised we have gone this long without one.

14/9/14
Not the warmest night I've had so far but one of the quietest, having no trains makes a huge difference! And it didn't rain so we were dry. Well we didn't have to worry about rain, but ……

I was woken up at about 11 pm with a splashing noise, thinking it was a big wave I looked out to check the boats and saw that across at our original site the water had risen so much that not only had the beach area been covered but that the water entirely covered the whole sandbar right up to the tree line. Back to sleep, as it does not affect us.

I wake up at 6 am, dress and bag stuff up while still in the tent, more to stay warm than anything, and start moving about at 6-20 am. I then opened the flap and looked out. To my horror the water had risen and was about 4 feet from the boats or 10 feet from the tent. And it looks to be still rising.

I shout to Grace to warn her and start to pack the tent and gear away. We both have everything away in record time and get away by only moving the boats a couple of feet. That was a close call. At least we learned a bit about camping on sandbars without getting wet.

After our enforced early start we get going and in 22 miles reach the '0' point for the middle section of the USACE maps. We are officially on the last section of the river and we now have 'only' 950 miles to go. Yippee! For some reason the flow has subsided, probably because of the width of the river. The Ohio River flows into the Mississippi just at this point as well but that does not make any difference. Suddenly it's hard work again.

As I look at the map and start to transfer to the lower section set, I realise that in my calculations last night I had omitted to include 60+ miles from the previous set of maps which puts my estimate for finishing in doubt. Grace thinks about this for awhile and says that as we now know we can do 40 miles a day with comparative ease, we can build some extras in to make up the distance. She has obviously thought about my intentions to finish on 4th October.

Water and supplies are the only problem we can foresee as the map is almost devoid of any signs of towns for quite some way. There is a town called Columbus, Kentucky, which is another state ticked off the list, with a state park and a boat ramp not very far away. After a short break, on a sandbar, again, for lunch we head for it.

The topic of conversation turns to our fund raising and we wonder if we can hold a lunch and call it the 'Sandbar Café' and as a menu feed the attendees the same sort of 'food' we have been eating. We decide against that but then invent all sorts of courses that are literally as described. Such as cheesecake; a cake made with cheese or house burgers; burgers cut into the shape of houses. This keeps us amused for a while. It has to, the scenery still hasn't changed much.

At Columbus we find that there is a boat repair yard and we talk to a man about supplies. He tells us: - They have a drinking water supply, good!
The town is not far way, good!
But everything closes on Sunday, bad!
The state park has a snack bar, good!
But it's a fair old hike because the recent floods have washed the direct path away, bad!

We pitch the tents at the top of the boat ramp on a grassed area with a lovely view of the river, and the boat yard. I am thankful that it is Sunday and they are not hammering and bashing but wonder if they have a nightshift.

We see various people coming and going to look at the river and find that many of them are looking along the riverbank for civil war artefacts. Apparently, the state park above us was the site of a large battle and after landslides they can find bullets, shells, parts and whole weapons and, sometimes, even buckles, buttons and cap badges. Rather like the First World War sites in France and Belgium.

One such visitor is a young man who stops to talk to us so I ask him if he would be kind enough to give us a lift to the state park which he agrees to do and we have burgers, fries and cokes like regular Sunday picnickers. It has been a lot further than the 'bit of a hike' that was described to us and I look around to see if I can find us a lift back.

The good old British accent to the rescue! A young man with a real Southern drawl and a true redneck truck. One where you have to open the window to use the outside handle to open the door AND you don't have to wind the window down first "'Cause it broke sometime back and I aint fixed it yet", gives us a lift back to the tents. His accent really is so 'country' that I almost think he is putting it on, until he tells me that he is in town for the annual family picnic. Then I realise he is the genuine article.

Grace comments on the change in accents from the way Tom Drennan in St Louis speaks, which is not that far away really, speaks to how the people we have met today talk. Welcome to the South y'all!

As we sit and enjoy the last of the day's sunshine a man, who introduces himself as John, and woman approach us and ask if the kayaks are ours and are we in Rotary. I tell him that they are and that I am and what we are doing. He tells me that he has a good friend who, along with his wife is in the Rotary Club in the next town down, a place called Hickman, Kentucky. He goes on to tell me that his friend is a Past District Governor and, unusually, so is his wife.

He rings his friend on his mobile phone and I get to speak to him briefly. He asks what district I am from and I tell him, 1040 Yorkshire. Just as I hear him call out "Honey he's from 1040 ..." the signal drops so I am left wondering at the significance of this. We can't get him back so I don't worry about it.
John asks us if we are in need of supplies and offers us a lift into town but then remembers it is Sunday and everything is closed. I tell him that we have seen that Hickman is about 17 miles downstream and that we had planned a stop there to do some shopping and he promptly offers to meet us and give us a lift. These nice people keep appearing.

When we check the maps we see that for the next few days there are occasional towns, so we may get real food and supplies, but coming up after that is a lot of nothing so we will have to see if we can put in some big mile days to get through. The weather is hot and sunny with little wind and we hope it stays that way. We will be leaving from mile marker 937 exactly, which at our current pace will leave us 137 miles short of our target

15/9/14
I went to sleep within minutes of climbing into my sleeping bag and woke up really refreshed and ready to go. I am just about to get up

and check if Grace is awake when I decided to check my watch. To find that it was 5 minutes past midnight. Back to sleep then.

I awoke again at 6 am and when I tell Grace about my initial wake up time she just looks at me. The look on her face is a mixture of 'what on earth did you do that for' and 'if you had woken me up pain would have followed'.

It is framing up to be a nice sunny day and we are away at about 7:30 am. We make it to Hickman for just after 10 am, the hardest part was going up the side channel past the commercial docks, to meet John. He's brought a lady he introduced as Ann Robertson with him, who, it turned out, was the wife of the man I had spoken to on the phone last night. She is a Rotarian and had been one of the first 8 female District Governors way back in the early 1990's. Not only that but she had been the Rotary International President's personal representative at the District 1040 conference in 1997. Coincidences keep happening on this trip! She knew many of the same people I did, sadly some of whom had died, and was familiar with our programmes and projects as she had friends in Yorkshire who she kept in touch with.

John and Ann take us to the shop, which is quite a way from the water so we were glad of the lift, and then take us to a local restaurant and treat us to an early lunch. This makes the stop almost 2 hours in length but we never refuse a chance not to eat the dried stuff. They also call at the local newspaper office to see if they have anyone free to interview us, but unfortunately they don't. John offers to send them a couple of pictures and see if they can use them and get details of the expedition off the website.

Fully fuelled up on good home cooking, including pecan pie with ice cream, we set off again. As we get to the mouth of the channel John and Ann are parked near a ferry ramp and blow the car horn and wave at us. Not sure what the ferry queue made of that.

We make it to the next town, New Madrid just after 5 pm, almost 49 miles from our start point. This has been the furthest we have covered in a day so far.

Not without drama though. A one point Grace took a different route to me as we negotiated some meanders in the river and she was at the other side of it. About a mile away. It took me some time to spot her; a small red dot low in the water, almost invisible against the riverbank. She was so far away that I couldn't see her at first and had a few moments of panic as to what had happened. This worried me, as if anything had happened I wouldn't know where she was never mind be able to help.

When we finally get close to each other again I make my feelings known and tell her that I am not happy about being so far apart. I don't know if it's the age difference or just that I always have had a cautious streak where personal safety is concerned, but she didn't seem to understand my concerns telling me that I am worrying about nothing. I don't agree and tell her so.

On arrival at the town of New Madrid I walk to the top of the boat ramp to scout out a campsite. There is a paved walkway along the top of the levee and a car park to one side. There is also a grassed area that has a wall toward the riverside that looks like it will be OK for the tents. All in all it is a nice area, which has the bonus of a toilet on site, and when I look over the walkway see that the town is right at the other side, so the shops and a 'mom and pop' place can't be far away.

There is a couple in a truck, what else, looking out at the river and they greet me, telling me that they have watched us come down the river and up the boat ramp. I ask them about camping in this area and they point to the flat area I hade first seen and tell me that, "You will be fine here". I also ask for directions to somewhere where we can eat and they direct me to a café alongside a fuel station that is "Just along the road and turn left". It's anybody's guess just how far that is given previous directions included phrases such as 'about a block away' when in a woodland area.

They ask the, by now, usual questions, about what we are doing and get the, by now, usual answers as we chat for a few minutes. Then out of the blue they tell me that they need to call back home but that they will come back in 30 minutes when we have set up camp to run us to the food place. I accept their hospitality and as they drive off go to tell Grace of the arrangements.

We unload, secure the boats and start to pitch the tents. As we finish I notice that there is a memorial plaque on the wall just beside us commemorating the life of a local Firefighter, who died in the line of duty, and that the wall to the side of the levee is actually constructed so as to have tiered seating facing towards the memorial.

The couple I have been talking to turn up right on the 30 minutes that they said they would and introduce themselves as Bobby and Tanya. They tell me that they have rung the local Police Chief to tell him about us, where we are camping and requested that the staff on night duty pay us a couple of visits during the night "Just to make sure everything will be OK overnight". He then takes me to the fuel station/café and brings me back with freshly made burgers, fries and cake as a treat. When we get back I find Grace talking to a couple of people who continue to talk to us as we eat.

It turns out that Bobby is an associate pastor at a local church and, like just about everyone else we have met so far they are just nice people. I'm beginning to wonder where these stories about having trouble along the route have come from. The people up north tell you to be wary of the southerners and city folk, the southerners tell you to be wary of the northerners and the city folk and the city dwellers are just amazed that you have survived the countryside in both north and south. They need to meet each other more.

Bobby and Tanya, and a couple of other people that have stopped by, say their goodbyes and we sit and write up our journals before turning in for the night. The various joggers, walkers, sunset watchers and river observers all wave and greet us as they pass by. I get the feeling everyone knows about us! Small town America at its best.

Looking at the maps it seems we passed into the state of Tennessee today, and then back out as the meanders of the river take us back and forth between the different areas.

16/9/14
Apart from the two women out for a walk and talking loudly as they passed by at 4 am, it was a good night.

We are on the water for 7:30 and it is soon apparent that the flow is good so we may make good time. As we set off I suggested we follow the channel as the map showed that the left bank swept quite a way out but, as we started round the first bend leading away from New Madrid we saw that there was a channel between the left bank and an island so we headed along it to cut the corner.

Too late I realised that this whole island is missing from the map and we end up grounding out on a sandbar. It would seem that the floods earlier in the year had created the 'island' and that as the water has dropped it is too shallow to take even a kayak. We have no option but to go round the spit of land, which actually requires us to backtrack a little and waste time and effort.

I find that at 9 am there is a US Coast Guard broadcast on the radio giving information for river users and a weather forecast. Obviously it is aimed at commercial traffic but is useful to us. It seems that the weather is pretty good with a warning about the river being in flood further North, which will cause it to rise in our area by quite a bit. The forecast is for it to be 12 feet higher in Columbus, Kentucky where we were a few days ago. With this in mind we keep going.

Back in the main channel we move fast, but it is a very winding route and taunts us with short cuts which contain whirlpools, eddies and lines of rough, boiling water, in areas that are between islands and the bank. Grace and I stray off the channel at one point into one of these 'short cuts' and we have to traverse a section that could be classed as rapids they are that rough. She gets through OK while I get caught in a very rough part and nearly capsize. She obviously has much better balance than I do as she sails through it with a huge grin on her face.

Lunch is another sandbar café affair consisting of reconstituted dried something and then back to paddling. Our aim for the night was the town of Caruthersville, which has a boat ramp, and a casino marked on the map. From information we have been given and previous experience there is usually a restaurant attached to casinos and often the chance of a hotel room at reasonable prices. We make it to the town in good time and as we pull onto the boat ramp a local comes to our aid. He introduces himself as Mike and tells us that he was born in the UK, as his father was in the US Air Force and had married an English woman. He is a bit of a character to say the least but gives us a lift to the casino motel, which is about a couple of blocks away. This method of describing distance is catching.

We had discussed this on the approach to the town and had decided that if a hotel was available we would use it rather than risk putting on another few miles and end up wild camping in possible flood conditions. The hotel is nothing to write home about but is more comfortable than a tent and has WIFI so we can catch up with home and Facebook to let people know where we are and how we are doing.

I take a walk back to the boat ramp to check on the kayaks. I know they are chained to a sign but I have a bit of a niggling doubt that needs settling. As I am walking I take the chance to speak with Doug Seagers and Marguerite Constantine about making arrangements for our recovery. Marguerite tells me that she has a few options involving Rotary Club members but wants to make sure that we are close before setting things in motion, while Doug tells me that he arranged for us to spend a night in Lake Providence, Louisiana with another friend of mine 'Treish' Treischmann who I met while over in 2000 on the Rotary Exchange. Again he tells me that he is watching our progress and will contact me with final arrangements as we get nearer.

Hearing their voices reminds me that even though we have met quite a few people over the last few days, overall, I have never felt so lonely and isolated in my entire life. This is not a reflection on Grace. She is a good friend and we have some laughs at times along the route, but the never ending 'sameness' of it all and the lack of signs of life along the way are wearing me down. Somehow talking with them brings it home more than the conversations I have with family members. Perhaps its because I have been able to see them on video calls as well as talk to them. Or perhaps it's that I know they are so far away in the UK and that there is no possibility of saying to them 'I quit, come and get me' and them doing it.

We had dinner in the casino restaurant, which was good value and big portions, and then visited the gambling floor, as Grace had never been in a casino. Not exactly the grandest of places but as it was modelled on an old Mississippi Paddleboat it was a 'must do' visit for us.

When I check the maps I see we are 110 miles from Memphis and wonder if we can make it in 2 days? It means 2 big days in terms of mileage but I think it's possible. There are less bends and the channel is well marked so we should have a good run and be able to maintain a decent speed. I hope so.

17/9/14
Not a bad night, well better than a tent. But only just! We both wake up with more bites on our legs than we had at the last midge infected campsite. I try to be charitable and suggest we brought them in by walking across the grass as we came back from dinner. Grace points out that getting more bites in proper beds seems to be the norm as she has been bitten at every hotel we have stayed at. On reflection so have I.

Breakfast was included, although I still cannot get the hang of how to make waffles, so that saves us some time. We have to carry everything back to the boats, load up and are on the water by 7:45, not a bad effort really, given the hard work at the start.

About 25 miles into the day we cut across a sunken sand area in error. The map showed the river bending round to our right and that the banks were a considerable distance apart. As we looked ahead the view corresponded, or appeared to, so we duly started to follow the curve. We had committed ourselves only to find that the floods had been at work again and that we were actually traversing an area that had been carved out by the water flow removing an entire chunk of land, leaving a passage about ½ a mile wide. We had to continue on our chosen route but only because it would have been almost impossible to get back upstream into the main channel from where we were.

Fully committed we continue and up pops the first wave-creating dam. There is lots of white water, well I say white, it's mostly dirty foam, but we are able to pass through without grounding out. There are a couple of whirlpools but they are OK to traverse. Actually they were a bit of fun as they speed you up on entry and then start to spin the boat on exit. I later read that some of these whirlpools have been known to cause barges to spin and subsequently sink as they have banged into each other in their units and become holed. It was still fun at the time.

As we continued I thought that I could hear a train or power station in the distance and asked Grace if she could. Yes was the reply so I thought nothing of it. About a mile later the noise was getting louder but no train hooters were heard, I spotted what was causing the noise. A ribbon of roiling white water that stretched across the entire river in front of me. There was what is called a 'Wing Dam', or weir in English, which was holding back the river at a point of two different levels and what we were confronted with was the entire Mississippi river falling over it. And we had first heard it over a mile away. So it was obviously quite a drop. This was the point of no return.

As we get closer to it Grace follows me, staying about 10 yards behind me, and starts to film my passage. About 10 yards away from the white water I saw that it was a drop of about 5 feet. The water flow started to increase and I accelerated towards the foaming lip. Just before tipping over the edge I could see that the whole thing was a man made construction, not a natural sandbar. It had been made by dropping huge rocks in a line. The pattern so uniform that it could not have been anything else.

I bottomed out on the upper layer as I went over and then bounced off the lower ones. I shouted "ROCKS" to warn Grace as I went over but of course she was already committed. I turned as the water smoothed out and saw her heading for a pyramid shaped stone as she dropped over the edge. I had visions of her boat being holed and her being thrown out into the rocks and white water. With a stroke of luck as she was being tipped one way another rock tipped her back upright and she came through unscathed. As we drifted and compared our feelings we both had hearts beating like steam hammers.

I made a 'Note to self': avoid doing that again.

Lunch at the sandbar café was an interesting combination. Half cooked pasta shells and a banana. Stops are also an opportunity to visit the 'restroom' (as opposed to doing it in a bottle on the move) and at most stops that we have made there has been some sort of tree or bush we can hide at the back of. Trees were not in evidence at this stop so there was much hilarity as we asked each other to turn our backs. The trees also used to hide the accompanying noises but not on this occasion. Might make for interesting conversations when we get home but as for now we seem to be less shy about this sort of thing.

My observation and commentary skills were also called into question, again, on this stop as I opined that we hadn't seen as many barges as we had been led to believe we would. Grace started to count them and pointed out we had 6 in a row and in total passed 11. She also reminded me that one was pushing empty units and the waves were like roller coasters. Fortunately not cresting, but big all the same. Seems like I am to be banned from predicting those as well. Perhaps it's as well given my weather predictions.

As we continue the map still does not reflect the reality of how the river changes the environment. There are whole islands and huge sandbars that are marked on the map but which have disappeared from the physical environment.

The shipping channel is relatively well marked and we find that it is wide enough for us to use, to take advantage of a flow that pushes us a good 2-3 mph quicker than outside it, and still be able to cut corners and avoid the barges. The short cuts we see often have evidence of dams across them so, inviting as they are, we avoid them.

We camp 50 miles from our start point, in a place so unremarkable that it does not even have a feature that it can be named by. I knew that we would be in a wilderness area but did think it would have some landmark to gauge our journey by. This has been the biggest day yet leaving us with something like 59 miles in order to reach Memphis tomorrow. I am sure that given good flow and an early start and we can do it.

As I am looking at the maps, to check the route, I note that the lower half maps have the longitude and latitude marked at much more frequent intervals than on the other set, which is a helpful guide to gauging our progress and noting our exact position when landmarks have changed.

Grace shows me the video footage of the crossing of the weir and as my boat goes over the lip the back half rises and comes clear out of the water as I tip over the edge. That is 8 feet of boat that is clear of the water and at an alarming angle. I am glad I couldn't see it happen at the time, I might have got worried.

18/9/14
We did get up early and we were on the river in double quick time and it was not much in the way of an eventful day really. Well other than covering 61.4 miles in order to get to Memphis, which is a huge

distance to cover. We had been doing the equivalent of almost 2 marathons a day, and using arms not legs for most of the journey, but today was a Herculean effort.

The channel was flowing fairly quickly, we managed to maintain in the region of 7 mph for most of the day, so the actual paddling was not as hard as it sounds but it was constant. On reflection I am possibly giving a false impression. It was hard work though, so don't think it wasn't, I just think we had got used to it.

We only saw a few barges today; honest it was not just my counting, so they were not a problem. One thing we did have to put up with was a fairly heavy rain shower that threatened to slow us down and discourage us. It didn't last too long and cleared at about 12:30 so we did our usual "sandbar café" when the sun came out again and had a 45 minute stop for lunch.

The only thing of note was me lining up to sit on a log we were employing as a bench and missing the damn thing entirely! I thought Grace was going to do herself an injury she was laughing so hard. I couldn't help but join in. What a fantastic noise laughter is and it's marvellous how it cures all ills even if only for a short time.

Small wonder that The Theodora Children's Charity and their 'Giggle Doctors' are so appreciated by the children they visit. There are times when we could have done with them visiting us on this expedition.

Mud Island Marina and the Memphis Yacht Club was our stop for the night, which is located in the heart of the city up a small inlet. They gave us a free berth and assured us that our equipment would be safe, as they had gated access, patrolling guards and CCTV coverage; I still chained them together to be sure.

Unfortunately they had no land to camp on so we had to get a taxi into town and check into an Econolodge, which is a cheap hotel chain. I had rung them from the marina to be told there was only one room left but when I tried to book they put me through to a recording that required Internet access. Not wanting to mess about I rang back and told them to hold it as I was on the way.

Cheap unfortunately equates to poor service in this case. The first room we were allocated was still a mess from previous occupants, for the second room the two sets of cards issued would not give access. By this time I had now had enough and was officially well angry and let them know my feelings when I presented myself at reception again. Third time lucky as it turned out.

So much for it only having one room commented Grace. I was so mad at them I had forgotten that.

After a quick shower we set off into town to find the famous Beale Street and a restaurant and ask directions of a man and his wife as we exit the hotel. To our surprise he is from Derbyshire and to his that we are from Yorkshire. Another small world conversation ensues along with congratulations on our expedition so far.

We ate in the 'BB King BBQ' on Beale Street, which wasn't really a BBQ and didn't have BB King singing for us. They did have some great food and a superb live band though and I couldn't help but think that at times like this the trip really is hard work!

I know that Grace in interested in Music and Drama, she is in amateur dramatic shows, the last as a Nun in the Sound of Music – no really, the same girl who has been using the outdoors as a toilet for over a month has tried to pass herself off as a NUN and stripped down to her undies in public but I promised not to mention that so hide this page if she is near you. I comment that I can never understand how people like the singer we are listening to is so talented but is completely unknown while some other 'celebrities' could not hold a candle to her. She tells me it is about being a showman rather than talent and cites Robbie Williams as an example. Not as good a singer as some but a real showman.

We could have been a million miles from kayaking the Mississippi and this is the city where I had said to myself that, if I did not think I could complete the journey, I would give up at and would push myself to here and no further. I look at what I have done so far and realise that I can do it.

NO I HAVE TO. I have come too far to stop now.

As we will be back into wilderness area again in short order tomorrow I propose another 55 miles tomorrow that will put as at a place where we can camp. If things do not go according to plan there is a fall-back position of a potential camp at 48 miles or even a casino, which is in the middle of nowhere according to the map, at about 35 miles. It will have to be bad to do so little if we end up staying there.

Week 7
Memphis, Tennessee to Newton Bend, Mississippi

19/9/14
Good night's rest, although again we both got bitten by bugs in the hotel beds. Let's get back to tents, its safer and more comfortable. Did I really just write that?

It wasn't until I saw the news bulletin on the TV in the hotel breakfast room that I realised the date, 19 September, and that it was my son, Kenneth's, birthday. The time difference worked in my favour for once and I managed to FaceTime him. Turns out he was in a pub, where else, having lunch with his wife, Helen, and our grandson, Thomas, so it was a bonus on the call. Once again they told me how proud they were of both of us and that they were looking forward to seeing me on my return. Thomas was more impressed with the fish fingers in front of him I think. The only bad bit was that I couldn't raise Pauline but some contact with home beats none at all.

Grace is in some discomfort with her wisdom teeth. A problem that flares up every so often she tells me, and despite mouth wash and pain killers the problem is not going away. I ask if she wants to try and find a dentist before we leave Memphis or if she can hold out for a few days till we get to Lake Providence, Louisiana where our Rotary friends can arrange one. She opts to hang on so I contact Doug Seegers and ask him to sort something out if he can.

One thing that is always assured, as a member of a worldwide organisation made up of business and professional people, is that if you need something the members of a local club will be able to help, if not directly then because they know someone in their community who can. I have had experience of this on both sides of the fence in the past and am always happy to help others in return for the help I have been given.

On checking out, the desk clerk tried to ring a taxi but couldn't get through, probably, he explained because it was the rush period. He did nothing more at this point than ask the night duty security man, who was just clocking off to go home, to run us to the marina. Different crew on duty from the shower that were (allegedly) in charge when we checked in. He was a nice guy and had been stationed in the UK as a member of the USAF so he knew something about our part of the world. A bit more than his chosen city of dwelling as I had to give him directions to the marina after he managed to get lost.

Pauline rang just as I was pushing off from the boat ramp so had a chat for a few minutes, which would probably be the last chance before she flies out. I wish her a safe journey and we set off. Only to stop again after about 5 minutes for a photo call with an authentic Mississippi Paddlewheel Boat. A real floating one, not a pretend one like the casino in Caruthersville. It is very big and appears to have about three decks of accommodation and entertainment. It looked like an elegant way to travel and, strangely, not out of place in the 21st century.

Just before we set off I get a call from Doug Seegers who tells me that the Trieschmanns have set up a provisional appointment with a local dentist for Grace. All we have to do is give them a date of arrival and, if possible, an approximate time. What made me think it would be anything else?

We fair zipped along, covering 35 miles in about 4 ½ hours, which was a very quick pace, taking us to where there was a casino at the Tunica River Park. The casinos are built on land owned by Native American tribes. They pay no taxes to the State or Federal Governments and are a great source of income for them. There was no town nearby so the casino had built roads specifically to give access for gamblers and the river park so that it could service boat traffic. As we approached we had been talking about trying to get references to the Books and TV series "Game of Thrones' worked into the narrative of our journals and had jokingly decided that we would call this casino "Winterfell' after one of the castles.

Imagine our surprise when the buildings came into full view to see that they had been designed to look like a medieval castle! Well, an American storybook version anyway. If anyone could have heard us laughing they would have thought we had finally and completely lost it.

As we pulled up on the obligatory, and very big, boat ramp we were watched by a guy at the top of the ramp who promptly drove his pick-up truck half way down to meet us. After a short exchange he offered to run us up to, and after we had eaten, back from, the casino. He was nice enough but obviously lonely and had had a few beers. From talking to him it seems people take a few days off work to visit casinos for shows they put on and for special "prize" nights. Tonight our new friend is looking forward to 'winning' a sports jacket in return for his patronage of the casino. It strikes me there is still only 1 winner. The casino.

He takes us up to the building and shows us through the gaming floor to the restaurant and then tells us where he will be when we want a lift back, or that he will come and join us later. The restaurant is rather large and is of the "Eat all you can" variety. They may regret offering us that option.

As we stand at the reception desk we must have looked like something from, well goodness knows where. Our clothes are now starting to show signs of wear as well as permanent stains and even after having had a shower that morning I am prepared to bet there is a certain smell around us. Everyone else looks reasonably well dressed so I wonder if we may get refused service. Of course not is the answer. This is America and who you are is more important than how you look. As long as you have the money to pay for what you want. The lady who serves us is quite taken by our English accents, we are near to Arkansas now and the Deep South is all around us so Grace and I are a very rare pair of birds indeed.

I decide to see if we can get a discount on the cost of lunch with my retired Police Officer ID and she tells me that it only really applies to Officers in Uniform. When I say "We are undercover and on a mission so be kind to us" she laughs and knocks slightly more than 50% off the total bill. I end up paying $10 instead of $23. The laughing continues when she asks us to wait until our server arrives and then walks round the counter and announces, "This way please". I ask her if she is stalking me now which produces sounds of great hilarity from everyone around.

We sample just about everything on the menu and generally chill. I have a couple of voicemails from friends back home and decide to ring a couple of them just to catch up and hear their voices more than anything. For a while the river is nowhere in my mind.

I have trouble understanding how isolation has become such a frequent topic in my mind especially when we have constant contact with others through mobile phones and the Internet. Or perhaps it's because we have become so used to instant contact that it merely magnifies the effect when we are truly out of reach.

As I check the web I find that the Rotary Blog was published a few days ago and has generated some considerable interest especially in the New Orleans area. They have sent a message asking to speak with me as they want to help in any way they can. I call the contact, Carl Michel, and he tells me that they have already set about securing accommodation in the city, have been in touch with media outlets, have a proposal for a place to stay south of the city and are working in conjunction with Marguerite to secure us a boat to bring us back from the mile zero point.

This is fantastic news as up to now I had no idea what we would do. Now it's being done for me. They even have a plan for us to attend a function on the 4th October and want some photos of the trip to show and possibly give us an opportunity to tell the group about the trip. Not sure we will be up for the last bit but we will see.

True to his word our friend comes to find us and takes us back to the boats. Not for the first time we look at them, then each other and say, "Damn, still there then" which produces some strange looks from people around us. Yes it is now plural, as more casino visitors have passed up the opportunity to gamble to come and see the crazy Brits in their kayaks. Oh, the fame and glamour of it all.

We had set a target of 55 miles today and achieved it, with a little extra added for leaving the Memphis marina and finding the casino. It was not any easy day but not a terribly hard one either, we have had worse, but with a 2-hour stop for lunch it was a long one.

Tonight we will camp in Arkansas, the 9th of 10 states we pass through and have less than 700 miles to do to complete the trip. In terms of time tomorrow sees us with 2 weeks of travel until completion.
Once again it's a very hot night, I hope that this is due to us being so far south and not that a storm is coming.

20/9/14

There was no storm today; in fact we had blue skies and hot sunny weather all day. Nothing remarkable really, just lots and lots of paddling. Another almost unforgettable part of the whole journey.

We stopped at a town called Helena, Arkansas at 10:30 am for a meal, a sort of brunch I suppose, and somehow it took just short of 2 hours. The town has obviously seen better days as most of the shops on main street are closed up. We found a small place that served some of the biggest portions of burger and fries that I have ever seen, which didn't stop me eating them of course. I asked if they could make us some sandwiches but they declined as they only produced hot food. The man on the next table asked what it was we wanted and offered to get them for us.

He was gone for almost 40 minutes, which even in the slow moving south was something of a record for not rushing. Or so I thought until I found out that he had driven about 10 miles to the next town to get them for us. Best travelled cheese sandwiches this side of the River!

Just before we set off I get a message from Triesch and he tells me that everything is set up for Grace to visit a dentist and we need to aim to be in north of their area just after 12 so they can meet us and take her into town. As things are going at the moment we should be OK with that.

We still managed a good day in mileage terms but it could have been better if we had had some scenery. The boredom of loneliness is creeping in and we are running out of topics of conversation. We camped on a sandbar just at the side of the main channel. There was absolutely nothing there. Nothing, just us a bunch of trees and our kayaks.

One of the things that has been with me throughout the journey is that when we do talk Grace is good company and we have some laughs and lively debates. But if she gets a phone signal I might as well be alone. I don't take it too bad as if I had the option I would take it, but lack of coverage and cost rules it out. I had received a message from O2 quite awhile ago informing me that I had incurred charges of £180 and that if I did not make an immediate payment they would terminate my service. I wonder how long it will take me to change suppliers when I get home?

I decide that I will not mention this as it will only make a rubbing point between us and we can generate enough of those just because of the journey itself. Better to rage in silence for a while when alone and then ignore it thereafter as Ranulph Fiennes comments in his book 'Mind Over Matter', his diary of an unsupported Antarctic crossing with Mike Stroud .

At the campsite it is HOT, so much so that the tent feels like a sauna but cools as the sun sets, and we have a comfortable night.

21/9/14
Not much to say about today other than it was a hot one and the river just kept going along in front of us. No change in scenery, not many barges and no dramas to report. The one thing that did give us concern was the rate at which we were going through our water supplies. It was very hot and we needed to replace fluids at a prodigious rate.

There were no towns anywhere near the river today but we did see some houses on the Mississippi State side of the river. Having checked how low the supplies were I proposed that we stop at one and see if we could fill our containers.

This was quite a laughable moment in itself. I pulled alongside Grace, pointed at the houses in the distance and said *"shall we .."* and before I could finish the sentence she said *".... pull up there and get water"*? This was followed by me saying *"and if no-one is ..."* and her finishing with *" .... at home we can see if they have an outside tap"* It's true! Great minds think alike. And fools seldom differ. We know each other well by now.

We pull up at the bottom of a very steep and weed overgrown concrete ramp and I manage to scramble to the top. There are signs of life but I don't immediately see anyone around, that is until a small boy jumps out of a car and says hello. I ask him where the house door is and he points and then says "It's Miss Debby's birthday today". I find the door and see a group of adults sitting down and toasting someone with champagne and when I knock and they open the door, I cannot resist asking for "Miss Debby". One of the ladies looks at me in surprise (well I am wearing full paddle gear including the spray skirt and knife on my left shoulder), acknowledges that it is her and then lets her mouth drop as I start to sing 'Happy Birthday To You' and tell her I am the singing telegram man!

Stunned silence for a few seconds. So I tell them what I am really doing and ask if can use their water supply. This causes even more of a stunned silence. Do people really think it is such a strange thing to do? Obviously the answer is yes.

They prove to be very hospitable not only helping us fetch the containers but giving us some cold beverages both to drink as we fill up the water carriers and to take with us. We are very grateful for their help, water is the one thing we cannot afford to run out of, especially in as remote an area as this.

That night we camped on an island that was in the mouth of the Arkansas River, which flows into the Mississippi. I checked the maps to see about our arrival in Lake Providence at the requested time of 12 noon and think it will be overly ambitious, not just due to the river distance but also because of the entry channel being marked as a commercial port. Doug has always joked that they will come out in a boat to harass, and taunt us with cold 'sodas' and beer as we get nearer so, if they do, we might manage a tow that will save a little time. I'm sure it will work out somehow; as long as we can put another big day in tomorrow we should be fine.

When we pitch camp there are signs that someone had used a motorcycle and a quad bike on the sand dunes at some point in the not too distant past so we began to wonder if it was an island as marked. The likely explanation was that the water level had dropped low enough at some time thereby allowing them to access the area, so we thought nothing more of it.

Not long after it had gone dark I was convinced that I could hear voices outside the tent and a banging noise from where the boats were pulled up on the beach. I jumped out of the tent and looked around. Nothing and no one to be seen. I walked down to the boats but they were still away from the water so that hadn't risen causing them to move and make a noise. I put it down to my imagination and return to my tent.

Only to be woken a couple of hours later by a pack of coyotes howling at full pitch. They sounded to be right next to the tent, almost as though they were at the door. I looked out again but saw nothing.

Except the most star filled sky that I had seen on the trip so far. Without any light pollution the night sky is an amazing sight. From horizon to horizon the entire vista is filled with a never ending series of twinkling diamond points that are suns for far off planetary systems, I could even see other galaxies standing out with their spiral arms visible to the naked eye. I couldn't help but wonder if we really are alone in the universe and will we ever find out.

Back in the tent as I was drifting back to sleep I heard the voices again. Only this time I put it down to imagination and ignored it. Or tried to. I didn't think we were alone after all!

22/9/14
It was a beautiful sunrise that heralded another glorious day. It was also another unremarkable one.

When I told Grace about the voices she admitted that she was relieved that I had heard them as well as she was also convinced that someone was talking nearby. At one point she thought that someone was trying to attract her attention by going "Psst Psst" at the door of her tent. Neither of us could come up with an explanation. At least she had heard the coyotes as well so I hadn't imagined them either.

Just another day in terms of paddling. We had a period of strong crosswinds that shoved us about a bit but they didn't last long. They probably cost us about 5 miles in lost distance/time. The scenery still didn't change much; with the banks being tree lined all the time and no signs of houses any more. We are starting to see more signs of industrialisation as we travel further south, with piers that stick out for barges to load and unload their various cargoes. Not all are grain or coal anymore either, there is growing evidence of chemical plants, usually agricultural ones, as well.

Lunch was at the sandbar café as usual and was the standard menu of rehydrated mashed potatoes and rice/pasta. As with other stops we try to minimise the effect of our presence by burning the waste packaging and today is no different. Except that today with the wind being a little high I elect to wedge the offending items in a washed up tree root. I reason that it will be wet wood and will come to no harm from the three little packets and few used tissues and alcohol wipes we have to dispose of. Well, that was my reasoning.

A few minutes after setting it alight and walking away Grace calls to me and tells me that, "The tree is burning quite well". I laugh but when I look round I can see she is not joking; it looks like a small forest fire! The 'wet tree root' has been washed up for so long that it is tinder dry just under the surface and as I have shoved the packets into the deepest cavity I could find it is now a roaring fireball.

I employ the toilet bottle to try and put the flames out but seem to be fighting a loosing battle for quite a while. With some relief I manage to put the flames out and convinced that it is extinguished hurriedly climb aboard OLLI and paddle away. I have only gone about 25 yards when Grace tells me to look back. The damn thing has burst into flames again. I don't think I could have paddled any harder and no, not back to the sandbar. For the rest of the afternoon I wonder if the U.S. Coast Guard, or who ever, will chase me down and charge me with offences under some obscure American law. This is a great source of amusement for Grace, till I tell her that I will name her as an accomplice. She tells me that she's never heard of me.

Towards the end of the day we pass the city of Greenville, Mississippi and see someone on the left bank of the river waving an orange flag towards us so we went to see what he wanted. When we get across to him he introduces himself as Park Neff, he is a Rotarian and another of the river angels. Park tells us that he has been following our website and Spot3 for some time now so is well aware of our progress and had planned to join us for a while on the river. Unfortunately the commercial traffic at his put in point was heavy and stopped him from setting out.

With that idea thwarted he jumped ahead of us and brought cold drinks, the offer of a bed at his house and a run to the shops for supplies. As we are stopping at Lake Providence tomorrow, and his house is quite a drive away he tells us, we decline. He fully understands our reasons, agrees with our decision and is most complimentary about the progress we have been making.

After we have chatted for a while then I leave Grace with him and see if I can get a signal on the mobile phone so I can ring Triesh in Lake Providence to check on arrangements. He tells me he has secured an appointment at 4pm for Grace and they plan to get the boat out and come to meet us. I wonder if they will be able to tow us, as the last time we met he had a 'float boat', which is a large square platform with two pontoons and an outboard motor.

He asks if we would like stay on Wednesday as well to have a day off as he has also been following our progress, and comments on the high mileage we have been doing for some time now, without any more than night rest. We will have to decide but it's nice to have been given the option. Did I really expect anything else?

Back with Park and Grace he is telling her how he has been listening to the barge traffic on the radio and that they have been commenting on the 'two crazy kayakers heading down the river'. He tells us that they are actually quite complimentary about how we conduct ourselves around the barges and use the flow of the marked channel. He adds that this is quite some praise as most of the time they are complaining about recreational traffic getting in the way so we must be doing something right. This is in marked contrast to the one who radioed us to get out of the channel when we were so far outside it that we were nearly on dry land!

Just below where we have been talking to Park is a huge bridge and I check with him our exact location. Mississippi on the left bank, Arkansas on the right and he confirms that there is a Casino just at the base of the bridge on the Mississippi side. This is it! THE bridge! The one that elicited the comment from Pauline almost 12 months ago of 'You are mad" as we went over it. I'm beginning to think she is correct.

Camp tonight is high on a sand island called American Point, which is exactly 527.1 miles from the Gulf as marked on the sign placed by the Coast Guard to tell commercial traffic where they are. The flashing red light on it does not disturb us at all. But the pack of coyotes does. At least the phantom voices are not following us tonight.

23/9/14

The coyote pack that was howling as we retired for the night was quite disturbing but they didn't start up again in the night so that was a bonus. Another real bonus was that the tent was dry when I woke up, as in not even condensation on the outer or underneath, so it got packed away dry. The day actually got off to a notable start in that we had Raman noodles for breakfast. That's a first. Not something I would recommend on a regular basis as they are mostly carbohydrate, or is that cardboardhydrate, with chemical flavouring to give them 'taste'. Taste like sh*t but won't kill you, as Crocodile Dundee would say.

Not a lot to say about the paddling, or the scenery, other than we made almost 30 miles, and got to Louisiana the 10th of our 10 states in just under 4 hours or about 11 am as we had set off early. We stopped for a quick lunch, the noodles had worn off, and set off again only to run straight into several lots of barges almost causing a traffic jam which slowed our progress.

We had only been going about half an hour from our stop when my phone rang. It was buried in the bottom of my deck bag and I didn't even know it was turned on. It was Doug Seegers and his timing was excellent as I needed both hands to negotiate the wake of a passing barge. So I had to cut him off and tell him I would ring back. He never even got a word in edgeways such was the situation I was in.

Eventually things settled down and I got through to him to hear him ask where we were? I could only answer 'about 15 miles or so North of Lake Providence' as that was the nearest I could tell him from the maps and landmarks, such as they were. He asked if I could identify an island and told him that I thought we were just north of one called 'Stack Island'. The call terminates as the signal drops and I get back to paddling.

The next thing we know is that we can see a powerboat heading towards us at great speed. Directly towards us. Our previous experiences with power boats has taught us to be wary as they fly along at a great pace, and with the bow so high up they cannot see directly in front of them and create a bow wave in front and a wake behind that are far more difficult to negotiate than anything the barges create.

As it gets closer it slows and sinks into the water I can see Doug Seegers, Triesch Trieschmann, Earl Lingle, a Past District Governor for the region and really good friend, another Rotarian friend called Ron, who is from Monroe, along with Triesch's wife Sandy and their exchange student from Germany on board all waving at us. So much for expecting a sedate float boat!

They pull up alongside us and without further ado we climb out of the kayaks and into the boat and then lift the kayaks into the boat. Then off we go at 30mph with our GPS and Spot3 working overtime. The funny thing was that when we checked the web page later it didn't really show that we had suddenly started to travel much faster. We arrive at Lake Providence in next to no time and once we have negotiated the side channel into the very busy port area, we find a problem.

The ramp for launching is too steep to take the boat loaded with the Kayaks; as they might slip off as the boat is pulled up, so Triesch decides to take the boat round to another ramp in the channel. Sandy is a little unsure of herself reversing the trailer at the next point so I go with her to drive the truck and trailer. The next ramp is a little less steep but we still strap the kayaks down before setting off up it, just to be sure.

We leave the ramp and drive to the Trieschmanns house where it is action stations for us to find kit from the boats as the dentist Grace is visiting is in Eudora, Arkansas, which is a bit of a drive away. She gets showered and I unload and clean the boats I then put the tents up, vacuum them out and clean kit that could be hosed down. I am staying in the guesthouse at the other side of the lawn, which has its own washing machine which I put to full use before showering and re-joining the others.

Back on the porch I get a big hug from Doug and that just about makes my day and nearly reduces me to tears. No, it did reduce me to tears. I confess to Doug, again, that I have never felt so isolated in my life as I have on this trip. He just hugs me again and gives me a cold beer.

One of those actions is manly; the other is what true friends do. Work out which for yourself.

I get handshakes and backslaps from Earl and Ron, more cold beer and start to relax. Then they tell me of the problems that Pauline has had. Her flights had been delayed and she had had to spend the night in Houston only arriving in Alexandria at 4pm today, 19 hours later than planned and about the same time as I was halfway through cleaning the boats, gear and myself. They didn't want to worry me until they knew she had landed with Marguerite safely. I got to talk to her soon after being told and although she sounded relaxed she confessed to be tired hanging about with nothing to do. I look forward to seeing her soon.

Grace gets back from the dentists and all is well. Sods law has applied, of course, in that she has not had any pain today, but she has been checked out, given some mouthwash, a prescription for antibiotics and sent on her way. It only cost $25, which is a lot less than we had expected.

The next issue is how long do we stay here! Option one is to have tonight and do the shopping for supplies in the morning and then set off at lunchtime so as to put at least some miles in. Option two is to do the shopping and then have the afternoon off and stop with the Trieschmanns another night and set off early the following morning.

One thing Triesch is keen to point out is that he prefers to put us in a few miles downriver to avoid the working dock of Lake Providence and the problems we had when we landed whatever time/day we elect to set off. As usual either will suit him and his family. I get the feeling Grace is not keen on the extra afternoon off but I think the rest would be good and helpful overall.

I get a quiet moment to myself and reflect that it really is good to have friends like Triesch, Doug and Marguerite and how distance and infrequent personal contact does not diminish the friendship. If anything it strengthens it and reinforces the commitment that people make to each other in an informal way. The old truism of being able to choose friends and not relatives springs to mind when I think about some of my family members.

It was really good to see Doug, even if I did get a bit tearful. No doubt more tears will follow later.

Arriving in Louisiana, the last state the Mississippi River runs through shows us that the end is in sight. But we still have a long way to go.

Dinner tonight was great, almost a family affair, with my Louisiana family of Doug, Earl, Ron and the Trieschmanns. Just a fun, relaxed evening, even if we did go out to a restaurant to eat rather than stay at home. Doug and the others from Monroe left after dinner and we went back to the house. Grace was stopping in the main house while I was stopping in the guest cabin at the other side of the lawn and had it all to myself. It seems strange to say that I enjoyed being on my own when I have been heard to complain about isolation, but there is something different about being in a house with all amenities, only 100 yards from the main house. It was my space and I didn't have to erect it. And it had a shower and a kitchen and real chairs and a table to sit at while I drink coffee. The simple things in life at work again.

24/9/14
I might have been in a house and not have anywhere to go in a great rush, but I still woke up at 6 am. It only took a couple of moments before I remembered where I was and what I was doing, so I rolled over for 30 minutes. On fully waking I had the luxury of a cup of coffee and a hot shower, sheer bliss, before going up to the house for breakfast. All the washing, repairs and other little jobs that needed doing had been taken care of yesterday so it only remained for us to go shopping for supplies this morning.

Sandy takes us shopping and we managed to spend $112 at Walmart on dried food alone. We worked out that the amount we bought is what we will need as a minimum. From here on in we only get 2 or 3 chances to stop in the next 9 days and, even then, it is not certain what facilities we will find.

The big decision still to make is should we set off today or have the rest of the day off and move on in the morning. We are just at the lumberyard owned by the Trieschmanns and visit with the head of the family, King Trieschmann (yes, his first name really is 'King') for a while. Although not a young man any more he works everyday and can probably tell you what the inventory is and how much it is worth off the top of his head. As we head to the door to join Triesch for lunch I ask Grace, who looks as tired as I feel, what she wants to do and she says

"I know what we should do which is not what I would like to do".

The 'should' is 20 miles this afternoon the 'like' is another night in a bed. She also says that she would like a chance to Skype everyone at home as we may not get many more chances. I do a quick add up of miles in my head and reason that losing 20 miles today is not that much of an issue given the speed at which we have been moving, so propose that we have the afternoon off which she accepts.

The bonus to this is that there is time to carry out some extra repairs. The most important was to my tent poles, as one had split a few days ago and I had done a temporary repair using a small kit I had bought in Grand Rapids. I had chance to take my time and fashion a sturdier repair that would last to the end of the journey. I had also found a couple of small holes and some areas that needed a few stitches and was able to repair these as well. I am impressed with the tents, we have probably had more use out of them on this expedition than most people would get in a couple of years. I also get chance for a snooze, which is most welcome!

I also get the opportunity to talk to Carl in New Orleans and he tells me that everything is set up for us; all we have to do is set a meeting point. I tell him that we will be in touch again when we are in the Baton Rouge area so that we can have a better idea of times and dates. Carl is to be the Team leader for his District Group Study Exchange to South Australia in early 2015, a role that first brought me to Louisiana, so we have something in common already. I look forward to meeting him in a few days time.

There are an extra couple of bonuses 1) Sandy has spent the afternoon preparing a small feast and we get that most Louisianan of dishes, Gumbo, for dinner and 2) We get visited by Wayne Parker, who is an agent of the Louisiana Wildlife & Fishing Department. He is responsible for policing the river and its immediate environs and is interested in our trip, not just in Louisiana but along the entire length of the river and has come to interview us for an article in their magazine that is published and sold all over the Lower United States. Fame is catching up with us again.

After dinner I sit and chat with Triesch for a while, mostly about how the area has changed since I was last there. The most startling thing is that a major employer has pulled out of the area, which has resulted in a 40% drop in overall population as they move away to find work. Lake Providence always was a relatively poor area, one measure actually placed it as the poorest parish in Louisiana, and things haven't improved for them.

As I walk across to my little house I look up and see the night sky in all its glory again and this time the Milky Way is in evidence. It is aptly named, as there is a central ribbon of stars, countless millions of them, weaving through the sky like a celestial reflection of the meanders of the Mississippi River. It really is milky in appearance, such is the density of them and as I lie on my back looking up at them I wonder again if we are alone and will we ever find out? The reality is that the distance between stars is such that it takes light hundreds of years to cross the void and that travels at 176,000 miles per *second*, so any living being is unlikely to make the journey. Unless 'Star Trek' and 'warp drive' become a reality.

It is looking at the sky that makes me realise that it has not changed over the thousands of years that human kind have been around and that someone had the idea of using them to navigate around the globe, a method that can be used today, if you know how and have not become dependant on the satellite based systems. It also stirs in me the desire to travel further and wider, undoubtedly the same as it has done for many others as well. I will never make it to the stars but I can find other places to view them from.

25/9/14
Strangely it was not the best night's sleep I've had on the trip so far, probably because of the richness of the food as we had been used to more bland meals up to now. Our diet of dehydrated stuff is anything but Haute Cuisine! As a result I was up at 5:30 am and took what might be my last shower for some time. After a big breakfast we load the truck and set off. Last night Sandy gave us some US Army ration packs called an MRE. This stands for 'Meal, ready to eat' but has been nicknamed 'Meal refused by Ethiopians' which is a bit cruel but typical of military humour. It remains to be seen if they are any better than what we have been using up to now. She has also given us several survival kits in sardine cans, various nibbles and several other bits of goodies including a Leatherman tool, to replace one I have lost. She

tells me they come from her 'anti zombie apocalypse survival bag'. I am not sure if she is joking or not, well she is ex-military and probably has a survival bag under the bed in case of a hurricane, but the zombie part?

We use an alternate to the commercial port we came in at, which is to the south of the town and right on the river edge, rather than up the side channel so all we have cut out is the long drag down to the river avoiding barges.

We are underway at 8:30 am, after some emotional goodbyes, and get back into the routine. Grace seems to lag behind a little and I think that she is still tired but, game as ever, she keeps going. Me? For some reason I have found a new lease of life and plod on like a Duracell powered toy.

We paddle steadily on again stopping for lunch at our usual haunt; the only difference today is the menu as we try out the MRE packs. OK so they are bulky and everything is in its own individual pack, which seems to produce a lot of waste but the contents are, well, amazing. I have a pasta dish followed by a sort of Angel Delight type pudding and a chocolate biscuit. There is a milk shake type drink and a 'cup' of coffee. The pack has a water-activated heater in a bag and there are cardboard sleeves to hold hot things. Grace finds a little bottle of Tabasco sauce in hers to add flavour and we both have plastic cutlery, napkins, wipes and chewing gum to act as mouthwash/toothpaste. The instructions also contain information about the high calorific value of the contents and how this meal will 'meet the demands of the soldier on active duty'. As long as it feeds me I'll eat it but I can imagine it becomes boring when on long deployments.

One other consideration is the bulk of them in the packaging. OK it scrunches up when empty and burns easily, without setting fire to nearby trees, but I am unsure that I would want to carry more than a days rations of three meals at any one time and wonder how the army actually do manage this aspect.

In what seems like no time we reach our stated goal of 50 miles. Once again we have "stolen" miles from the river by cutting corners and straightening bends out. The campsite we have found tonight is right by the river marker and does not have a marker light, so searchlights from the barges will probably illuminate us as they make their way upriver and seek to check their position. Tonight is also the first time we have actually hung the food bags away from the tents as we are in bear country, according to Sandy who was backed up by Wayne Parker, and it is not worth taking the risk of keeping them near the tents.

I get a text message from Sandy telling us that tomorrow we have been offered a chance to camp in the church compound in the town of Vidalia, Louisiana and has sent me the number of the resident Pastor, Father Bill, so that I can ring him and make full arrangements as we get nearer. A check of the maps shows that this will mean a 55 mile day but if we make a start no later than 7:30 am, and only have a short lunch stop, we can do it as we have some real assistance from the river flow now. Hopefully we can find somewhere to eat at Vidalia as well so that will be a bonus.

We are both in our tents for 7:30 pm, the insects had a big hand in that, perhaps they will scare the bears away, and it is completely dark not soon after. We are at 32° North above the equator and the effect is to give almost balanced days, in terms of 12 hours of light and dark, at this time of year. I resolve that I must try to visit the equator some day to see what it is like.

Week 8
Newton bend, Mississippi to Belle Chase, Louisiana

26/9/14
The coyotes were not as loud last night. The owls were though. As predicted the barges used the searchlights to illuminate the marker board we were camped next to. There was no sign or sound of bears, or trains, so overall it was a restful night.

With another big day in the offing we get up, set off and are on the water for the target of 7:30 am. Lunch was an MRE, again. On a sandbar, again. Then back to paddling, again. The monotony of paddling only broken by us discussing what Grace can use as the topic for her Masters Dissertation. I find this very interesting as she tells me more about the science and art of sports coaching. She describes it less as physical instruction of technique and more as psychological warfare. This is more interesting than the alphabet game or even when we planned her wedding, house size and style and even her children's names. Not that she has any plans for those just yet but it kept boredom at bay for awhile.

We are coming across more, and much bigger, barge units, some of them approaching the 45-unit maximum allowed on the river. It's interesting to hear them talk about us on the radio, most are merely warning each other of our presence and some are even complimentary. Except one who decided to give us another lecture on keeping out of the channel. I begin to think it was the one from further up the river that had the same attitude; did he think we didn't know to keep out of the way? And if he had bothered to look close enough he would have seen that we were outside the channel anyway. I tell him that we are fully aware of his presence and that we are quite able to comply with regulations and safe methods of travel. This shuts him up and I wonder if someone on the bridge with him had pointed out that we were OK.

A little further on I had a radio conversation with one barge set up that had 2 engine units. I asked if they were from the same company and that if going the same way ran on one engine to save fuel. It turns out that one had a steering problem and was unable to make safe progress so they joined together to get him to a place of repair.

About 4:30 and just upstream from Vidalia I called our contact, Father Bill, to let him know we would be there shortly after 5:00pm. As she listens to me talking to him Grace starts to laugh and pulls away a little so after I have completed arranging a meeting point I catch her up. She is still laughing and when I ask she tells me that it sounded strange listening to me calling someone 'Father' especially given that I have no religious views. Apparently I had said "Bless you for your kindness' at one point and this really struck her as amusing. I wasn't even aware that I had said it.

As we passed a riverside conference centre and medical facility (why the two were together was not clear) we saw Father Bill waving at us and pointing us a little further downstream to where there was a boat ramp, right under the main highway bridge that connected Vidalia with Natchez, Mississippi. We pulled up and a man and wife with their small son helped us to drag the boats to long grass where we could fasten them up. I never did get their names but they were impressed with our expedition and the fact that a Minister of Religion in his 'working' clothes had come to meet us. He also advised us that the area was closed off after 9 pm and that the Police would be visiting the area to check it out. He never did explain why, probably a crime prevention action.

Father Bill explained he is the minister in charge of the Episcopalian Church in town, he and his wife helped us to load his car and we set off. As we set off he tells us that he has already alerted the local police to the fact that we will be camping in the church grounds and where the kayaks are, so we will be looked after during the night and not bothered by anyone. He then asks if it 'is within the rules' for him to take us to dinner. When I assure him that it is he comments that he only asked as he assumed that there might be some rules about being self sufficient and only using what we can carry on an expedition of this sort.

Thank goodness we hadn't set a rule like that is all I can think!

After we had pitched camp in the church grounds, and had a wash in the kitchen bathroom and changed clothes, we set off for dinner. The first thing he told us was that we would be eating at a place known as 'Natchez Under The Hill' on the other side of the river as the food was better over that side. I assumed at that point that he was not a native of Louisiana as they assert that they have THE best food on the planet.

At dinner I found that Father Bill is an interesting guy. He is a former US Army (Infantry) officer who studied for and became an ordained minister and then returned to the Army as a Chaplain serving all over the world. On retiring he became a civilian minister. One thing he told me was that they had lived in approximately 45 houses during their 40 plus years of married life. He also told me that the majority of the moves were because of his military service and that he had been posted all over the world.

Dinner was interesting, especially the grace he intoned and the looks we got as he and I swapped notes on the beers we were drinking. I could have spent hours with him. Sadly, planning for tomorrow and bed calls so we have to curtail the night, which ends with me losing the argument about who should pay the bill.

I managed to speak to West Constantine, as we would be nearing the area where he and Marguerite live and tell him where we are and that we intend to put in a 50-mile day tomorrow, and ask if this is anywhere near for him to visit along the way and perhaps bring some food. Oh and Pauline, so I can see her. He tells me that he has checked the maps and that this will put us very close to the State Prison, Angola and that camping would not be a good idea. His daughter, Shannon, used to work as a guard at the prison and she advises that we may even get moved on by the prison or police authorities in the area.

He proposes to pick us up and suggests the prison ferry landing as a suitable place. I tell him that this might be a bit longer than we could manage to do and suggest a boat ramp that is marked on the map. He is not familiar with it but says he will check and see if he can meet us there. It would be helpful to have a night in a proper bed, as long as we can find him and that the drive to their house is not too far from the river. It might mean doing 55 miles again, perhaps, so we will have to see.

As we start to bed down for the night Father Bill tells us that he will pick us up at 7 am so that we have time for breakfast before we get back on the river.

27/9/14

The second attack by wildlife took place last night! A semi feral cat that has adopted the church (someone feeds it so it won't go away) makes several attempts at trying to share my tent. I manage to discourage it without resorting to violence.

We are up at the usual 6:00 and packed away, so that we can have breakfast and be ready for Father Bill to take us back to the boats at 7:00. He, and his wife, arrived at 6:30, just before we break out the bagels and chocolate spread and immediately asked if we would like a 'proper' breakfast. In less than a heartbeat we both said, "Yes please", so we load the car up and set off. We went to a small café and got a 'Texas skillet' breakfast. Bacon, eggs, sausage and shredded potato in vast quantities. No wonder Texans are so big if that's how they start the day.

As we eat I ask Father Bill how he knows Sandy Trieschmann. He looks quizzical and says. "Sandy who"? I explain about our friends and their offer to help source safe stops along the last part of the journey and he says, "I got a call from the Bishop telling me that you were coming this way and to expect a call from you and that he had offered help from the church". I almost choke on my fried egg on hearing this and wonder if Sandy has any more shocks in store for us.

As a consequence of this meal we are not under way till 8:30, but stopping for an hour for a meal is worth it as miles covered equals calories expended.

Back at the boats and after we have loaded up, Father Bill gives us each a personal blessing and a short prayer before waving us off. As we back away he calls out "Don't forget – only name, rank and number, give nothing away". I must meet him again some day and look forward to it.

The morning passes discussing ideas for Grace's dissertation again and I suggest that possibly some sort of visit to Louisiana State University and their diving team might be something that can be arranged. Another quest for Marguerite, but one that I am sure she will be able to complete. Quick lunch stop along the way, do I really need to say where? And then off we go again.

During the afternoon session we reached the point where we had covered 2000 miles travelled. As it happens there is a barge passing so I radio the captain and tell him who we are, what we are doing and what we had done. I then told him that we didn't have a 'hooter' to celebrate with and asked if he could sound his horn for us so that we could record it and post it on YouTube, which he did. After thanking him and him wishing us well for the rest of our journey I hear him talking to other boats in the area about us. One of the other captains comments was *"Did I hear that guy right? They have done 2000 miles in a kayak! I wouldn't do that in a tow boat!"* and then another said, *"I wouldn't do that pushing a control stick never mind paddles."* Its nice to know that the professional river users admire what we are doing even if we cannot get the media in the UK to give us any coverage.

I have trouble contacting West by phone to see if he has located the boat ramp and I am getting concerned that he will not be there. During a call at lunch time he tells me that there are two ferry crossing points and that one is nearer to the boat ramp, as long as we are talking about the same place, and that it is where we should aim for. I am not sure that there are two as only one is marked on my map and I have asked a passing boat if they know of more than one Angola ferry. He told me that there is only one at about mile 300, or some 15 miles/2 ½ hours further down the river, than where we are aiming for.

This is further than we can travel today and we would be arriving after dark as well. This will not be an option for us so I start to plan an earlier stop. I finally manage to get through and he tells me that he has located the boat ramp at mile 315, right where I thought it would be and we will be able to make it. Better still he tells me Pauline is with him! Mind you I am wet and smelly so I am not sure what sort of reception I will get. There is one last hurdle to overcome before we can get to the ramp and that is passing three side channels that lead to a hydro electric power plant located on the right bank. The same bank that the boat ramp is on and the third of them is only about 50 yards from it. They are clearly marked on the map and there is a box containing the following warning printed adjacent to their location:

CAUTION
OLD RIVER CONTROL STRUCTURES

Very dangerous currents in and near beginning of inflow channels when structures are in operation. Flashing amber lights and horns are located on the south points of the inflow channels of the Low Sill and Auxiliary structures. The inflow channels are NOT navigable channels, therefore, under no circumstances should any vessel attempt to enter. Tows andother vessels should navigate as far as possible from this area and asclose to the left descending bank of the Mississippi River as safety will permit.

In other words, get over to the other side and stay there until you are past this point. Not an option for us.

Passing them is quite a challenge as the water is turbulent, swirling and with waves that are cresting in places. As I navigate the last of them I trust the stability of OLLI my new found skills and hope that I do not capsize, especially given the audience that is standing watching my approach. Fortunately I make it and with a nonchalance that disguises my relief pull up onto the ramp.

The reception is a lot less emotional than I imagined but it is good to see Pauline after all this time. I do feel sorry about meeting her when Grace cannot meet Phil at the same time. We have been through so much together. I just try not to be too overt in my happiness to save her feelings.

It is a 40-minute drive to the farm and after we clean up we head out for dinner. The restaurant owners placed a bottle of wine on the table that sports a huge bow and label stating how many miles we have left to go. At another table are other diners who have been following our progress on the website and come across to meet us and tell us how amazing they have found our journey. They greet us like long lost friends, even though I have no idea who they are, and it seems that we are celebrities in town. Well, in the 'Brown Bag Gourmet' restaurant at least.

The meal is a strange affair as I feel that I would have preferred not to have had it. Not that I am ungrateful, quite the opposite, but I am aware that everyone around me knows who I am, most of them are like family, and Grace only knows Pauline and me.

In many ways I would rather we had just had dinner at the farm or that we hadn't been picked up at all and had settled for a dehydrated bowl of mush. Such is the bond I feel with Grace, even if we disagree at times.

I will be sharing a bed tonight with Pauline and that will be strange, as I haven't done that since getting up at 4 am on 1 August. I am sure that it might be hard to leave in the morning but as the end is now so near I can almost touch it, nothing is going to get in the way.

28/9/14
What a restless night! I had someone in my bed and they were real <u>and</u> kept moving about. That would be Pauline then.

I was up and about at the usual time, 6 am, and had my gear packed away ready for the drive back to the kayaks in no time at all. Funny what a difference being in a building makes. The really odd thing is that I have not left a single thing behind, either by design or accident. By design because I cannot be sure that there is not something I will need between here and mile zero, by accident because I have managed to leave a trail of equipment behind me almost all the way.

As we ride back Pauline is quiet and obviously worried about me but I try to reassure her that I will be OK. I just hope that she listens. Back at the boat ramp there is a Coast Guard employee checking the river water levels and taking note of readings on equipment that is nearby. We never did ask him what the equipment was for, the level readings we knew were a way of gauging the rise and fall so as to give commercial traffic information on the channels and riverside towns advance warning of potential flooding. He joins our little group and it turns out he lives just down the road from Marguerite and West.

We drag everything out of the truck and pile it between the boats and as we pack it away everyone is amazed, as usual, as to how it all disappears. The Coast Guard guy said "I'd have bet my paycheque that it wouldn't all get in!" as we put the last few items in and get ready to push off. Shame he didn't, it would have made a nice donation to the funds.

The start of the paddle today is not a very happy one. Bit of a tearful set off and a plod of a journey. And then to cap it off it rained, steady and relatively heavily, for about an hour. At least there was no wind to hold us back.

I am not sure if seeing Pauline has been a good thing or not. She has seen that I am OK, a bit thinner and somewhat scruffy, but OK. However it has reminded me of the length of time I have been away from home and the relative loneliness that I have felt since arriving in the USA, especially since setting off on the river with its vast distances and lack of other people. It has also been a hardship for Grace as I feel that having one of my family members so close has reminded her just how far away hers are. Add that to the number of people I have already known, who we have met in the last few days, and I feel guilty about how she must feel about my relative easy time of late.

As we started to look for somewhere to stop for lunch we saw a canoe slightly in front and to our right, which had two occupants. We wave at them as we aim for a stopping place and they cut across to join us. They turn out to be two US college graduates travelling by canoe to New Orleans, called Susan and George. They may be the same age as each other but they are the same as Grace and I, not related or in a relationship, they are just two friends who decided to undertake the journey.

They are the only other people we have seen on canoes or kayaks since we left 'The Critters' on day 2 way up at Pine Point in Minnesota.

We take photos with our respective national flags; swap stories for awhile, then all set off. It doesn't take long before we have not only left them behind but cannot even see them. It is a sharp reminder not just how much faster our kayaks are than canoes but just how invisible small craft are on such a vast body of water.

Our target today is the town of St. Francesville, which is located at mile 265 where there are three boat ramps, and possible camping areas, marked on the map. Things have been going OK and then it starts to rain quite heavily which always has a bad effect on anyone, even more so when you are tired, like we are.

The first place we find is actually the ramp for the old ferry across the river that used to serve the town and, although we find a suitable place that is at the top of the ramp, I see a man in a pick up pull up and then notice that there are several others approaching. I walk across to talk to him and he tells me that although it may seem OK the area is something of a gathering point for launching fishing boats and other 'activities' that he does not describe with any more than a raised eyebrow. I ask if he knows if the next ramp is any quieter and he tells me that it is and is only a couple of hundred feet down the river.

I tell Grace and she agrees that we should move to the next one to be sure of a safe night. Only to find that it has disappeared under a pile of building equipment that has been dumped by the USACE who are carrying out works on the levee. With more hope than certainty we move to the last of the boat ramps marked on the maps. It turns out to be accessible from the river but the top area has been blocked off so that it cannot be used to launch boats. There is a flat area that we can camp on and fortunately it has stopped raining so we can set up in relative comfort.

We are getting ready to 'cook' our 'dinner' when a truck appears and approaches us. It contains two gentlemen of indeterminate age showing obvious signs of having consumed several portions of 'adult beverages'. Two middle aged drunks in other words. I wander across to talk to them and once again it is the British accent, and the policy of the US Government of maintaining Air Force bases in the UK, to the rescue as they enquire what we are doing. I think they make the usual comments of amazement at our actions but it is hard to tell through their drink altered Deep South accents.

It becomes hot and muggy as we finish our meal and soon the rain is belting down again. At least we had shelter sorted out and gear stored away before it started.

Sandy Trieschmann has been in touch about stopping in Baton Rouge and declares it is a real no-no, but suggests that if we stretch our schedule and put in a 55-mile day it will see us to the town of Plaquemine. Once again she has worked her contacts and has secured us the offer of camping alongside the lock that leads from the bayou or a room in the Best Western hotel in town. She tells me that if we decide to camp to let her know as she has obtained permission from the Mayor's office for us as the site is right in front of the council offices and is not normally allowed. I tell her it is likely that we will go for the hotel option if we can make it. She tells me she will continue to try and sort something at a lesser distance if possible.

I can hardly believe that if we do five more 50-mile days we will have completed the expedition. I also remind myself that we must **not** become complacent. One option for tonight had been for West to come and pick us up again as by road they live just over an hour away. I am glad I didn't accept the offer, not just because it would have been a bit of a bind to load and unload again but I am not sure that I would be able to continue if I had spent another night with Pauline. It would have been too hard to give up the comforts of company. It would also not have been fair on Grace for the reasons I stated at the start of the day. It has been hard on her today and I feel a responsibility for some of the cause.

As the barges go past they are the noisiest they have been so far on the trip and they are actually further away than they have been for a while. I cannot explain why, so close my ears as well as my eyes and go to sleep.

29/9/14
It was another night I woke up really refreshed and ready to go, only to find that it was half an hour past midnight. I manage to roll over and the next time I wake it was 4:30 am to the, oh so gentle sound of rain. Great! I doze for a while and stir myself at about 5:30 am. It was still raining and continued to do so all through breakfast. Then it stated to rain even harder as we pack everything away and take the tents down. Just about everything was soaked; the tents weighed twice as much as normal and didn't fit into their storage bags easily so all in all it was a miserable start to the day. We couldn't afford the luxury of waiting for the rain to stop so we wore our raincoats under the buoyancy aids and put the splash skirts on to keep the rain out of the boats. It was still not fully light when we set off, just before 7 am and the rain did not help with the gloomy atmosphere.

We started to follow the channel and I suddenly realised that Grace was on a different track to me. I called to her and asked if she had seen the next channel marker and she pointed off to her right. As I looked round I saw that I had lined up on a buoy that had obviously come loose and was at the wrong side of the channel. This could have been dangerous for me as had I continued I would have been in the shipping lane, and in the low light conditions, would have been all but invisible to the barges. It also presented a significant danger to the barges as if one of them was to make the same error they could end up out of the dredged channel and could run aground.

About 2 hours later the rain had stopped and the sun made an appearance so we made a quick stop to put our coats away. We had pulled up on a small beach area in a little cove just below a big house. Getting ashore was easy; much easier than getting back out. A combination of the river flow and a passing barge created some big waves. It was Grace's turn to have to bail out and try to set off again as a particularly large wave rose up and dumped a lot of water on her lap.

We had not gone far when I saw on the left side that there was a large inlet that went due south and looked like it would cut out quite a distance if we took it. I checked the map and saw that it was indeed a side channel round a big island but that it had another of the boxed warnings: -

Warning
An underwater stone dike has been constructed across Profit Island chute approximately 0.5 miles downstream of the inlet. The chute is permanently closed to navigation and under no circumstances should any vessel attempt to navigate the length of Profit Island Chute.

As we looked at it, it was tempting, very tempting, to go down it but then we heard the muted roar of the water rushing over the dike (weir) and saw the water foaming as though boiling. I even considered getting close and portaging round the dike and suggest this but as we looked it seemed less of an option. Wary of our last encounter with a similar structure we shrugged and stuck with the marked route.

We had 'only' been moving along at 6mph, how quickly we had become used to a slightly faster pace, and the trip round the island seemed to take an age. Especially when we got to the point where the channel joined the main river again and we could see that it was calm, in contrast to how it had been at the top. Just over 5 miles on, the river took a large bend to our left and the map showed that we would be on a straight run south into the city of Baton Rouge so we decided that it would be a good place to stop and have lunch, especially as we may not find anywhere in the city.

As we pulled up and beached we both commented that it was a shame that we didn't have a view of the city skyline in the distance. Grace joked that with our luck there was probably a beach another half mile on that had such a view but, if we moved, there probably wasn't. Guess what? Correct, she was right there was a beach half a mile round the corner that did have a bit of a view of the city.

Everyone had been full of tales of woe about Baton Rouge. About how we would be robbed if we tried to camp there; about how we would be trampled by the huge grain and container ships as they made their way to berths; how the tugs would dash from bank to bank as they serviced the ships creating wakes that would swamp us and how the maximum sized barges ploughed down the middle of the river causing waves that were tens of feet high.

We had planned to avoid the camping bit as that might have been partly true but as for the rest we decided that we would see what would happen and take care as we passed through. Plenty of other people had passed this way and survived so we reckoned that we could do it as well.

We passed down the approach and rounded the bend to head due west and traverse the docks. We could see the huge road and rail bridges that crossed the river and the impressively tall State Capital Building along with the usual glass towers that inhabit cities all over the world. We could see the warehouses lining the banks and the piers and unloading points jutting out into the river.

What we couldn't see were ships. There were some, but the docks were mostly empty and the river was almost devoid of moving traffic. Given the warning we had been given, and the horror stories that had been told, it was a bit of a disappointment really. Oh well, better quiet than so busy we cannot get through.

The frontage for the city is about 3 miles in total but the docks run for almost 10 and the whole way was completely built up with industrial areas and what were obviously chemical and oil processing/producing plants. Even when we left the city area the frequency of commercial activity on the river's edge continued and it looked like what it is. A scar on the landscape and a despoiling of the riverbanks. Not only were there buildings and frameworks blighting the area but also there was much evidence of spills of various sorts that had polluted, no poisoned, the land and subsequently the river.

Suddenly, and with about 6 or 7 miles to go before we reached Plaquemine, the river flow all but disappeared and we were reduced to working very hard to make 4 mph. It was as bad as being back on the dam and lock pools in the upper reaches, especially as a headwind had got up from nowhere. There is no other way to describe what we had to endure but a slog and bloody hard work! It felt like we were going backwards at times, the boats wouldn't keep a straight course as the wind veered and they turned into it.

We were not just tired but bone weary. It had been a long journey today and with the rotten start to the day this was something we could do without. I could hear Grace talking behind me and thought that she was using her phone while paddling, which impressed me, but later found that she was flexing her vocabulary and cursing everything in sight.

Sandy had sent me a text telling me that if we entered the town by the lock that was the outlet for the bayou to the river, we would be right where we needed to be for either camping or the hotel. There was no doubt that we would opt for the hotel. I start to look for the lock, which was not marked on the map, but as I travel further and further cannot find any sign of one. I did find a boat ramp that was shown on the map as being past the bayou and we pull up onto it.

I walk up to the top of the levee and see that the town is below us but there is no sign of a bayou or lock anywhere near. Or a lawn in front of the town hall. Or a hotel. I see a young woman in the distance who is out jogging towards me so I wave. She waves back, runs about another 5 paces, touches a light pole and turns to run the other way. I call out to her saying "Can you wait please I need your help" as I walk towards her and she turns and runs back. Thank goodness, I would never have caught her.

I quickly tell her about Grace and I and ask if she knows of the lock, grassed area and hotel in town. She tells me the lock is about a mile away in town, but is just an ornamental feature now as it was closed off many years ago. She thinks it has not been used since before she was born. She is about 23. Sandy has failed for the first time.

I take a chance and ask if she has a truck and can she give Grace and I a lift into town with our equipment. She tells me that she doesn't have a truck but will go and get her car. I have been most careful to make sure she knows that Grace is a young woman so that she feels safe and hope that she does help us.

Back at the boats I tell Grace what I have found out and that I have asked someone for a lift, so we begin to pack the gear away and secure the boats at the side of the ramp. We have finished doing this and the young woman has not turned up so I begin to think that this is the first time we will be disappointed. I tell Grace of my thoughts and she says "Well it will be on her conscience". No sooner has she said this than a huge pickup truck comes over the levee and approaches us. It is my new best friend! It turned out that she had driven to the other side of town to get her father's truck and that her mom had come with her. Either for safety or to meet the two crazy English people. Matters not to me, the lift is most welcome.

At the hotel we find that they have our names and have reserved a room for us. With the 'police' discount applied we get into the room and spread the tents, and other wet stuff, out on the floor. We must be the only people in the entire hotel using the air conditioning units to heat rather than cool their room.

We phone out for a Pizza Hut delivery to the room and I obtain a fistful of coffee packets from reception while I wait to collect it. We have ordered two large stuffed crust pizzas, the size normally reserved for a family, and a treat of a chocolate cake for supper. Great way to end the day. It turns out even better when I get home and check the credit card statement, as the charges never appeared. Which is good as it was the most expensive meal we had had. Even more expensive than the posh place in St. Louis!
30/9/14

We have breakfast included in the cost so that is one less chore for us to do before we pack up and set off. I manage a quick chat with everyone at the Constantine's and Grace puts a quick call in to home and we are set for the day. First challenge is getting back to the boat so I ask at reception if they can call us a taxi. Only to be told that it will be a 45-minute wait as it will have to come from Baton Rouge. Plaquemine doesn't have a taxi service of its own. Welcome to America where EVERYONE has a car.

Without any further ado the duty manager gives his keys to the receptionist and tells us that he would be delighted to assist by taking us to the boats. And without being asked. The angels are here again. He drops us off with a cheery wave and best wishes for a safe journey. I forgot to mention that he is Indian and commented that he had an uncle in Rotary back in his hometown, which is near Calcutta in India, so perhaps the Rotary baseball cap had a hand in the offer and is still working its magic.

The weather today promises to be hot and sunny without much of a wind and we set off comparing notes about how much we are looking forward to the other half of our pizza rather than the cardboardhydrate stuff.

The question for today is "Where did the flow go?" Yesterday we had a slow spot that we blamed on the weather, but today? What can we blame? Even in the channel the best we could do is 5.5mph and because of river traffic we can't always get into the channel. The barges have got smaller but more frequent and the ships are huge. We can get close to some of them as they are moored up at the side of the channel waiting to be taken into the port for loading. They tower above the river and when we get up close they are sheer slabs of steel that intimidate us.

The photos hardly do their size and impressive bulk justice. Thankfully all the ones we came across were moored but still have to be avoided as they are 'parked' in rows and we do not know when one of them might start up its engines and haul up the anchors. This has put a big dent in our plans as we have only managed around 45 miles.

It seems funny to write "only" and "45 miles" now but for 2 weeks we have been zipping along at 7+mph and more than 50 miles is relatively easy. Well not THAT easy. Added to that, it starts to get dark at 7:00 pm and days are just not long enough.

Grace tells me that she can feel her face burning as the sun gets higher so we had to stop and dig out the spare wide brim hat. Being bald has advantages; I've worn (and lost 2) one right from the start and know their value. We both put on long sleeved shirts as well at this point as it is better to be hot than burnt.

As it approached 5:30 pm we start to review stopping options and look for campsites when a barge captain, aboard a boat moored on our right, hailed us to tell us about a ship behind us. One of the really big ones and it is moving at more than 12 mph. In absolute silence. This thing weighs about 250,000 tons, is creating a wave about 3 feet high around its bow and, either the engines are that far away that we cannot hear them, or they are barely turning so are not making much noise.

As it passes we look up and nearly fall over backwards craning to see the top, the wave it creates is not a real problem, the ones from the jet bikes are more dangerous, and the engines make barely a gentle hum as the stern passes. The barge captain asks if I have a radio and I tell him that we have and ask what channel to use. It is a different one to above Baton Rouge so I alter the setting and call him. Nothing. Several attempts later it is obvious that it has failed. He tells me that the ships do not have lookouts at the bow, or CCTV systems, and that we will not show up on their radar systems, as we are just too small.

Nothing for it but to keep swivelling our heads every so often and keeping our distance. We thank him for his help, he wishes us well and we are off again looking for somewhere to stop for the night.

It is about 6 pm when we spot a small flat area on the left bank just above a barge marshalling area that has a beach we can use to access it. The 'beach' is actually made of seashells not sand, a bit rough on the feet and definitely different, but safe and away from the wash of the passing boats. We pitch camp and settle down for the night.

Craig Michel in New Orleans texts me a proposal for meeting up in New Orleans but the place he suggests is almost 60 miles downriver from our current location which, given the slow progress today, would be too far for us to be certain of managing. I ring him and we arrange a new one at about 45 miles in an area that is marked as having a boat ramp.

He tells me that the change will be no problem and that he has arranged for us to stay at a Rotarian friend's house for the night. We will have to take the boats out of the water and put them on a vehicle as leaving them where we have planned to meet will not be a safe option. Big cities again I suppose.

He also tells me that he is in discussions with the authorities in Venice, the last town before the Gulf and mile zero, to arrange transport back upstream when we finish. He will have a definite answer when we meet tomorrow. He also has feelers out for another host between New Orleans and Venice if we feel the need not to sleep in a tent. What a great friend he is and all from an article in an online blog published by Rotary International.

Grace and I have agreed to be on the water by first light, which is about 6:30 am to make sure we can cover the miles. As we lie in our tents I ask if she is feeling the heat that is building and tell her that my teeth are sweating. She laughs and says she is hot and feels like she is melting but that after the trouble she has had with her teeth she is trying not to think of any new ailments for them.

When I make the end of day observations I note that the river is shown as being less than 100 feet above sea level, and has been for five days now, and surmise that this is the reason for the lack of flow assisting our progress.

1/10/14
We got up at 5:30, eat breakfast in the dark and started getting ready to leave as soon as it was light enough, just so we could make the miles we needed to hit our pick up point given the relative lack of flow again.

Grace was loading her kayak and I was attending to a call of nature behind a bush when I heard a man's voice calling out "Hey Ken, Grace, how are you?" I then heard Grace's voice as she talked to someone. We were in the middle of nowhere, who on earth could it be? Wondering if it was the farmer, who owned the land we were on, who had come to throw us off, and how he knew our names, I completed the task in hand and walked across.

It was not the farmer but a chap who introduced himself as Doug. He told us that he lives nearby and that he surfs the web looking for people who are undertaking journeys by kayak/canoe on the Mississippi and then follows their progress on Facebook, or in our case, via our website and Spot3 page. He had fbeen following our progress and located our overnight stop and when he found that we were only a few minutes away from his house decided to come to see us! And he brought doughnuts!!! What a superstar he is. Not a Rotarian, or on the Mississippi paddlers page, he is just a keen supporter of people who use the Mississippi River for recreation and offers to help in any way he can.

He tells us that his family have a cabin and some land about 15 miles further down the river which, if he'd been able to contact us before, he would have invited us to camp on. He adds that when we get to that camp he would like nothing better than to break off work for a while so that he can join his 2 uncles, who are at the camp now, to 'visit' with us. He takes his leave and sets off for work telling us to be sure and look out for the sign on the left side as we pass through.

We get going and it is framing up to be a hot day again. There is not much in the way of flow to assist us so the paddling has become hard work again.

Right on the 15 mile mark from our departure point we spot two chaps standing on the left bank waving enthusiastically at us and as we paddle across we see a truck pull up. It can only be Doug and his uncles. They are clearly delighted to be able to chat with us and ask all the usual questions. Usual in so far as we can almost predict the answers we will give, it is only the phrasing that has changed as we have travelled down the river. The looks of amazement have not changed. They celebrate our arrival by passing us cold cans of Coke and Root Beer

The bank was deep mud and not really suitable for climbing out for a short stop, their words not mine, so we conduct the visit with us in the kayaks and them on the bank. After the offers of trips to shops and the like we take our leave and they pass us the remainder of the cans of coke and root beer that they have brought down to the rivers edge.

We set off with 4 cans each and an offer of ice to keep them cold. There is great hilarity as we all comment at the same time that ice in the bottom of the kayaks would not last long and cause more problems for us. They are such nice people that it is a shame to have to leave them, and again it is a kindness that has been shown without asking or expecting.

I cannot help but think, as we paddle away, that if there were more friendships like the ones we have just made around the world then we would live in a much better place. Then on reflection I realise there is. It's just that we allow people with the loudest voices to overshadow it all with rhetoric and the language of hate to such a degree that some think that they can only change things with the path of violence. I decide, yet again, that if we had less politics and religion in the world we could all get on a lot better. Simplistic? Idealistic? Guilty on both counts. But don't tell me that I am wrong.

Progress continues to be slow, painfully so, and it was made worse by having to avoid a lot of shipping. Getting out of their way means getting out of the channel and what bit of flow it offers. Frustrating barely covers it.

There is absolutely no let up in the industrial landscape as we continue down the river. We might have complained about the unchanging vista of the trees further up and the 'green hell' at the top but at least they were natural not these man made monstrosities. We had settled on a boat ramp that was shown as being just under the bridge carrying Interstate 310 over the river into the city of New Orleans as the pick up point and, as we rounded a bend, we could see the bridge and knew that we were not far from our stop for the night.

As we pass under the bridge I could see people on the levee using the area as an open air gym and some of the bending and stretching they were contorting into made me extremely jealous of their flexibility. They are an amusing diversion. As we straighten out and start to look for the ramp pick-up point, we see a northbound ship approaching us. It is one of the 250,000 ton leviathans and by the way it is sitting in the water is fully loaded. The bow waves it was creating are huge, looking to be about 10 feet, fortunately they are only rolls and are not cresting or foaming so we can ride them with, comparative, ease.
Then we notice that there is a southbound barge overtaking us and that

he will carve through these bow waves and break them up. Again it is a comparatively easy thing to negotiate as the flow of the river, even slow as it is, will help smooth them out before we get to them. Then we find that the worst part is yet to come.

The waves that were created by the two different vessels were intersecting causing cross-waves and rolls to 'attack' us from different directions all at the same time. A sort of 'V' shaped wave. Then the riverbanks, which had concrete sides, and the slab sides of moored barges started to have an effect by bouncing the waves back into the river channel. This is now creating multiple waves from multiple directions and some of them are starting to crest and foam at the top. They are an absolute nightmare to negotiate and cause real heart stopping moments.

My kayak rolled and pitched and the walls of the wave presented a steep climb followed by a sharp descent that caused the bow of the boat to bury itself into the bottom of the trough. The only thing to do is paddle hard to try and maintain as straight a line as possible to the wave immediately in front and to constantly shift direction to face each new wave as it forms. Not for the first time am I grateful for the inherent stability that OLLI has.

Grace tells me later that at one point the waves were so high that she saw me disappear over the crest and could not see even the tops of my paddles as I went down into the trough. I hope she has it on video, as I am amazed at surviving this incident intact and upright. Perhaps we can consider ourselves experienced kayakers now?

With no time to bask in the glory of mastering huge waves we take another hit to our confidence. We couldn't find the boat ramp. It was supposed to be less than a mile after the bridge but we had gone almost another 5 miles and still had not found it. I selected one of the piers that served as a discharge/loading point for a chemical plant as a point where I thought we would be able to get out. My reasoning being that if there was a pipeline and pier then there would be some sort of service road to it. It turned out that there was but not without difficulty.

I pulled up under the pier and almost immediately the boat grounded on the muddy edge. I got out and sank straight away up to above my knees in soft, squelchy and glutinous mud. It held on to me as I tried to wade through it, it was like having a thousand slimy hands holding my legs and trying to stop me walking. The gentleman that I am I offered to pull Grace a bit further in, well there was no point in both of us being slimed half to death, and then went up to see what I could find on dry land.

The levee was just a short walk through some scrubby trees and on the top was the access road I had hoped for. I was able to see the name of the chemical company that was acting as our temporary host and rang Carl Michel to tell him where we were. He had found the top of the boat ramp, had seen that it was overgrown and disused, actually where it was supposed to be, and was sat waiting for me to call.

There was a moment of great humour when we went down to the boats to pull them up and I said to Grace "I found these two blokes up top and they are going to give us a hand" and when they had helped haul the boats up the levee slope she turned to me and said "Where's Carl then" I said "Here" and introduced them. She looked at me in a strange way and said, "I thought you meant that these were just two random blokes that you had pressed in to service, given that you just ask for help off anyone that is around". Well, it had been a hard day.

We load the boats onto the ubiquitous pick up truck and set off to drive to our host's house. I swear we went over the river at least 5 times and thought that we were actually lost, but it turned out that the one-way system is such that it curls round itself to deliver you about a mile further on than when you had started. At the house we meet our host, Adele Bergman, and a whole host of other people. It turns out that they are all Rotarians and considerably younger than the ones in my club. We had a great dinner, after we had showered of course, and some great conversation not just about the trip but other things as well which made a great change for us

Carl tells me that it is all arranged for us to be picked up from the mile zero point by the Venice Harbour Authority boat and accommodation has been fixed up further down the river in Belle Chase, so we don't have to worry about camping on the outskirts of the city or in the swampy beginnings of the delta area. Where there might be alligators. And other things no doubt.

2/10/14
As Adele only had one spare room at her house I elected to sleep on the couch rather than the floor. It turned out to be the most comfortable thing I had slept on in weeks. Or was it that I was just very tired?

What we didn't know was that Adele had gathered up our paddle clothes that we had just piled up in a corner of the bathroom and had washed them before she went to bed. Hospitality indeed, especially given the muddy state that they were in.

The only bad news for me was that for some reason I had stiffened up around the chest area and upper shoulders, so much so that it was an effort to raise my arms to put my shirt on. The exertions of the previous few days' hard work had finally caught up and I was in quite a lot of pain. This didn't ease off when it came to lifting the kayaks out of the garage and onto the truck for the trip back to the river. I knew I would be in for a bad day overall but had to battle through, I hadn't come this far to give up now.

Carl and his friend took us to a park not far from Adele's house and a put in point. He had told us the night before that it probably wouldn't be a good idea to return to the area where they found, not least because of the traffic in New Orleans. He had hinted at other reasons but didn't expand on them at dinner.

As we drove along I asked what the other problem was that he had mentioned. He somewhat reluctantly told me that the area where he had met us was notorious for chemical spillages and that it was locally known as 'Cancer Alley'. He immediately told me that it was given that name because of the long-term effects on residents in the area rather than any risk that I had been in, but that he wanted to err on the side of caution in case there had been a fresh spill overnight that may have caused problems. Like chemical burns or, well anything really. I am really glad that he tells me this AFTER I've ploughed through the knee-deep mud. It was even more reassuring when he tells me that they didn't even want to go there again to launch us. We haven't missed much in the way of mileage but, again, I am certain that they had our best interests at heart and I am not keen on suffering any of the things he has described as happening to other people over the years.

We launch from a nearby park and use the pier reserved for the US

Coast Guard. Not before the park security/police approach and ask what we are doing and tell us that we shouldn't be here. Carl starts to explain that the gate was unlocked so he thought it would be OK, I hope they say it is as the boats are in the water and that was a struggle! Then I hear him tell them that we are from the UK and what we are doing and suddenly their attitude changes completely. To the point that we are in danger of being there longer than we need as they want to talk to us. So we work round them and they get the idea.

We said goodbye and thank you, see you at the weekend, and then set off. My chest is still stiff and sore to the point that I consider painkillers to reduce the effect. They start to loosen up as we get going so I decide to see how it goes without tablets. We set off at a nice steady 5mph easy paddle but after awhile the work rate increases but the speed drops, due to lack of flow we suppose, and my chest starts start to ache again.

We go through the centre of the city and I am able to point out some of the places that Grace and Phil should visit if they decide to stop in the city when we finish. She tells me that one of the guests from last night, Bart Shank, has offered to host them for the weekend at his house. His philosophy, he tells them, is travel cheap, eat well. She confesses to not being sure if she wants to but I assure her that the offer will be genuine and that it is up to her.

As we pass by Doveton, a suburb of New Orleans, our host from the night before, Adele, has come out of work to meet us on the riverbank. Nice touch, I feel humble at the thought of all the people following and helping us and hope that I can repay them somehow.

As we keep going it becomes obvious to me that if we are to make Venice (Louisiana not Italy) and keep to time arrangements, without any more delays or injuries then we will have to cut some more miles. I know Grace will not like it, but I do not believe I will make the mileage needed to finish on the appointed day given the river conditions and my physical condition.

About 15 miles into the day I had been OK, even my chest was not giving me too much of a problem. But the possibility of things getting worse started to weigh heavy on my mind and all I could see was complete failure. After so far and so much it was all I could think of. I can't make it; I won't make it; How can I make it; Will I make it?

OK, so cutting miles again is not good but I keep reminding myself that the aim is to reach mile zero, not injure myself or not be able to avoid boats, ships, barges or waves because of being too tired or in pain, any or all of which could be a bigger problem than a sore chest.

I'm not really happy with the decision but it has to be made. Another factor is that if I enter into a discussion with Grace it will lead to an argument and one that I know will end with me capitulating and taking on miles that I am not sure I have in me. Add to all this that final arrangements have been made, and set in motion, for our collection from the end; for family to meet us; for transport back to Moreauville and rest before we fly home. After considerable argument with myself I reach the decision and decide to look for a suitable place on the maps and take the consequences, blame or whatever else anyone wants to call it.

We get to the ferry crossing where we are being met and find that they will not let us lift the boats onto the pontoon and up the loading ramp, so we have to manhandle the boats across a field. Which did nothing for my chest muscles or mood.

Our host is called Heidi Lee and she comes to get us in her husband's pickup truck. She has brought her friend with her to help and it turns out she is ex military and well used to hauling stuff about. Thank goodness. We get the kayaks into the truck, well the front half anyway. We end up riding in the back with them and sitting on them to hold them down. We pass several Police cars but not one occupant even glances in our direction.

As we ride I tell Grace about my dilemma and that we will have to miss some miles and the reasons for my decision. I thought that I had conveyed how many but before we can discuss it we arrive at the house.

What a beautiful home it is and in a nice area. After showers and changing we set off for dinner with Heidi and her husband Robert. We both notice that they didn't lock the door as we left. When we comment on this they tell us that they never lock the door as the town may be a suburb of New Orleans but is a really safe place and has a great Police

Department. Another advantage is that there are only three ways to gain entry to, or exit from, the town. One is the ferry, the other is a swing bridge and the third is a tunnel. If there is a problem all they do is close the roads. And wait for the bad guys to come to them.

Obviously I was wrong about my earlier assumption as at dinner with our hosts we have a mini argument when Robert starts to mention potential put in places we can use and is talking in terms of 30 plus miles. This is further than I had thought and cut our discussion short saying it will wait till we get back.

When we check the maps with Heidi and Robert, there is a ferry landing at 35 miles and a garage at 40, both of which we can possibly use.

When we get back I go to Grace's room to explain the situation. I tell her that I understand that she is angry, as she will not have wanted to miss so many miles and find that she is angrier at the way I have imposed the decision. I suppose I have in her eyes, and try to explain that I did it for all the right reasons.

I really do not think we will make it and tell her so. I accept that responsibility for the errors and the decision even if some people will see it as a cop-out. I also tell her that I will ensure that everyone knows that it was my decision.

I also tell her that I am disappointed in myself for not planning this part properly, failing to take into account our potential physical condition at this point in the trip. A potential that has become a reality. Another factor is that I didn't ask the crucial question about flow in the areas we are in now as I had accepted that it would remain constant once out of the controlled areas. I had looked at the maps briefly with Robert before dinner and tell him about our previous progress and flow rate, and the way it seems to have disappeared. He tells me "It is high down here, but only in Spring when the first snow melt swells the river".

That starts to make sense as the Spring thaws would affect here before the north as the ice/snow on the land would not melt till later and then at a measured pace rather than the initial push that then subsides with the channel depth and lack of 'slope'.

Overall not one of my finest days but I believe that I have done my best to keep us on track and safe. I am disappointed in myself and feel Grace's frustration. This is not an electric storm, it's bad planning, poor research and pushing myself beyond what is good for me.

It is a measure of her temperament that she tells me that she accepts the decision but not the method in which it was imposed. She tells me that she would have supported me had I stuck with my original plan of incorporating both our views in decision-making. I am so grateful that we have not had a major fall out over this and get a bit tearful at what good friends we have become. A hug sorts this out.

She really is a good mate and this just serves to underline it for me.

This sorted out I sit with Robert and the maps for awhile and he points out a ferry crossing that is shown as being 35 miles from Venice, this would save us about 35 miles and make the finish entirely achievable. It is not as much of a saving as we could make but I am happy that it is enough of a help.

Week 9
Belle Chase, Louisiana to Mile zero, Mississippi River

3/10/14

The day started badly, it was lashing down with rain as we went out to the truck, and then got worse. I drove the pickup as Heidi was not keen on handling it with the boats overhanging the roof, and we went about 20 miles down the, one and only, road towards Venice and the put in point.

When we got there the first thing I realised was that we hadn't filled the water containers before we set off. This was the first time we have made such a simple error. We may be near the end but we still need water and in the heat of south Louisiana, lots of it. This led to a delay as Grace went with Heidi to get water, after we had unloaded the boats and gear.

I asked a young man, who was waiting for the ferry, to help me get the kayaks to the river edge and he was only too glad to help. Grace came back with water and we loaded up and set off. So far, so good.

As we set off I looked at the GPS and map and realised that the longitude and latitude readings did not match up. After some swift calculations and examination of the data I determined that we were 49 miles, not 35, from Venice so our journey was 14 miles longer. Great! Another fine mess I'd got us into. With the potential for a night in the tents we set off.

Progress was not brilliant but we managed an average of 5mph and having set off at 9:30 am the possibility of making the marina in Venice before dark was getting thinner.

At 12:30 we stopped, on what was probably the smallest sandbar area we had seen so far, to eat. We had a discussion about our progress so far and the potential for making our target and decided that we should go for it, even if it meant covering the last bit in the growing dark. This was not as bad as it sounds, we concluded, as the marina is up a side channel and away from major traffic.

I had the number for the Cypress Bend Marina and Motel at Venice so rang and reserved a room. I had to pay for it up front by credit card, which acted to concentrate our efforts. They asked for an estimated time of arrival and I said that we would be there at about 6:30pm.

The lunch area was not big enough for complete privacy for toilet requirements and all I shall say about that is that Grace made fun of certain noises that I made. We set off again about 1pm and set a good pace. We were doing 5.7 to 6.1mph in places. That was great and convinced us that we will make it.

Then the crosswinds and waves on bends and wider areas arrived. The kayaks kept turning away from the intended direction of travel, the waves kept rolling over us, the pace slowed right down, it was horrible.

We both had a rant at the elements but, of course, it does not a blind bit of good. We kept going through. I must confess at one point I even contemplated not fighting the elements and allowing myself to capsize just to get off the river. Get off the river and then find a passing truck to take us to the marina. Grace pulled alongside and confessed the same feelings. Sods law says that if we had then there wouldn't have been a truck for days. We felt our luck was that bad.

We paddled and talked about anything and nothing, just to distract ourselves. It has worked before for a variety of situations and it did for this one. Suddenly, and just as quick as it had appeared, the wind and waves died down and we speeded up.

We found the channel that led to the marina just as the sun started to set and it was great to be paddling. Why could it not have been this enjoyable all day then?

The information we had about the motel was that it was a mile up the channel but we seemed to have gone that far and still not found it so I had to ring to ask for a landmark. Having just finished the call a passing boat, loaded with fishermen out for a day's play, asked if we wanted a lift. You bet, was the reply. So the kayaks, and us, got hauled aboard and we arrived in style. It turned out that the guys on the boat were all travel writers so there is a chance we may get some more publicity, it wasn't for the lack of telling them about ourselves and the expedition.

We book in, shower, dress and go out for food. Then comes the worst news of the day. The harbour authority patrol has been told no one but us can travel on the boat for the recovery from mile zero.

This is a major disappointment, now the finish is just us. I try to console myself, and Grace, by stating the obvious; it's only ever been us right from the start. In truth I don't kid anyone, not even myself. I am saddened by this and it takes the last of the shine off what has been not the best of days.

We chat to some of the guys in the bar who are in the area for the fishing, about our expedition and Grace tells them of our situation concerning family members. She thinks that one of them just might take our family and supporters on his boat, judging by the way he kept asking questions. I think it depends how hung over he is in the morning and how much he remembers.

Back at the motel I have a message to ring Kerry Crosse, the head of the Harbour Patrol, about arrangements for tomorrow. I make one final plea about Phil and Pauline but he tells me that the insurance would not cover them; he appreciates why we are asking and would if he could, but can't. We agree that we will leave his berth area at 10am with an ETA at mile zero of 12:30 to 13:00.

He apologises again about not being able to take the others, but says if we drop off a camera with them they will take pictures for us. He sounds almost upset for us but he obviously has orders.

Tomorrow is the last day. The last 10 miles. How will I/we react I wonder. Probably not the same as we would with an audience. We'll see what happens.

4/10/14
It was strange to wake up and not have to rush, so much so that I wanted to rush, if that makes sense. We have breakfast and I see the lady called Kindred, who was on reception when we checked in last night, along with another woman who is obviously the manager. I tell the manager what we are doing and ask if we could use the room to have a shower when we get back as we have to drive to, at least, New Orleans and it would be nice, for the other occupants of the car as well,

if we could get cleaned up and changed. The manager says only if we are back early enough and the room hasn't been serviced. Kindred looks at me over the manager's shoulder and winks at me. I know then that it will be OK; as she will make sure that the room is last on the list to be made up.

As we are putting the last few bits into the bags we have the news on and with impeccable timing there is an item about a kayaker being attacked by a shark. It has taken a big bite out of his craft and it was only by luck that a boat was nearby and able to get to him to pull him from the water. We are, and shall be, eternally grateful for the news service we were watching that morning for their coverage of that incident and the gruesome photos they showed of the kayak. Or what was left of it.

We pack everything into the kayaks and set off. It seems a bit strange to be taking everything with us, especially when we could probably leave just about everything with the motel and save ourselves some work. It's a bit like not leaving anything in New Orleans, we have carried it this far that it has become routine.

The wind is quite strong but said to be from the North so once out on the river proper it should be coming from behind us and be something of a help.

We have to negotiate the channel back to the main river against current and wind before we can put ourselves back on track. Not only that but we have to negotiate the weekend fishing boats, including the idiots that don't slow down as is good manners and/or required. There seems to be some sort of competition starting at the same time as we set off and whilst nearly all of the boat drivers go slowly past us there is one fool in a bright yellow, twin outboard powered penis substitute that flies past at maximum throttle. I yell some very choice words at him but, obviously, he cannot hear me.

A chap in a nearby boat going slowly past looks across and calls out "Sorry about him". "That's OK" I call back "it's not your fault, but if you catch up with him give him a lead injection in his nostrils from me. About .22 calibre". He laughs and wishes us well. I'm not laughing, I'm serious. The buffoon could have killed us.

To get from the marina to the Harbour Authority post is 0.7 miles, which took us 45 minutes, and all of it bloody hard work. If I stopped the GPS read that I was going backwards at 2.5mph! I just hope that this improves once we get out into the main river. It also makes me glad that we have arranged the collection, as we would never be able to get back upstream in this wind.

When we get to the Harbour Patrol station to drop the camera off and check in with them they insist on taking us to the main channel, because of the wind and river flow. We accept of course. They haul the kayaks onto the back of their boat in a flash and it is obvious that they have done this before. The boss, Kerry, is not around and is not answering his phone so after a short wait they decide to take us out and come back for him.

They take us almost to the left bank and advise that we stay on this side to avoid the shipping and take advantage of the lee of the land. The wind is north eastern in origin, quite strong, and will be coming at us from the side, rather than being behind us, as the river does not run exactly due south at this point.

We launch off the boat and set off. Just 10 miles to go. It is not as easy as we had imagined it would be, not at all. The wind causes the boats to turn, taking us to the left all the time while the rough water and waves bounce us about something rotten. It is harder than we could imagine or, quite frankly how I can describe.

Grace has a paddy about the kayaks turning into the wind all the time and not responding and stopping her from getting anywhere and I respond by shouting at her. Falling out on the last day? In the last few miles? That is tiredness and emotion coming to the surface.

About half a mile or so later we join up and apologise to each other. That's friendship.

We keep going and I keep checking the map against the land based signs and we are definitely getting closer. We are just less than three miles from the end when one of the huge ships seems to be bearing down on us instead of cutting across the river in the main channel. We start to pull further to the left to avoid him and suddenly a small speedboat cuts across in front of him and comes to ask if we are OK.

We assure him we are but he still places himself between the ship and us as it passes about 300 yards to our right. He is proof that not all speedboat owners are idiots; some do care about fellow river users.

The end of the river is almost in sight. Which is more than the Harbour Authority boat is. We keep looking round but cannot see it, I am not that worried about that as they have the Spot3 details and lots of experience when it comes to this sort of thing. I continue to hope that they will be there to capture the moment we cross the line.

We see various signs that declare the names of company berths, mile signs and the like but unfortunately realise that there is no actual sign that says "You are now leaving the Mississippi River, please come back and see us" or at least one saying "Thank you for visiting the USA". I would have thought some wag would have done that by now.

The maps show that 29°09.000' north is the actual line of latitude that marks the official end of the river and the last of the marker boards is just past that on an island that marks the edge of the shipping lane. Beyond this point the Mississippi delta starts and the river has ended.

The 2-mile board is passed and I concentrate on the GPS as it counts down our progress ever southward. Suddenly it displays the figures 29°09.000' and as we cross the latitude line that is it. We have completed the expedition. We have travelled the length of the Mississippi River. We've finished. We've done it.

I feel, well, I'm not sure what I feel, Elated? Deflated? Triumphant? Proud? Overwhelmed? Emotional?

The best description is probably all of those and some that I haven't listed. I did video myself as I crossed the line and my reaction seems to reflect this. I cheer, shout and wave my arms, then my head slumps and I fall silent for a few moments. I see that Grace has done much the same.

I can scarcely believe it. After 2 months of hard work, untold paddle strokes; never changing scenery; campsites that have been insect infested, secluded beaches or mud filled holes; hotel rooms that have ranged from luxurious to insect ridden; food that has been home cooked, served by jacketed waiters in fancy restaurants, delivered in a cardboard box or reconstituted using nothing more than boiling water and emotions ranging from wide eyed optimism through gales of laughter to the deepest troughs of depression imaginable, it's all over.

Well almost. We still have the small problem of getting back to Venice and the Harbour Authority boat isn't in sight. As the land has diminished, and flattened to a large degree, the river has started to spread out into the delta. There are three main channels at this point. The one to the right is the deep water channel for the ocean going ships, the one to the left leads into the eastern bay below New Orleans while the centre on, the one we have selected, runs straight south into the Gulf of Mexico.

As the land has flattened the wind has increased in strength and, would you believe it, the flow seems to pick up as well. Suddenly we are zipping along faster than we have for ages and there is a distinct possibility that we will be swept further down the channel than we planned, possibly to a point where the boat cannot immediately see us.

We manage to paddle to the small island that hosts the channel marker sign as it has a series of wooden piles driven into the seabed, I think it may have been a mooring point at some time in the past for boats to await a pilot. After a considerable struggle with the water and wind we manage to hold on to them. Grace manages to get to the north side while I try and grab hold of it to the south side, so that we are together, but the current is too strong and I have to let go and find another holding point a little further down the row.

Once I have managed to secure myself I get the phone out and ring Kerry, the Harbour Authority boat captain, and only get his answer phone. Great, he is out of signal range or busy on something else. The first thing that crosses my mind is that they have been called out to an emergency, they are a rescue service as well as a police function when all is said and done, and we will have to wait for them to come and look for us. It crosses my mind that it may take hours for them to come and I am not sure that we can remain at this point for that long; we will get cold and tired in a very short time.

We have been there about 15 minutes, and I have tried to call a couple more times without any success, when I spot a passing boat that has four men in it obviously setting off for a days sport fishing. I remember that the area is advertised as being a good place to catch big game fish like Marlin and Sharks. Various different types of Shark, all of them big. Including Bull Sharks that are said to be very aggressive and have adapted to life in the waters of the Mississippi River for quite a way up from the seawaters of the Gulf. There is never a good place to capsize, and this location tops my list.

I wave and call to them and at first all they do is wave back! Is it normal to see a pair of kayakers clinging onto wooden piles in the middle of a river delta? I manage to call them over and when they get to me hurriedly explain our situation and ask if they can tow us about a mile and a half back upstream to where the Pilot boats moor up while waiting for the ships to arrive and need assistance. Called 'Pilot Town', they are at it again with the imaginative names, it is marked on the map and can be clearly seen from our position as it is a series of off white painted buildings raised up on stilts to allow for the flood waters to pass underneath it. One of the guys says, "Sure, where is it?" I can hardly believe my ears; I am being rescued by someone who doesn't know where he is. Fortunately the boat driver does and I manage to pull alongside. Two of the crew hold the boat front and back while we head upstream at a very slow pace.

I tell them that Grace is just above where they saw me and ask if we can approach her so that she can be towed as well. The skipper tells me that he cannot see her. Neither can I because of the boat so I describe where she is and he tells me that he can see the front few feet of her kayak sticking out from behind the posts. Thank goodness as I had all manner of visions and situations running through my head.

I look ahead and see the Harbour Authority boat coming towards us and tell the fishermen who they are. They let go of me and I paddle over to them, made a bit easier by them offering shelter from the wind, while the fishermen go to help Grace. I did not see the operation but she told me later that she had been pushed so far back into the piles that she couldn't use her paddles and didn't have enough hand holds to pull herself out. They pulled her out and brought her near to the big boat and with a wave went on their way.

The fishing boat and crew will always be anonymous to us as we did not get their names but I shall be forever in their debt. Even to the end human kindness showed up when it was needed.

The Harbour Authority crew take photos of us flying the Union Flag and smiling like crazy people and then haul us and our boats up onto the deck and we turn and set off back up the river to Venice. As we set off Grace and I have one last 'Got Here Hug', something we have done at the end of each day, and then start to see if we can contact our families. I leave Grace to talk to her parents and go onto the bridge to talk to Kerry to apologise for the note of desperation in my voice when I called his phone.

He tells me that it doesn't matter and that he will never actually hear the message anyway. He then looks sheepish as the crew start to grin and tells me he has managed to leave his phone in a container that they searched late last night, which is probably on its way to China by now. I thank him for his assistance and the kindness him and his crew have shown us. He tells me that they would rather help in this way than have to go looking for people who radio for help or who are reported missing when they fail to return. He asks that I tell people this and that all they have to do is contact the Authority office and make arrangements. It goes unsaid but is understood that they have had to recover bodies before now and they really don't like having to do that. As a former Police Officer who has done that many times I understand the hidden text of his, unspoken, message

It seems surreal as Grace and I sit on the boat, almost as if we had just been out for the morning and were now heading home for lunch. I honestly do not know what I think or feel. When we arrive back at the marina we can see our reception committee of Pauline, Phil, Marguerite, West and Michelle (their granddaughter) standing on the dock edge watching as the boat rounds the harbour wall. We are waving and holding the Union Flag aloft when the siren and flashing light on the boat comes into full operation. I wonder how many other people on the dockside know what it is we have done. Probably all of them as if they didn't hear it from us they will have from our reception committee.

It seems to take an absolute age for the boat to travel the length of the harbour wall, then turn round so that they can back up to unload. Everyone is so near yet still so far away. This is torture. As a joke Grace and I wait until we are about 10 yards away and then turn and walk towards the front of the boat. It falls flat for everyone but us as they think we are collecting equipment. Oh well, it amused us.

As we get off the boat, and the river for the last time, there are many hugs, a few tears and many words of praise. Unfortunately we cannot sit and just relax, as we have to unload the kayaks from the boats, unload the kayaks and then load the kayaks onto the truck for the journey home. Grace and I have this part of the journey down to a fine art now, so much so that any 'help' we get is actually a hindrance. Sorry everyone.

The reception lady, Kindred, tells us that she has managed to leave our room from last night until last for cleaning but that we only have about 30 minutes until the manager comes back. Grace first and then me and we are showered and on our way.

As we drive away I realise that it may take some time to sink in, just what I have done.

And some time to get over it.

That night we stayed in New Orleans, Pauline, Michele and I with Adele Bergman; Grace and Phil with Bart Shank. The Rotary Club had arranged a fund raising evening, for the Rotary Polio Eradication Programme, at a local bowling alley and wanted us to go and meet some of the members who had helped in the background as well as their District Governor, who wanted to meet and congratulate us.

Amid the noise and clatter of the bowling, the laughter and shouts of encouragement for the bowlers, the stream of well wishers wanting to talk to us, Grace and I really just wanted to be with our family. Don't get me wrong it was a wonderful evening with some really nice people but at one point I saw Grace sat to one side and went across and sat with her. After a few moments silence I said "This is a bit overwhelming for me, how about you?" She said "Yes, it feels strange to be around so many people". I know just what she meant even after complaining of being isolated for so long it will take time to adjust.

Grace and Phil stayed in New Orleans for another night and we arranged that I would drive down and pick them up on Monday afternoon, so that they could be together and see the city while Pauline and I went back to the farm with Michele. I spent all Sunday afternoon sorting and cleaning gear, not all of it could be taken back to the UK so West gladly put some of it into his 'Zombie Apocalypse Survival Bag', it seems that they all have them, and packing for posting the equipment that Jim Lewis had lent me.

The boats were cleaned and wrapped in tarpaulins and stored on the farm. Sadly we couldn't take them home, the shipping and import tax charges made that impossible, and they were to be put up for sale in the US. The buoyancy aids, neoprene boots and gloves, hats and splash skirts were all left to soak in a tub full of water with lashings of clothes washing liquid. I did wonder if the smell would ever come out but it did.

It was then time to relax, visit with friends and eat proper food more than once a day before flying home.

The final word goes to the anonymous man on the bridge at Lake Itasca who, from the brave shield of a crowd, loudly told us "You won't make it" as we commenced our journey. Well Sir,

WE DID IT!

And it only took (aproximately) 1,460,000 paddle strokes.

Post script:
Remember the man on the bridge on the third day? The one who took our photographs?

The day before this book was delivered to the printers he tracked us down via our local newspaper with the folloewing message: -

I am a resident of the American state of Minnesota. Last August, I was on a bridge over the Mississippi River taking photos of the scenery. It was a lovely shot of the river, the reeds, and the pine trees beyond. When I spotted on the water two kayakers approaching, I asked if I could take their picture, because it was such a nice addition to the shot.

Our conversation was very quick before they passed under the bridge, but I learned that they were from Halifax, England, and that they were on a kayaking journey down the length of the Mississippi.

I must tell you that I was a little concerned for their welfare, as it seems to me that such a jouney would be quite an undertaking.

So if they or people who know them could assure me that they are alright, and that they enjoyed their stay in my country, I would by most grateful.

Thank you,
K. William Jones
Ramsey, Minnesota

Thank you Mr Jones you have summed up the warmth and friendship we received throughout the journey and we are grateful for your concern. I am equally grateful to the Halifax Courier reporter, Laura Tacey, for taking the time to contact Mr Jones to assure him that we are well and for passing his details on.

Ken Robertshaw

Physiological and Psychological effects

Any long term physical endeavour such as Grace and I undertook is not without consequences.

We knew that it would be hard work, both physically and mentally, and that we would have difficulties along the way. We also knew that it would be hard to explain to people just how difficult it was as, to be frank, it is outside the experiences most people will ever have in their lives. That said, I do not want anyone to gain the impression that we were in mortal danger at all times. Yes, there were times when we faced difficulties of both a physical and psychological nature but we did not, and still don't, dwell on them.

Overall it was a tremendous experience, taught me a lot about myself (you really are never too old to learn something) and one that I hope will serve to inspire others to achieve.

One of the most important aspects of the expedition was nutrition. We knew that we would require a high carbohydrate diet to provide the necessary fuel and provisioned accordingly. Even though we had been advised that we would need a higher than normal protein intake we did not get this quite right. The constant exercise not only burnt fat reserves but also muscle, which did not have the building blocks it needed to replace and build as we journeyed.

The following table shows an analysis of my body measurements taken before and after the expedition (All measurements are in inches)

Chest 44/42　　　　　　　Waist 38/34　　　　　　Tummy 41/37¾
Hips 41/39½　　　　　　　Thigh 2¼/ 22½
Bicep 14/13¼　　　　　　　Shoulder spread 45¼/42½
Body fat 29.5%/23%
Weight 210 Lbs.(15 Stone) / 180Lbs.(12Stone 12Lbs.)

The most surprising of these is the reduction in bicep size and shoulder spread as it would be normal to assume that constant use of these areas would have an increasing effect.

The reduction in weight only serves to underline the old adage of eat less and move more to lose weight.

After the first few days my hands started to develop callouses and the constant gripping of the paddles, albeit as loose as possible to prevent strain, resulted in fingers stiffening up during the night. This remains a problem almost three months after my return as I find that I am constantly flexing my hands to relieve stiffness.

Although the weight loss was a welcome side effect it also had a downside to it. The reduction of the size of my bum made sitting in a kayak all day grow uncomfortable as the days passed. It also means that very few of my clothes still fit me. This does not mean that I will return to my former weight as I have become determined to keep my new found self.

One physical aspect that cannot be overlooked, but one that we did during planning, are legs. They are used to help stabilise the kayak in rough water, by bracing under the sides, and to help increase stroke power, by pushing against the footrests. However the vast majority of the time they are laid out in front, giving the body a right angle bend, and doing very little. This led to them being 'rubbery' when we first got out of the boats and making us unsteady for the first few minutes on dry land.

This was a particular problem for me as I have a replacement knee and nerve conductivity issues with my left leg. In short I have a heavy limp and a weak leg, the result of various injuries and hospital stays. One of the reasons behind supporting The Theodora Children's Charity is the time I have spent in hospital.

A frequently overlooked psychological condition is the effect of being clean and wearing clean clothes. I think we all know that it is important to keep ourselves, and clothes, clean, to prevent sickness and be fragrant around others but do we realise just how it affects us?

Water was for drinking and cooking not having showers and at most of the campsites there was no opportunity to wash. Basic cleanliness came from washing hands and faces with alcohol based liquid or 'wet wipe' cloths at meal times whilst baby powder was employed in other areas. The single biggest boost to wellbeing in terms of cleanliness came from brushing teeth.

Even if no other part of the body could be washed we always took the opportunity to brush our teeth. I cannot describe how this simple act has an uplifting effect. A fresh tasting mouth makes the rest of the body feel clean and raises the spirits.

There was not much we could do about changing clothes, as we simply did not have any with us to change into. I never did get used to the way they generated an almost indescribable odour, which remained even after being washed on the occasions we were able. I burnt them before I came home.

Other psychological effects are harder to quantify and explain.

To the outside world we all appear as a completely different person to the one that we know ourselves to be. I know that I display confidence, appear relaxed and in control of most situations and that I can stand and address an audience of any size without displaying any nervous traits. I know that I appear to be laid back and not worry about anything, equally I know that my temper and 'get on with it' side can arrive almost without notice. To the outside world I am a 'people person' who gets on with life and just enjoys what is happening.

The truth is that I constantly battle against depression and at times have an internal dialogue that lasts for hours over what can be insignificant detail or incidents. Not an easy thing to put out into the public domain and one that will cause some people to actually question why I have.

The answer is simple. I control my situation; my situation does not control me. It does not make me any less effective in what I choose to do; it does not prevent me from doing what I want to do.

I have not disclosed this for any sensational reasons or even to gain sympathy. I have disclosed it so that people will understand that mental health is as important as physical health and that they should not judge others when they occasionally find that they are 'not just themselves today'. This is especially important for young people as often we merely put their moods down to hormonal changes as they grow up.

I hope that the above will help put the following into perspective. Every day was a new challenge. We never knew where the river would take us, what the scenery would be like, if we would see anyone else, if we would come across dangerous waters. That was what made the expedition so exciting. It also made it mundane, as frequently the days would be the same relentlessly boring view of tall trees, slow flowing water and not one single soul to talk, or even wave, to.

The feeling of isolation was complete. Especially in the first few days when we couldn't see anything but the narrow strip of water directly in front of the kayak and tall reeds to either side. The wider stretches down south were as bad. The banks of the river were that far away that seeing anything smaller than a large building impossible.

I spend most of my day in conversation with other people, frequently I am in company and enjoy just sitting with them and have an active social circle. Suddenly this was removed from me and I couldn't even pick up the mobile phone to speak to them as A) I needed both hands to paddle B) There was no signal half of the time C) O2 charged me a fortune for the privilege when I did get a signal.

Perhaps the hardest thing to endure, psychologically, was the frustration that contact with the 'outside world' brought. Conversations were stilted; what did I have to tell them? They had no idea what we were going through and anything they said inevitably was, if not wrong then not quite right. Then there is the problems that are unique to modern communications, signals dropping out without warning, getting time differences wrong and catching people as they are waking up or going to bed, or worse still them holding the iPad or IPhone at the wrong angle so that I could not see their faces.

Trying to get them to understand that actually seeing them was more important than hearing them was probably the most frustrating thing of all. To the point that it was almost not worth making contact as it had the opposite effect.

One aspect of my psyche is that I have difficulty in asking people for help, whatever the task or situation. I also have difficulty in accepting help when it is offered. The number of times that we received help from people along the route, often at their instigation, has finally

drummed this out of me. People will help and are willing to do so, all you have to do is ask or accept.
We all need to remember that

Strangers are friends that you haven't met yet

The will, and determination, to continue is sometimes the only thing that we have to keep us going. We all have reserves of energy, both physical and psychological, that we can draw on but how many of us draw on that every day for several weeks on end? I did. And it was hard.

When we got to the point where we knew we could succeed, when we knew we had beaten the river, I made a confession to Grace. I told her that on more than one occasion that as I was walking about and getting ready for the day's journey I had thought about falling over and spraining a wrist so that I couldn't continue. A ridiculous thought, of course. Imagine my surprise when she told me she had considered the same thing.

It was our sheer will and determination that prevented us from doing this. We both rose above our internal doubts and conquered them. Then we laughed at that piece of disclosure. Laughter makes most things go away, everyone should try it a bit more often.

Don't imagine from reading of the dark moments of the journey and the sense of failure that crept in occasionally that the expedition was the most depressing thing I have ever done. Far from it. It was the most fulfilling thing I have ever done and one that was worth every ounce of effort.

I found that the entire expedition, from concept to execution, has made me examine my personal outlook on many things and has shown me that I have a mental toughness that I believed had deserted me. I also believe that it has been strengthened as a result of this experience.

Ken Robertshaw
January 2015

Printed in Great Britain
by Amazon